THE
unofficial GUIDE®
ᵀᴼ Mall of America

1ST EDITION

COME CHECK US OUT!

Supplement your valuable guidebook with tips, news, and deals by visiting our websites:

theunofficialguides.com
touringplans.com

Also, while there, sign up for The Unofficial Guide newsletter for even more travel tips and special offers.

Join the conversation on social media:

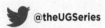 @theUGSeries

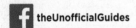 theUnofficialGuides

 theUGSeries

 theUGSeries

#theUGseries

Other *Unofficial Guides*

Beyond Disney: The Unofficial Guide to Universal Orlando, SeaWorld, & the Best of Central Florida

The Disneyland Story: The Unofficial Guide to the Evolution of Walt Disney's Dream

Mini Mickey: The Pocket-Sized Unofficial Guide to Walt Disney World

Universal vs. Disney: The Unofficial Guide to American Theme Parks' Greatest Rivalry

The Unofficial Guide Color Companion to Walt Disney World

The Unofficial Guide to Disney Cruise Line

The Unofficial Guide to Disneyland

The Unofficial Guide to Las Vegas

The Unofficial Guide to Universal Orlando

The Unofficial Guide to Walt Disney World

The Unofficial Guide to Walt Disney World with Kids

The Unofficial Guide to Washington, D.C.

THE *unofficial* GUIDE®
to Mall of America

1ST EDITION

BETH BLAIR

Please note that prices fluctuate in the course of time and that travel information changes under the impact of many factors that influence the travel industry. We therefore suggest that you call ahead or check websites when available for confirmation when making your travel plans. Every effort has been made to ensure the accuracy of information throughout this book, and the contents of this publication are believed to be correct at the time of printing. Nevertheless, the publishers cannot accept responsibility for errors or omissions, for changes in details given in this guide, or for the consequences of any reliance on the information provided by the same. Assessments of attractions and so forth are based upon the authors' own experiences; therefore, descriptions given in this guide necessarily contain an element of subjective opinion, which may not reflect the publisher's opinion or dictate a reader's own experience on another occasion. Readers are invited to write the publisher with ideas, comments, and suggestions for future editions.

The Unofficial Guides
An imprint of AdventureKEEN
2204 First Ave. S., Suite 102
Birmingham, AL 35233
theunofficialguides.com, facebook.com/theunofficialguides, twitter.com/theugseries

Cover design by Scott McGrew
Cover photos © Mall of America
Text design by Vertigo Design with updates by Annie Long
Index by Ann Cassar

For information on our other products and services or to obtain technical support, please contact us from within the United States at 888-604-4537 or by fax at 205-326-1012.

AdventureKEEN also publishes its books in a variety of electronic formats. Some content that appears in print may not be available in electronic formats.

Many of the designations used by manufacturers and sellers to distinguish their products are claimed as trademarks. Where those designations appear in this book and the author is aware of a trademark claim, they are identified by initial capital letters.

ISBN: 978-1-62809-034-5; eISBN: 978-1-62809-035-2

Distributed by Publishers Group West
Manufactured in the United States of America

5 4 3 2 1

CONTENTS

LIST *of* MAPS

ABOUT *the* AUTHOR

BETH BLAIR lives in the Minneapolis–Saint Paul area and is a travel and lifestyle writer. She is also author of the international title *Break into Travel Writing* (Hodder Education, 2012, and printed in the US by McGraw-Hill, 2012). Her articles have been featured in *BBC Travel, Forbes Travel Guide, AAA Traveler, Destination Weddings & Honeymoons, Global Traveler, St. Paul Pioneer Press,* and numerous anthologies, including the *Chicken Soup for the Soul* series. She was the 2013 *Shape* magazine Weight Loss Diarist and was named first-place winner in the 2010 Writer's Market "Freelance Success Stories." Her co-owned travel blog **TheVacationGals.com** won Gold in the prestigious 28th annual Lowell Thomas Travel Journalism Competition (2012). Beth is a member of SATW (Society of American Travel Writers).

ACKNOWLEDGMENTS

MINNESOTANS TAKE THEIR STATE VERY SERIOUSLY, including their sentiments on Mall of America (MOA). Every time MOA is mentioned, our ears perk up and we lean in and take the words to heart. Much like the quintessential Minnesota hotdish (casserole to non-Minnesotans), we approached this book with a concoction of local, tourist, and firsthand perspective, and thank everyone who has offered their thoughts and approached us in the mall and parking lot asking for advice or directions. Their confusion was our learning opportunity.

Thank you to Leif Pettersen, Tourism Communications Manager at Mall of America, for his willingness to answer questions about this ever-growing monstrosity; Linda Kramer and her children for offering a longtime local's perspective; Kristin Bianchi for her endless optimism and patience when taking our Girl Scout troop to MOA's Build-A-Bear and Microsoft for scouting opportunities; Michelle Schlehuber for offering her wisdom on hosting a successful fund-raiser through MOA events; Steve Wright for sharing his fifth-grade class's creative insight on the mall; and personal shopper Carly Gatzlaff and fitness expert Emily Christie for offering their personal expertise.

With much gratitude to the entire Blair family: my husband, Jeff, and children, Jeb, Maddie, and Maisie, for always being onboard when asked to try the latest food, rides, and activities at Mall of America. Your enthusiasm, curiosity, annoyances, and opinions are what this guidebook is all about.

Endless gratitude to all of the brilliant publishing pros for their talent, efforts, and ideas: Bob Sehlinger, Molly Merkle, Tim Jackson, Holly Cross, Amber Henderson, Emily Beaumont, Annie Long, Steve Jones, and Liliane Opsomer.

INTRODUCTION

▌ UNOFFICIAL DECLARATION

THE AUTHOR OF THIS GUIDE specifically and categorically declares that she is and always has been totally independent of the Mall of America; Nickelodeon Universe; Sea Life; and all other attractions, stores, and restaurants within Mall of America.

The material in this guide originated with the author and has not been reviewed, edited, or approved by the Mall of America.

This guidebook represents the first comprehensive guidebook and critical appraisal of Mall of America. Its purpose is to provide the reader with the information necessary to experience Mall of America efficiently, economically, and smoothly.

In this guide we represent and serve you.

▌ LARGEST MALLS *in the* UNITED STATES *and* WORLD

CURRENTLY, ACCORDING TO the International Council of Shopping Centers, there are approximately 109,500 shopping centers in the United States, and Mall of America (MOA) is the largest—for now. In early 2015 it was announced that MOA's owner, Triple Five, is planning to build the largest retail and entertainment complex in the world, America Dream Miami. As of this writing, ground has been broken, but plans are still developing. In October 2015 it was announced that Triple Five submitted plans to the city of Bloomington regarding the next phase in MOA's growth. The price tag: $500 million. MOA's Phase II began rolling out in late summer of 2015 and into 2016. Future plans include a 180-room luxury hotel and 120 residential units, Collections at MOA (a 1-million-square-foot upscale shopping district), additional office space, and another parking area.

When word spread about the Miami mall plans, the media seemed confused. Over recent years, images of abandoned shopping malls and theme parks have been trending on social media. A search for #abandonedmall on Instagram portrays a selection of vacated mall images, some of which are artistically staged. The eerie ambience of dreary, desolate buildings that were once booming commercial epicenters appears to be setting the stage for the future, as online shopping encroaches on the shiny shopping mall.

However, there are thriving malls, and MOA is one example. Plus, it isn't a one-time success story. The Minnesota-based megamall was inspired by Triple Five's Canadian shopping center, West Edmonton Mall (opened 1981), the largest mall in North America, and crowned king for many Guinness World Records:

- World's largest indoor amusement park (25 rides and attractions)
- World's largest indoor triple loop roller coaster (1,285 meters of track)
- World's largest indoor lake (complete with a replica of Christopher Columbus's Santa Maria)
- World's largest indoor wave pool (12.5 million liters of water)
- World's largest parking lot (with room for 20,000 vehicles)
- World's tallest indoor permanent bungee tower (30 meters up and 30 meters down)

While MOA doesn't quite reach this Canadian mall's scale—for one, there isn't a water park yet—it does boast some pretty impressive fun facts. One lap around the mall equates to 0.57 mile, and while that may not sound like much, these visuals might impress you: Seven Yankee Stadiums can fit inside MOA, as can 32 Boeing 747s, while 258 Statues of Liberty could lie inside the mall. Finally, imagine 28 theme park rides in the center of the mall. Yes, there is plenty of space for MOA's 42-plus million guests to enjoy.

The largest malls in the United States, when looking at retail space boasting more than 2.5 million square feet, are only a handful. That list is whittled down to the following: Mall of America (opened 1992) in Bloomington, Minnesota (and the reason you are holding this book), has 4,870,000 square feet. Until MOA's Phase II happened, King of Prussia Mall (opened 1963) in King of Prussia, Pennsylvania, held the largest-mall title in the United States with more than 400 stores and over 3,779,242 square feet. Aventura Mall (opened 1983) in Miami-Dade County has 2,700,000 square feet and 300 stores, and South Coast Plaza (opened 1967) in Orange County, California, has 2,700,000 square feet and about 250 stores.

Looking at the world's largest shopping malls based on gross leasable area (GLA), you'll find New South China Mall in Dongguan, China, which boasts 7.1 million square feet. However, the mall is considered a flop because of its location and other factors, such as out-of-reach prices for local citizens. Does a 99% empty mall count? We say no.

Since New South China Mall is mostly empty, that puts Golden Resources Mall in Beijing, China, in first place with 6 million square feet. Again, reports say this mall isn't thriving either. Moving over to the Philippines, the SM Megamall in Mandaluyong sits at 5.45 million square feet, and business seems to be going well there. Next in line is SM City North EDSA in Quezon City, Philippines, at 5.2 million square feet.

FUN FACTS ASIDE, LET'S TALK SALES

WHILE THE NATIONAL AVERAGE SALES for healthy malls are $475 per square foot, some malls are raking in profits well beyond that. In recent years MOA has averaged $701 per square foot, and West Edmonton Mall has come in at $745 per square foot. These two malls aren't alone, as many malls are still profitable. In the summer of 2015, Green Street Advisors real estate research firm released a top 10 list of the estimated most profitable shopping malls.

Bal Harbour Shops (opened 1965 and holding at 450,000 square feet) in Florida held the number one spot at $3,070 sales per square foot. The Grove in Los Angeles (opened 2002 and at 600,000 square feet) ranked second with $2,140 sales per square foot. Forum Shops at Caesars in Las Vegas (opened 1992 and taking 636,000 square feet) made the list in fifth place with $1,616 sales per square foot.

As you can see, when it comes to shopping malls, size is not a factor in success. The secret sauce is much more, and Triple Five knows the recipe.

MALL *of* AMERICA HISTORY

MUCH TO CONTRARY BELIEF, Mall of America is not in either sister city Minneapolis or Saint Paul. It is located about 1.5 miles from the Minneapolis–Saint Paul International Airport in the southern suburb of Bloomington. Similar to how Orlando gets credit for being home to Disney World—it's actually located in Lake Buena Vista—Minneapolis frequently gets the glory of being home to the nation's largest indoor shopping mall. Naturally, the two Twin Cities and surrounding suburbs like to claim some kind of connections to the mall that draws all. Hotels, restaurants, local water parks, and even tattoo parlors love being able to claim they are "only minutes from Mall of America." It's true; if you removed all traffic from the highways, getting from Bloomington to the epicenter of either downtown would take roughly 20–25 minutes. Traffic, weather, and construction make for a different story, however.

On April 24, 1956, Metropolitan Stadium "the Met" opened in Bloomington and was home to several sports teams. First came the Minneapolis Millers minor league baseball team (1956–1960), then the Minnesota Twins and the Minnesota Vikings played there from 1961 to 1981, while the North American Soccer League's Minnesota Kicks shared the space from 1976 to 1981.

In January 1982 the Twins and Vikings relocated to downtown Minneapolis's Metrodome. After the move the Bloomington stadium sat vacant, occupying 78 acres, for several years until demolition began and was completed in 1985. The Bloomington Port Authority began tossing ideas in the air about what to do with this space. Location, location, location rang true with the site, considering it was only a mile and a half from the Minneapolis–Saint Paul Airport and it sat at the cross section of Interstate 494 and MN 77 (Cedar).

The proposals boiled down to four ideal options: office complexes, multi-residential possibilities, a new convention and visitor center, or a retail and entertainment complex.

You can probably guess which straw was drawn. In 1986 the opportunistic Ghermezian brothers, the men behind the world's largest retail and entertainment center that had recently opened (West Edmonton Mall in Alberta, Canada), signed an agreement with the Bloomington Port Authority to develop the United States' largest retail and entertainment complex.

Ground broke on June 14, 1989, with Ghermezian's Triple Five Group leading the endeavor. It was a blustery day, with 35-mile-per-hour winds, proving that this attraction was what Minnesota needed. Regardless, many cynics threw money on the table saying this enterprise would never take off, let alone succeed.

Slightly over two years later, on August 11, 1992, Mall of America was officially opened to the public. We weren't there, but opening weekend looks like a success when you watch a video on YouTube entitled "Mall of America Opening Weekend 1992." The video shows thousands of people filling the multilevel space, riding roller coasters, inline skating in the Rotunda, and creating with LEGOs. We notice that most of the stores in the video are long gone. Anchor stores included Bloomingdale's, Macy's, Nordstrom, and Sears and were included in the 330 new stores. The best part, 10,000 people were taking home paychecks.

Since opening day, MOA has seen many stores and restaurants come and go, including original anchor Bloomingdale's. MOA attracts a wide variety of offerings, including the dueling Apple and Microsoft stores situated directly across from each other in the South Court. In recent years one-year leases have been offered to retailers to "sample" MOA to see if the mall is a good fit. Some retailers move on when the lease is up, while others have re-signed and stayed around.

In 2015 the 750,000-square-foot Phase II rollout began, and while the unveiling was slow, the sparkle was bright. The new grandiose front entrance revealed a colorful new Mall of America star logo, the perfect photo op for visiting tourists.

The new expansion included over 150,000 square feet of retail space. Of the new portion, Level 1 was designed to attract luxury tenants, Level 2 was reserved for home-inspired shops, and Level 3 welcomed Culinary on North, the new food court. JW Marriott opened in November 2015, followed by a stream of stores and then office buildings in spring 2016.

Shopping is the tip of the iceberg when it comes to what draws people to MOA. Celebrities frequently show up for book signings, concerts, and other publicity appearances. Holidays bring a bounty of festive events, while fund-raising walks are held year-round. What especially makes MOA outshine its counterparts across the country is its numerous big-traffic-driving attractions. The most prominent by far is the 28-ride theme park, currently called **Nickelodeon Universe.** Other popular attractions include the 70,000-square-foot **Sea Life Minnesota** (formerly Underwater Adventures), 2,500-square-foot **Amazing Mirror Maze, Theatres at Mall of America,** and specialty stores such as **LEGO, American Girl,** the newly updated **Build-A-Bear,** and the brand new **Crayola Experience.**

THE PAST REMEMBERED

LOCATED IN THE NORTHWEST CORNER of Nickelodeon Universe, in front of the SpongeBob SquarePants Rock Bottom Plunge ride, is a brass marker in the shape of home plate. The plaque is printed with "Metropolitan Stadium Home Plate 1956–1981" in honor of the site's sport history. Even more remarkable is a red stadium chair bolted to the eastern wall of the theme park. This represents the precise location of Harmon Killebrew's 520-foot home run on June 3, 1967, a record for both Killebrew and Metropolitan Stadium. In honor of the beloved baseball player, the street on the south side of MOA is named Killebrew Drive.

In the northwest Nordstrom Court is the Tom Burnett 9/11 Memorial. Burnett was one of the heroes who helped stop the terrorists on United Flight 93 that crashed in Pennsylvania. Bloomington, Minnesota, was his hometown.

WHERE IS *the* WATER PARK?

OCCASIONAL FIRST-TIME VISITORS who didn't do their research are sometimes confused when they discover Water Park of America is not inside Mall of America. As the crow flies, Water Park of America (1700 American Blvd. East, Building B; Bloomington, MN 55425;

☎ 952-854-8700) is about a half mile from MOA, but you will find it to be closer to 2 miles or less depending upon your starting point and driving route. There is good reason for even more confusion. MOA has teased over the years that growth expansions include a water park and an NHL-size hockey rink. In the meantime, Water Park of America will have to do. It is certainly Minnesota's biggest and best water park.

As you can tell by the water attraction names, Water Park of America is Minnesota-themed through and through: Fort Snelling Zero Depth Activity Pool, Cascade Falls FlowRider, Lake of the Woods Activity Pool, St. Croix Lazy River, Lake Superior Wave Pool, Eagles Nest Family Raft Ride, Eagles Nest 7th and 10th Floor Body Slides, Eagles Nest 5th Floor Tube Slide, and Isle Royale Hot Tubs. While this isn't the largest water park in America, it's up there in size, with about 70,000 square feet of water attractions. Locker rentals are available, and towels are included with admission. Guests can trade in a wet towel for a fresh one anytime. In our experience, the staff does its best to maintain tidy locker rooms, but we've read reports that during peak times the chaos can spill into the locker rooms because more people equals more mess. Again, we haven't seen this first-hand, but if you have, please let us know of your experience. In addition to the water park, visitors will find the on-site Northern Lights Arcade, with 75 games across 5,800 square feet.

Whether you plan to visit the water park or not, the attached Radisson is one of the most family- and group-friendly hotels in the area. We've stayed in the Queen Deluxe Room, which has a queen bed and two sets of bunk beds with a TV in a separate cove.

NICKELODEON UNIVERSE OVERVIEW

WHILE THERE ISN'T A WATER PARK YET, Mall of America does have Nickelodeon Universe (NU), with almost 30 rides and attractions, ranging from preschooler rides to thrill rides to the new 8-minute Fly-Over America, a spin-off of Vancouver's FlyOver Canada and similar in technology to Disney's Soarin' attraction. The park is open to all guests, but tickets must be purchased to board rides. Looming 55 feet overhead is the longest indoor zip line in North America, Barnacle Blast, with a length of 405 feet and a ropes course. These attractions are not included in ride wristbands and points: Dutchman's Deck Adventure Course ($15.99 One Time Pass), Anchor Drop Spiral Slides ($3.99 One Time Pass), Barnacle Blast Zip Line ($13.99 One Time Pass), and Ghostly Gangplank Ropes Course ($11.99 One Time Pass).

Food stands with classic theme-park concessions, such as Dippin' Dots and popcorn, are set up around NU, while a Caribou Coffee occupies a spot in the center of the park. Face painters have booths out in the open, as do spray paint artists, with merchandise consisting of hats and T-shirts.

Overall, NU is easy to navigate, clean, and offers a nice assortment of rides for all levels of thrill seekers. For more information, see Part Seven: Nickelodeon Universe.

MOA SHOPPING COMPETITION

THE NUMBER ONE TOURIST ATTRACTION in the State of 10,000 Lakes isn't water-based, as license plates declare (actually, some say there are more than 12,000 lakes, but that's for another book). Instead, the top Minnesota tourist attraction is Mall of America. An estimated 42 million people visit the mall each year, and that number is likely increasing with the new Phase II addition. People who don't have an appreciation for retail therapy will say MOA is "like every other mall in America—only bigger." It's true that this mall houses all of the expected stores found nationwide, and in many cases duplicates stores and restaurants. There are two American Eagle Outfitters, three Claire's, five Caribou Coffees, two Champs Sports, two GameStops, and the list goes on. What is nice, though, is it's unlikely you will need to visit another mall after a trip to MOA. As our 7th grade neighbor Mason says, MOA is one-stop shopping. More good news for shoppers: Minnesota does not tax on shoes or clothing. Best of all, the mall offers shipping from MOA to your front door, so you don't have to worry about airline baggage fees.

Being that MOA dominates Minnesota as a megamall and tourist destination, outsiders are surprised to discover there's more to the Twin Cities in the way of shopping. Shopping here is big business, and retailers know they have steep competition, not solely from MOA. As of 2014 Minnesota had 102 million square feet of shopping-center space (the United States has a total of 7.5 billion square feet). Shopping malls run the gamut and range in size from small convenience centers to large regional malls.

OTHER POPULAR TWIN CITIES MALLS

Burnsville Center (1178 Burnsville Center, Burnsville, MN 55306), located southwest of MOA (off I-35 West), is a traditional mall catering to the southern suburbs with Macy's, Sears, Gordmans, JC Penney, and Dick's Sporting Goods. Take I-494 west to Exit 6B (France Ave. S) and head north to find **Galleria Edina** (69th St. and France Ave., Edina, MN 55435), which focuses on luxury shopping. North of the Galleria is the first of the three "dale" shopping centers, **Southdale Shopping Center**

(10 Southdale Cir, Edina, MN 55435). This mall has been around for decades (open since 1956 to be exact) and actually boasts a bit of American history as the first indoor shopping mall. **Ridgedale Center** in the western suburb of Minnetonka is located off I-394/US 12. Anchors include JC Penney, Sears, Macy's, and the newest addition, Nordstrom, which opened in 2015. In the typical fashion of keeping up with the competition, **Rosedale Center** (10 Rosedale Center, Roseville, MN 55113), a favorite with northern suburbs, is in the midst of a 140,000-square-foot expansion. Current anchors include Macy's, Herberger's (formerly Montgomery Ward), and JC Penney, but this new addition is making room for the newly announced Von Maur. **Eden Prairie Center** (8251 Flying Cloud Dr., Eden Prairie, MN 55344) is located in the western suburb of Eden Prairie. Anchors there include JC Penney, Kohl's, Sears, Target, and Von Maur.

POPULAR TWIN CITIES OUTDOOR SHOPPING VENUES

THE EASTERN SAINT PAUL SUBURB of Woodbury has it's own epicenter of shopping (and the traffic to prove it): **Woodbury Lakes** (9020 Hudson Rd., Woodbury, MN 55125). Many other outdoor shopping centers can be found throughout the Twin Cities, but one of the most notable is the 11-block **Nicollet Mall** in downtown Minneapolis. This strip boasts a typical display of urban activity, with restaurants, bars, shopping, and hotels, and is where you formerly found *The Mary Tyler Moore Show* statue of character Mary Richards tossing her hat in the air. Her new home is the Minneapolis Visitor Information Center on Nicollet Mall. Minneapolis's **Uptown** (Lake St. and Hennepin Ave. intersection) has lots of shopping and dining action. Across the river (the Mississippi River, that is) Saint Paul's **Grand Avenue** has about a mile of boutique shopping, restaurants, and coffee shops. We recommend the local **Red Balloon Bookshop** geared toward children's books (891 Grand Ave., Saint Paul, MN 55105; ☎ 651-224-8320; redballoonbookshop.com).

OUTLET MALLS

THE TWIN CITIES AREA has a handful of outlet malls, the newest being a quick jaunt south of MOA right off MN 77 in Eagan called **Twin Cities Premium Outlets** (3965 Eagan Outlets Parkway, Eagan, MN 55122). Of the 100 shops, most are upscale and carry designer brands, as does the 100-store **Albertville Premium Outlets** (6415 Labeaux Ave. NE, Albertville, MN 55301) located west of Minneapolis. **North Branch Outlets** (38500 Tanger Dr. #214, North Branch, MN 55056) is located north of the Twin Cities and has more than 30 shops. These three outlet malls are outdoors, so dress according to season.

ANTIQUES SHOPS

ANTIQUES SHOPS HARDLY COMPETE with the modern trends of MOA, but antiques lovers will find plenty of shops to browse in both

Minneapolis and Saint Paul, as well as surrounding areas. Of particular interest are **Stillwater,** the St. Croix River town west of Saint Paul; the town of **Rogers,** northwest of Minneapolis; and the quaint southwest Minneapolis suburb of **Hopkins,** which features the **Hopkins Antique Mall** (1008 Mainstreet Hopkins, MN 55343).

Retail 101:
UNDERSTANDING RETAILING

WHILE THE GENERAL PUBLIC UNDERSTANDS the terms "shopping" and "sales," most shoppers don't think about the world behind the merchandise. In order for a store to stay open, many goals must be met. In other words, the shop must be profitable, and today achieving profitability is much harder than it looks. In addition to the expected costs, such as rent, operating expenses, and inventory, today's shops are up against online shopping and the temptation of overseas competition, including the dirt-cheap offerings from China alongside free or minimal shipping on eBay.

While we shoppers are surfing our phones to see if we can get a better deal elsewhere, store owners are watching inventory like a deck of cards Kenny Rogers–style. Instead of holding, folding, walking away, or running, the questions of price tag (mark items up, down, or neither) and buying more inventory come into play.

Shopkeepers know their next move by monitoring their Key Performance Indicators (KPI). Watching days of supply, turnover, and speed of sales provides insight on how their businesses are doing and the next steps. KPIs include returned merchandise, units sold per transaction, out-of-stock items, sales per hour . . . all that the layman understands. Also analyzed are details such as how often a product sells out and sell-through percentage, which means the units sold divided by inventory available. KPIs explain clearance racks and blowout sales as stores make room for new or seasonal inventory. Such factors reveal why hot items or name brands rarely go on sale or are not included in store coupons. Today, many of the top-tier stores are struggling because of Fast Fashion. The best explanation is summed up in a few words: cheap runway fashions. Teens and young adults looking for the latest styles are keeping up with the latest trends at a fraction of the price, while the usual, pricier brands are struggling to stay afloat.

Twin Cities locals are accustomed to the high turnover at Mall of America. Yes, some of the stores and restaurants mentioned in this book have already met their MOA demise as the ink was hitting the page. Only a handful of stores can boast being present at MOA since opening day in 1992. Anchor store Bloomingdale's closed in 2012 after a 20-year run. Do you remember Soul Daddy restaurant, the winner of *America's Next Great Restaurant* reality TV show? That hoorah lasted only eight weeks.

PSYCHOLOGY OF SHOPPING

BESIDES PUTTING MERCHANDISE on the shelves and selling it, mall stores must rely on tactics to draw shoppers in and get them to open their wallets. Sales, BOGO (buy-one-get-one free or half-price), coupons for future use, and social media interaction are some of the ways stores draw in customers.

While newspaper, radio, and TV ads are classic forms of advertising, social media tactics are becoming more prevalent. Stores ask shoppers to post a picture or some kind of status update along with a hashtag in exchange for discounts or giveaways. Why not, it's free advertising!

It's a well-known fact that grocery stores are laid out in a specific fashion. Nutritionists tell clients to shop the perimeter for fresh, whole foods and avoid the inner aisles, which are filled with processed junk. Products appealing to children are strategically placed at kid-eye level, while candy and other sweet treats are placed by the checkout line for those last-minute splurges as customers wait in line.

The same goes for mall-shopping retail. Have you noticed you have to walk through the entire store to reach clearance items? Last-minute accessory splurges can be added on at the checkout counter. Visual aspects have their place in storefront windows. Have you ever fallen into the dressing room trap? You know, you try on an outfit and feel all confident as you check yourself out in the dressing room mirror while feel-good music plays overhead. Then, you get home only to realize the outfit looks nothing like it did when you were at the store. There are bumps and creases and, well, the new outfit is simply unsightly. That's because the store played a "gotcha!" with strategically placed lights, mood music, and even elegant decor.

While mall retail may not have rows of cereals to choose from, there is still a psychology to the madness, and it appeals to the eye and the emotions. Trends, sales, styles, and lifestyles all come into play as far as apparel retail goes. Store windows beckon shoppers and appeal to their ideal demographic, along with signs announcing sales and can't-resist discounts.

For shopper Jenny Holmes, MOA's aroma lures her:

There's something about the smell of Mall of America that gets me every time. The minute I walk in the doors, it's that familiar smell. Almost like chlorine at a pool. But it's so welcoming and familiar, as crazy as it sounds. It's the best place for retail therapy and a closer version of Disney World for this shopper.

KNOWLEDGE IS POWER

THANKS TO THE INTERNET, shoppers can hop online for instant product and price comparison, as well as creative ideas that can turn into an instant purchase. In 2015 Pinterest hopped on the "buy now" bandwagon, and now any item with a dollar sign can be bought on the spot. Shoppers avoid shipping fees by mall shopping, but another advantage brick and mortars have over online competition, regardless of location, is tempting the compulsive shopper. Instant-gratification shoppers and trend followers naturally find themselves with full shopping bags after a day at MOA. Retail therapy is real, and in some extreme cases it places people in 12-step recovery support groups and credit card pay-off plans. However, shoppers who prefer to scrutinize their spending and shopping habits can find benefits shopping MOA. In addition to avoiding shipping costs, shoppers are also able to inspect and compare items, as well as enjoy a huge selection from which to choose.

TYPES *of* MALL *of* AMERICA SHOPPERS

MALL OF AMERICA DRAWS ALL AGES, personalities, and types of shoppers. People-watching can be fun when you need a break and decide to relax on one of the many benches throughout the mall.

FASHIONISTA This stylish, hip, and unique shopper doesn't follow trends and obviously has his or her own style.

TREND SHOPPER This shopper knows every brand, latest fashion, and seasonal color, and is usually dressed like everyone else in the same age range.

BARGAIN HUNTER If there is a free membership option, this shopper has a card, along with coupons, saving codes, and sale dates listed on the calendar. There's a good chance you will also find this shopper at the Twin Cities Premium Outlets in Eagan.

MAN OR WOMAN ON A MISSION Shoppers on a mission refuse to get sidetracked by the shiny things on the side and often have a purpose or certain product in mind.

RESEARCHER Wondering what product is best and what store has the best price? The research shopper is your man or woman.

THE MOM Visit on a Tuesday morning and "the mom" is easy to spot since Toddler Tuesday draws hundreds of caregivers. The mom uses MOA to shop and entertain her little ones.

ARE YOU MORE CREATIVE THAN A FIFTH GRADER?

We asked a local fifth grade class what they think about Mall of America. Their answers are peppered throughout the book. Their bright teacher, Mr. Steve Wright, went a step further and asked them to write creatively about Mall of America.

- Mall of America is like an ant hole; there are always a lot of people.
- Mall of America is like a spiderweb; once you get caught, you can't get out.
- Mall of America is like a beehive because it is always busy.
- Mall of America is like rush hour, with people rushing from store to store.
- Mall of America is like a car crash; people and stores are everywhere.
- Mall of America is like a zoo; there is always, always a new place to be.
- Mall of America is a beehive filled with sweetness.
- Mall of America is like seeing fireworks because of all of the rides going at once and it is bursting with excitement.
- Going to Mall of America is like entering a popcorn machine because there are always stores and people popping everywhere.
- Going on the rides at Mall of America is like being in a washing machine because they toss, spin, and flip you.
- Mall of America is like a stack of giant elephants stacked up.
- Being at Mall of America is like being a hockey puck; you're always getting passed around to different stores.
- Mall of America is like the George Washington of Malls.
- Mall of America is like a cornucopia; you never know what'll come out of it.
- Mall of America is like heaven; it is as awesome as a place where ice cream is free.
- At Sea Life the fish were racecars swimming around.

BROWSER The "just looking" response is common with this breed, as browsers are not usually tricked into marketing schemes but still like to know what's out there.

NONSHOPPER This person would never go to MOA if it weren't for all of the fun attractions, such as rides, miniature golf, and a mirror maze, or unless his wife makes him. Sometimes even the attractions don't do it for him and you will find him asleep on benches around the mall. (See Part Eight: Other Attractions for more things to do for nonshoppers.)

HOW *to* CONTACT *the* AUTHOR

DESPITE LIVING MINUTES from Mall of America and spending countless hours shopping, dining, and playing there, I also understand that our readers will have their own experiences, expectations, and encounters. Therefore, I want to hear from you. Do you have something fun to share? Have you had a memorable positive or negative experience? Do you know of a better, cheaper, or more efficient way to experience Mall of America? Has there been a change since this book came out? There is a good chance we already know about it, but we may not, so let us know. You may contact the author, Beth Blair, at UGMallofAmerica@gmail.com.

PART ONE

PLANNING YOUR VISIT

GATHERING INFORMATION

THERE IS NO DOUBT MALLOFAMERICA.COM is a wealth of information. Updates are made daily, and you can sign up for weekly event updates. Future guests can visit **mallofamerica.com/visit/visitor-information** to download the latest Mall of America Visitor's Guide in English, Chinese, Japanese, and Spanish or order a free Visitor's Kit that is delivered by mail and includes a Visitor's Guide, Map & Directory of stores, and a Destination Bloomington Travel Guide. Arrival usually takes a few weeks. If you don't have time to order the information, you can pick up a Map & Directory at Guest Services.

If you want to keep up with what's going on at Mall of America (MOA) and other shopping venues in the Twin Cities, **alishops.com** is a terrific resource. We're pretty sure Ali has surveillance cameras in every corner of every mall in the area. Ali is a style editor for *Minneapolis St. Paul* magazine and host of Shop Girls on mytalk 107.1, but it's her mobile guide to MOA that you want to keep tabs on. Ali keeps up with grand openings, store closings, restaurant scoop, and celebrity sightings.

IMPORTANT MALL PHONE NUMBERS

MALL OF AMERICA likes to keep the experience simple for guests, and that's why the "One Call for the Mall" was created: ☎ 952-883-8800 connects shoppers with Guest Services, which can connect you to anywhere in the mall. For direct access to Security Dispatch, call ☎ 952-883-8888. Finally, if you have a question and prefer to use text messaging, the mall text number is ☎ 952-955-9243.

unofficial **TIP**
Starbucks (E164, 952-854-1922) located off the east Rotunda is open Monday–Thursday, 6 a.m.–10 p.m.; Friday and Saturday, 6 a.m.–10:30 p.m.; and Sunday, 7:30 a.m.–8 p.m. for store employees and walkers. The other Starbucks location (W276, 952-853-1274) is open Monday–Thursday, 7 a.m.–9:30 p.m.; Friday and Saturday, 7 a.m.–10 p.m.; and Sunday, 8:30 a.m.–8 p.m.

OPERATING HOURS

MALL OF AMERICA retail hours are Monday–Saturday 10 a.m.–9:30 p.m. and Sunday 11 a.m.–7 p.m. Most retail stores are closed Easter, Thanksgiving Day, and Christmas Day, but as Black Friday transitions to late-night Thanksgiving, those times may continue to roll back into Turkey Day. For exact hours, call ☎ 952-883-8800 or check mallofamerica.com. The same goes for Halloween and New Year's Eve, when restaurants and attractions may be open later.

WHEN *to* GO *to* MALL *of* AMERICA

BEST TIME OF YEAR

IN OUR OPINION, September, October, April, and May are the best months to visit Minnesota. With school still in session, the crowds are minimal, and the weather is nice if you plan to venture outdoors. If you have no interest in the weather, then anytime during the school year, Monday through Friday, is great, with the exception of the holiday season, simply because of the crowds. But even then, the mall is so massive it's not a horrible experience, unless you shop during the madness of Black Friday or the days leading up to Christmas. Not only is the mall packed, but also parking is insane. If you visit during the holiday rush, it's best to stay in a nearby hotel and take the free shuttle.

Winter

Warning: Minnesota winters are long and cold. However, Mall of America has changed the way people look at Minnesota in the wintertime. That is, those people who do not care to ice fish, ice skate, play hockey, ski, tube, sled, snow mobile, or build snowmen. We have all of those activities up here, and the cold temps and feet of snow do not phase offspring stemming from the Scandinavian gene pool. However, those of us who prefer a comfortable 70-plus degrees appreciate MOA all the more. Despite the outdoor temperatures, MOA makes it easy to forget the icicles. If you stay in one of the two connected hotels, Radisson Blu or JW Marriott, you can leave your coat in the room. Drivers can leave their coats in the car and make a mad dash for the closest entry or rent a locker at one of the many locations inside the mall. Hotel guests relying on shuttles may want to consider hauling coats since catching the hotel shuttle means braving the elements, especially now that new ground transportation for hotel shuttles, taxis, and tour buses is located in the north MOA parking lot (north of Lindau Lane and east of IKEA). Guests exit through the new North Entrance (where the new oversize MOA star is located). Signs offer directions for the various locations.

TWIN CITIES WEATHER AND DRESS CHART			
MONTH	HIGH	LOW	DRESS RECOMMENDATIONS
January	24°F	8°F	Full winter gear: coats, hats, gloves, and boots if you're going to spend any time outside
February	29°F	13°F	Full winter gear: coats, hats, gloves, and boots if you're going to spend any time outside
March	41°F	24°F	Full winter gear: coats, hats, gloves, and boots if you're going to spend any time outside
April	58°F	37°F	Full winter gear: coats, hats, gloves, and boots may be needed in the early days/weeks; jacket or coat likely necessary at the end of the month
May	69°F	49°F	Sweater or jacket
June	79°F	59°F	Possible jacket for evening in early weeks
July	83°F	64°F	Dress for the heat. Prepare for mosquitoes if outdoors.
August	81°F	62°F	Dress for the heat. Prepare for mosquitoes if outdoors.
September	71°F	52°F	Dress for the heat early in the month. A jacket or sweatshirt is likely needed later in the month.
October	58°F	40°F	Jacket or coat. Full winter gear possibly needed mid- to end of the month.
November	41°F	26°F	Full winter gear: coats, hats, gloves, and boots if you're going to spend any time outside
December	27°F	12°F	Full winter gear: coats, hats, gloves, and boots if you're going to spend any time outside

Note: Mystic Lake Casino Hotel still picks up and drops off at the Transit Center lower level of the east parking ramp. The other exciting news is MOA now offers car valet service that offers communication via your mobile device. The best part: drivers will bring the car to you at three separate locations. For more information on parking, see pages 62–68 in Part Three.

While MOA sits at a pleasant 70 degrees, Minnesota still has the etched face of Old Man Winter. The chart above covers the highs and lows of Minnesota, with tips on how to dress. We skipped the average daytime temps because oftentimes the wind chill dips pretty low in the fall and spring months. We'd rather see you prepared. In 2014 schools and some businesses across the state closed due to below-freezing temps. The coldest wind chill temperature we saw here in the Twin Cities was –48 degrees.

If MOA is your only destination and you're staying at an on-site or nearby hotel, you won't need or want to pack heavy boots or bring

unofficial **TIP**
One warning we cannot push enough is looking out for black ice on roads and sidewalks. Parking lots are especially notorious for bad slips and falls. Fortunately, MOA has ample covered parking, but still pay attention if you park along the edge because rain and snow will blow in and freeze.

your long down coat, although you can use a locker if you do. If you're in town for the Saint Paul Winter Carnival or Red Bull Crashed Ice, both during the winter months, you will certainly want to dress for the extreme: warm layers, coat, hat that covers the ears or hat and ear-muffs, scarf, mittens or gloves, and boots. Did we mention layers?

BEST DAYS AND CROWD AVOIDANCE

TUESDAYS AND WEDNESDAYS are the best days to visit MOA during regular nonsummer or nonholiday weeks. With that said, we locals can see a difference on Wednesdays versus Friday–Sunday during the summer. While midweek at MOA is busy, it's not nearly as high volume as the weekend. Because Friday and Monday bookend the weekend, expect a higher volume of people on those days. Visit midweek during the school year and you will pretty much have the mall to yourself. The biggest week-day draw is Toddler Tuesday (10 a.m.–noon), and that crowd is usually near the Rotunda before splitting off for shopping, dining, and rides. If there is a big draw such as a concert or dance event, forget everything we've said. The mall will be crazy, and the east side of the mall will be loud and challenging to maneuver. Our best suggestion is to check the event calendar ahead of time and plan accordingly at mallofamerica.com/events.

A parent of four who lives outside the Twin Cities but knows MOA well says:

> We went to Build-a-Bear for my daughter's birthday, and there was a dance competition in the Rotunda. The music was awful and loud. We wanted to leave, but we'd already made the drive. People who might be bothered by this will want to look at the calendar and avoid days like that. People who don't like kids might want to avoid Tod-dler Tuesdays. People who don't like crowds or waiting in line should avoid Valentine's Day, especially if it falls on a Saturday. Prom sea-son means lots of teens in fancy clothes traveling in groups. If you have to park on the very top level of East to find a spot, it's going to be very, very busy inside.

SHOPPING SEASONS

WE CONSUMERS NORMALLY THINK of life in the way of seasons—fall, winter, spring, and summer—but in the world of retail there can be as many as 20 shopping seasons, and they're all tied to holidays and special events. Does back-to-school shopping ring a bell? How about Valentine's Day, Mother's Day, and Spring Break? Take a good look at storefront windows, and the current shopping theme will be obvious.

Naturally, the end-of-the-year holiday season is the peak, starting with Black Friday the day after Thanksgiving and running through Christmas. After Christmas, the traditional sales run rampant until the New Year, when a new healthier, fitter, goal-oriented season launches.

What does this means for shoppers? Something new is always on the way in, and something is always going to be marked down, then pushed to the clearance table. As bargain hunters know, shopping the after-season can be rewarding.

MAKING *the* MOST *of* YOUR MONEY

SERIOUS BARGAIN HUNTERS

FOR VISITORS TRAVELING TO MALL OF AMERICA on a mission to get the best deals, we suggest designating an e-mail account for MOA stores and attractions. If you're going to MOA tomorrow, this won't help you. However, assuming you're planning weeks or months in advance, you'll appreciate this tip. Here's why: Many of the good deals arrive via store newsletters. Many of the options are print-and-cut coupons or can be scanned from your smartphone. Other times, e-newsletters are filled with sale announcements. The mall has a capacity for more than 520 stores, so you can subscribe to a lot of e-mails. But we warn you, if you use your normal e-mail, you will be inundated with advertising. We are speaking from experience. If you don't have time to open and deal with a separate account, create a folder to dispense your MOA e-mails.

DISCOUNTS, SALES, AND MALL OF AMERICA COUPON BOOK

FINDING DISCOUNTS AT MOA can be tricky, if you don't know where to look. The thick **Mall of America Coupon Book** ($9.95) is filled with 250 coupons and offers, ranging from 10% to 20% off purchases to saving a few bucks with a minimum purchase ($15 off when spending $100) to buy-one-get-one offers. If you order the book online, expect to pay shipping and handling. Before you purchase, find out if your MOA hotel package includes a coupon book, as most do.

In our experience, the coupon book has been worth it, but we have heard from other shoppers that it's a waste of money. Why is that? It all depends on your agenda. Because we live in the Twin Cities and frequent MOA often, we're able to keep the book in our car and reference it every time we need to go shopping. With that said, we did spend a weekend shopping, including two nights at a local hotel, and found that we saved quite a bit of money by using the dining coupons at every meal and taking advantage of store discount codes. Therefore, even if you're there for a short visit, you can make the Mall of America Coupon Book work for you. Regarding online coupons, the Deals page on the MOA website (mallofamerica.com/deals) is hit or miss, again, depending on your shopping goals.

Other than that, following specific stores on social media, signing up for brand newsletters, or downloading apps are the best way to find bargains. For discount apps, we recommend the **Malltip.com** app for finding current deals. Plug in Mall of America (not to be confused with Mall of the Americas in Miami) for current discounts and sale dates. Logging on today, we're finding 40% off everything at Ann Taylor, $25 shorts at Abercrombie & Fitch, $6 tops at Aéropostale, two stuffed toys for $35 at Build-A-Bear, 40% off at Clarks, and many, many others. The Locate Store button at the bottom of each store discount offers a marked map of the mall and outlines the store you're looking for, along with the floor number.

Another place to keep an eye on specials is the Bloomington Convention and Visitors Bureau site: bloomingtonmn.org/deals-packages. Not only are there generous hotel packages and restaurant deals, but there are also store discounts.

BARGAIN RACKS

MALL OF AMERICA IS NOT, generally speaking, a bargain mall. It's pretty obvious, considering the mall is hoping to continue its expansion of luxury retailers when Phase IIB opens in 2018. However, budget shoppers looking for trendy yet affordable clothes will appreciate the nice selection of fast-fashion stores (the fast food of fashions): **H&M** (W117, ☎ 952-858-8888); **Charlotte Russe** (E141, ☎ 952-854-6862); and **Forever 21** (E144, ☎ 952-854-1890), where we have seen tank tops for under $2. All three stores are on the first floor. Up a floor is **A'GACI** (E248, ☎ 952-854-1649), flaunting the latest styles, but it's the shoe department you will want to stay for.

On the upscale end, **Nordstrom Rack** (W324, ☎ 952-854-3131) is hands-down an all-time favorite as the off-price shop for Nordstrom. On the opposite side of the mall is hit-or-miss **Marshalls** (E320, ☎ 952-851-0750) designer discount store.

Nearly every store in the mall has a clearance rack of some sort, but some shops are known for their bargains. Already affordable **Old Navy** (E138, ☎ 952-853-0100) has a bargain room in the back left of the store, where we have discovered racks full of steep discounts for the entire family, including shoes, dresses, tops, and bottoms. Tech shoppers will appreciate **Best Buy's** open-box deals. We have scored a number of electronics browsing the open-box and clearance items. Most of the items have been returned. If that's the case, each is inspected and tested to ensure it can be sold like-new before being put back on the floor. Our favorite feature is that Best Buy offers a full manufacturer's warranty for an open-box product. This is a great perk because it's like buying a factory-sealed product, and Best Buy's Return & Exchange Promise applies. Best Buy clearance products are usually discontinued, overstock, or end-of-stock items and are sold in new, unopened, factory-sealed packages. **DSW** (W124, ☎ 952-876-0991) shoe store has a clearance room in the back where shoes are marked down as much as 30–70%.

CREDIT CARDS AND STORE REWARDS

RETAILER CREDIT CARDS COME WITH SOME PERKS, such as discounts, birthday bonuses, cardholder events, special offers, and even private sales. One downfall of opting for a store credit card is being limited to that specific store or stores under a limited umbrella. Such credit cards frequently come with a higher percentage rate, anywhere between 24% and 29%. Ouch. However, if you play your cards right, meaning pay off your cards regularly, credit card offers can work to your advantage, and the rewards can be worth it.

Along with the perks mentioned above, many stores will offer a nice one-time percentage off your purchase. If you're watching your credit score or have a big purchase on the horizon (for example, a house or car), where your credit score matters, remember that inquiries can put a ding in your credit, especially when applying for multiple cards.

MOA has many stores with their own credit cards. Do your research before blindly applying for a credit card. Some salespeople can be pretty aggressive, as they receive bonuses for each new cardholder they rope in.

Department stores Nordstrom, Macy's, and Sears each offer their own card options and carry benefits. Sears cardholders can shop at Sears, Kmart, Sears.com, and Kmart.com, while Macy's has a store credit card and American Express options. Both card options come with regular special cardholder-only discounts. Nordstrom has various levels for cardholders, with rewards equivalent to spending amounts.

The following MOA stores offer credit cards. Sometimes the specials or offers change yearly. Therefore, read the fine print on the application to note any changes or updates.

- **American Eagle:** 15% off first purchase and birthday month
- **Abercrombie & Fitch:** No annual fee
- **Ann Taylor and LOFT:** Earn 5 reward points for every $1 in-store/online at Ann Taylor; $20 for every 2,000 points earned; $15 birthday gift
- **Banana Republic:** 15% off first BananaCard purchase; $10 reward card for every $200 spent; $10 for every 1,000 points earned
- **Best Buy Master Card:** 5% back in rewards on Best Buy purchases with standard credit; $5 reward certificate for every 250 points
- **Brickmania:** Offers an elite membership ($50) for yearlong discounts and special member-only sales
- **Christopher Banks:** 15% off your first purchase; no annual fees; auto-enrolled in Friendship Rewards—get 15 rewards points for every dollar spent, $10 reward certificate for 2,500 earned points; birthday bonus

- **Eddie Bauer:** Earn 5% in rewards for every dollar spent; $750 in a calendar year, earn 8% in rewards; free return shipping; $15 off any one purchase during your birthday month
- **Express:** 15 points for every dollar spent on card; $10 reward for every 2,500 points; birthday gift; A-List credit card offers exclusive benefits after earning 7,500 points within the program year
- **Gap:** 15% off GapCard or Gap Visa Card purchase online; $10 reward for every $200 spent
- **J.CREW:** 5% off your first purchase; $25 rewards card for every $500 spent; birthday surprise; complimentary personal shopping, styling services, and standard alterations on in-store purchases
- **J.Jill:** 10% off your first J.Jill credit card purchase; 5% off every card purchase; 10% off entire birthday month
- **Justice:** 15% off purchase at the time of applying/approval; 15% off next credit card purchase in the store/online
- **The Limited:** $15 reward for every 300 points earned; free hemming on regularly priced pants; birthday savings
- **L.L.Bean:** 3% off at L.L.Bean, 10% off at L.L.Bean Outdoor Discovery Schools, and 1% off everywhere else Visa credit cards are accepted; every $10 earned brings a $10 L.L.Bean coupon in monthly statement; free returns; free monogramming
- **PacSun:** $10 reward certificate for every 100 points earned; birthday bonus
- **Victoria's Secret:** $10 Angel Reward for every 250 points earned; $10 birthday gift each year Angel Card is active
- **Williams-Sonoma:** $25 Williams-Sonoma gift card after your first purchase; free online shipping when W-S card is used.

SENIOR, STUDENT, AND MILITARY DISCOUNTS

THERE AREN'T ANY REGULARLY hosted discount days for seniors, students, or military at MOA stores or restaurants. However, with a current or official ID, most of the attractions do offer a discount.

MOA has been known to throw a **Holiday for Heroes Party** in December. A military ID lands free rides in Nickelodeon Universe for members of the military and their families (up to four people). This event is usually advertised on mallofamerica.com and pushed out on the mall's social media channels.

The rest of the year Nickelodeon Universe gives $10 off an Unlimited Ride Wristband with military ID for up to four family members. This offer does not work online. Military ID must be presented at Guest Services located on the north side of Nickelodeon Universe.

The Theatres at MOA (S401, ☎ 952-883-8900) offer $6 tickets to seniors and military all day/every day.

Sea Life (E120, ☎ 952-883-0202) offers a $4 discount to military personnel and $2 off to college students with a current college ID. The most generous of all discounts is Sea Life's free family membership for military families of a currently deployed soldier. The family must bring valid or current deployment papers to receive the family pass.

ATTRACTION DEALS

WE HAVE AN ENTIRE CHAPTER dedicated to Nickelodeon Universe (Part Seven) and Other Attractions (Part Eight). Knowing what you want to do and when you want to do it can save you a bundle on attractions. For example, if you plan to hit Nickelodeon Universe, an all-day unlimited wristband is $31.99. Sea Life on it's own is $22.99 per adult and $16.99 per child. Opting for the MOA Entertainment Pass, which includes an all-day unlimited wristband for Nickelodeon and admission to Sea Life, for $41.99 saves up to $10 per person. The only con of this option is both attractions must be used the same day. On the other hand, some combos do offer savings with a bit more flexibility. Add on Moose Mountain Miniature Golf (N376, ☎ 952-883-8777) and you will save a few bucks in addition to being able to use the golf passes any day. See Parts Seven and Eight to learn more about your options.

The Official Twin Cities Adventure Pass

Family travelers looking to see more than MOA will want to consider the Bloomington Convention and Visitors Bureau **Big Ticket,** a three-day adventure pass that provides 30% savings on two MOA and four other Twin Cities attractions. The pass is good for one year from date of purchase, but all three days must be used consecutively. Cost is $89 for adults and $79 for children (ages 2–13) and (ages 1–13 at Water Park of America). Attractions include an unlimited ride wristband for **Nickelodeon Universe;** general admission to **Sea Life;** all-day admission to **Water Park of America** (☎ 952-854-8900, waterparkofamerica .com); general admission to **Science Museum of Minnesota** (☎ 651-221-9444, smm.org, parking not included); general admission to **Minnesota Zoo** (☎ 952-431-9200, mnzoo.com, parking included); and admission to **Great Clips IMAX Theatre** (☎ 952-431-4629, imax.com /minnesota). This offer can be combined with a hotel via the Bloomington CVB website. Is it worth it? The answer is certainly, if these attractions appeal to you. It is, after all, a 30% savings.

MAKING *the* MOST *of* YOUR TIME

BEFORE PHASE II OPENED, Mall of America reported that if a guest spent 10 minutes in each store, then the total time spent would be 86 hours. It is reported that the average MOA shopper spends about 4 hours at the mall. Of those shoppers, 40% are visiting from outside the Twin Cities. Obviously, that means the remaining 60% are locals. If shopping is your only reason for being at MOA, and you only have one day, you can zip through each floor over two hours with plenty of time for browsing. If you plan to try on clothes, you will want to add on at least another hour, especially if it's a busy day and there are long lines for the dressing rooms. If you are with the family, and they are hitting the attractions and have their own agenda, we strongly suggest you find the stores you want to visit before your trip to MOA and plan out your route.

The first time I went to MOA in 2001, I was accompanying my husband on a work trip. While he was in Saint Paul, I spent the day at MOA from 11 a.m. to 5 p.m. In hindsight, I saw only half of the mall: the east and north sides of Levels 1–3. I recall browsing stores and spending about an hour and a half in Nordstrom Rack. That day I spent about 6 hours at the mall and left with only a Calvin Klein coat, Clinique makeup from Bloomingdale's, and a Red Hat Society statue for my mother. I didn't realize I could enter the then–Camp Snoopy theme park or I would have explored more. To make matters worse, the only food I found was the mall food court. I seem to remember eating a burrito. Little did I know there were many full-service dining options. I laugh at what a waste of a day that was. Today, I know a lot more and hope you learn from my experience.

FIRST THINGS FIRST: DOWNLOAD THE APP

IF YOU EVER EXPLORED the former online MOA Trip Planner, you will quickly see that the new Mall of America app blows it away. It is intuitive, easy to navigate, and extremely helpful. There is a fantastic map, events list, and parking assistance. You can take photos, record a memo, or write reminders of where you parked, as well as the text number for when you're ready for valet parking to retrieve your car. As for shopping, not only can you add places to visit under My List, you can also select coupons and deals (see Deals category), chat with the mall for shopping or dining advice via text or phone (both numbers are in the app), and even view photos of the latest styles and trends. A Mall Info section offers a variety of information, including strollers, lockers, and even the Parental Escort Policy. This interactive app is a must-have and will save you precious time at the mall.

SHOPPER TRAFFIC PATTERNS

SHOPPER TRAFFIC PATTERNS are pretty predictable at MOA. Shoppers in browse mode often start on Level 1 and work up the levels throughout the day. By lunchtime the elevator lines get long as hungry people head to the Level 3 food courts. If you're a browser, or have a long list of stores to knock off on all levels, we recommend you start on Level 3 and work your way down as the day goes on, ending your shopping spree on the same side where you parked or in the shuttle zone. However, if you have certain stores in mind, sometimes it's best to plan out your route ahead of time. Here are a few examples and recommendations.

HIGH-END HUNTERS Luxury shoppers can park in West Parking by **Nordstrom,** home to top brands such as Balenciaga, Chanel, and Prada. Entering from parking Level 4 will bring you into Level 3 without any stairs. Nordstrom Café is on Level 3 and offers a contemporary menu with sit-down service, or you can order a coffee or baked good to go. In the mall, on Level 3, shoppers will find the spacious **Nordstrom Rack** (W324, ☎ 952-854-3131). **Williams-Sonoma** (W262, ☎ 952-854-4553) is located outside Nordstrom on Level 2, while Level 1 has Nordstrom's eBar coffee shop, with plenty of tables and chairs. Taking a left out of Nordstrom, regardless of level, takes shoppers along North Garden. Halfway down is the entrance to Phase II. Level 1 of Phase II holds promises of luxury retailers; upscale fast-fashion Zara is reported to be moving in at the end of 2016. Level 2 is supposed to offer housewares. Level 3 is the new food court called **Culinary on North.** Looping around to the southeast corner is our favorite section for luxury shops such as the new **kate spade** (S106, ☎ 952-854-1003); **Michael Kors** (S184, ☎ 952-814-1900); and **Burberry** (S178, ☎ 952-854-7000).

SPORTY GALS These shoppers will want to stick to Level 1 for athletic attire: **Calvin Klein Performance** (S130, ☎ 952-854-1318); **Athleta** (S145, ☎ 952-854-9387); **lululemon athletica** (N106, ☎ 952-854-6785); and both **PINK** (N120, ☎ 952-854-1615) and **Victoria's Secret** (N178, ☎ 952-814-9289). The newest addition is Kate Hudson's **Fabletics** (S142, ☎ 651-583-5511).

FARMERS AND OUTDOORSMEN Parking near Sears is convenient. **Carhartt** (N144, ☎ 612-318-6422); **L.L.Bean** (S100, ☎ 952-854-1017); and **The North Face** (S166, ☎ 952-854-1493) are on Level 1. The trendy T-shirt shop **FBFG Farm Boy/Farm Girl** (N380, ☎ 952-854-1311) is on Level 2, while **Bootbarn** (N386, ☎ 952-854-1063) is on Level 3. Shoppers with an active young man won't want to miss **JM Cremp's: The Boys Adventure Store** (N240, ☎ 952-854-9105).

SHOPPERS WITH A SWEET TOOTH MOA has a nice variety of sweet treats. Cold cravings can be quenched at **Paciugo Gelato & Caffè** (W392, ☎ 952-814-3528), the heavenly gelato shop with a daily changing selection of more than 300 rotating flavors. **Northwoods Candy Emporium** (N312, ☎ 952-373-4959) is our favorite place for fudge, as well as its awesome variety of candy from yesteryear. **Godiva Chocolatier** is now down to one location (W126, ☎ 952-858-9306). **Peeps** (NU, ☎ 952-854-5130) provides a buffet of Peeps flavors that change with the season, along with other popular candies such as Mike and Ike and Hot Tamales. Locally owned **iCandy Sugar Shoppe** (E154, ☎ 952-767-0224) is under the same umbrella as the trio of Minnesota-themed stores, including Minnesot-Ah!. The mall's newest candy shop, **It'Sugar** (N270, ☎ 952-854-9245), carries classics such as Pop Rocks and the "world's largest box of Nerds." **Great American Cookies** (S336A, ☎ 952-858-9814) is one cookie shop we can vouch for. While there are various choices, the three for under $5 is a great deal. The Oatmeal Walnut Supreme and Double Fudge rank as favorites with my gang. On the other side of the mall, **Nordstrom Café** (1000 NW Court, ☎ 952-883-2121) has its famous Lemon Ricotta Cookie (aka "be still my lemon-loving heart"). Families with toddler to tween girls will want to spend time at the **American Girl Bistro** (5160 Center Court, ☎ 877-247-5223). The experience is girl-centric, with cutesy decor and perfect girl treats. **Nestle Toll House** (W152, ☎ 952-767-7760 and E283, ☎ 952-853-0272) has a couple of busy locations that offer their famous mouthwatering cookies. Finally, head to Level 3 to visit locally owned **Cupcake** (W384, ☎ 612-760-1200) for championship-winning cupcakes from the popular *Cupcake Wars* reality TV show.

CALLING ALL BUILDERS   LEGO lovers won't want to miss the obvious **LEGO store** (S164, ☎ 952-858-8949) on Level 1 off Nickelodeon Universe or the Level 2 **Brickmania,** a supplement to LEGO products featuring various warcraft and military LEGO enhancers.

HOW FAR YOU WILL WALK

PART TEN IS DEDICATED to health, fitness, and beauty, as MOA is loaded with wellness opportunities. However, we're going to give you a sneak peak here because we think it's important to warn you how much walking you can and likely will do at MOA. To start, one lap around the original MOA is 0.57 mile. If you walk a lap around each of the original four-sided levels of the mall, you will walk about 1.71 miles. When you start weaving in and out of stores, backtrack, run into the theme park to chat with the family, then go back to pick up that sale item before heading to the food court, those tenths of a mile start adding up—and you haven't even explored Phase II yet.

We've hit the mall for a day with a Fitbit pedometer attached to our jeans and managed to get in approximately 7 miles. Even if you're browsing slowly or running from ride line to ride line (read more in Part Seven about Nickelodeon Universe), you will be on your feet most of the day. Again, read Part Ten for more on mall activities.

BLISTERS AND SORE FEET   In addition to wearing comfortable shoes and good socks, bring along a small foot-emergency kit if you or your children are susceptible to blisters. Your kit should include gauze, antibiotic ointment, disinfectant, moleskin or Johnson & Johnson blister bandages, scissors, a sewing needle or something else sharp (to drain blisters), and matches to sterilize the needle. If you develop a hot spot, cover it ASAP with a blister bandage. Cut the material large enough to cover the skin surrounding the spot. If you develop a blister, air out and dry your foot. Next, drain the fluid, but don't remove the top skin. Clean the area with disinfectant and place a blister bandage over the blister. The bandages come in several sizes, including specially shaped ones for fingers and toes; they're also good for covering hot spots. If you don't have blister bandages, don't cover the hot spot or blister with Band-Aids (they'll slip and wad up). Remember, a preschooler may not say anything about a blister until it's already formed, so keep an eye on things during the day.

MALL *of* AMERICA FAQS

Is Mall of America Safe?

In early 2015 a video was released revealing terrorist group Al Shabaab calling for an attack on Mall of America, along with two other malls, West Edmonton Mall in Canada and the Oxford Street shopping area in London. MOA did not take the threat lightly and immediately amped up security and training for employees. Since the threat, we have noticed an increase in police security and K-9s (police dogs). While we cannot offer insight on the threat or chance of future threats, we can say with confidence that we have been to the mall dozens of times since the threat and will continue to go. As in any public place, pay attention to your surroundings and report anything you consider suspicious. The mall urges all visitors to report any suspicious activity. Mall Security may be contacted at ☎ 952-883-8888 or you may visit Guest Services located by main entrances on Level 1.

How Do I Lodge a Complaint?

All MOA concerns, complaints, or comments are handled by Guest Service desks found at all main mall entrances, or you may call ☎ 952-883-8932. If you need to file a complaint with a particular store, restaurant, or attraction, contact the business directly.

May I Bring My Pet to Mall of America?

According to the MOA website, only trained and working service animals are permitted in MOA. With that said, a couple of evenings over the holiday season are reserved for pet photos with the Professor Bellows Santa. The website says "pets of all kinds" are welcome, so apparently you can tie a red bow around your llama's neck and head on down to MOA for that special photo op. This Santa, from Professor Bellows, is one of two in the mall and usually books appointments. However, reservations are not taken for pet nights; instead, it's first come, first served. There are official event guidelines with complete event information and a waiver that must be signed in order to enter MOA and participate. If you do bring your pet to MOA, see Part Three, page 70, for boarding and day-care options.

What Should I Wear to MOA?

Believe it or not, MOA has adopted a dress code. Don't worry; it's nothing extreme. The classic "no shirt, no shoes, no service" is in effect, and clothing must be deemed appropriate, meaning no obscene language or gestures, as well as no racial, religious, or ethnic slurs or phrases that could be considered offensive. Bulletproof or simulated bulletproof vests are a no-go. Clothing that deliberately obscures the face, such as hooded tops and ski masks, is not allowed. (Since there are no ski hills within the mall, that shouldn't be a problem for shoppers; plus the mall is kept at a comfortable 70°F year-round.) In our experience, religious-inspired head scarves and veils don't seem to be a problem, as Minnesota is home to many Muslims.

SHOULD YOU DRESS TO IMPRESS? Being that MOA was our local mall for five years, we've experienced customer service of all ranges. Remember the scene in *Pretty Woman* when Julia Roberts's character, Vivian Ward, enters a boutique and is dismissed for not looking the part of the upscale store's clientele? You won't encounter that level of stuffiness at MOA. Minnesotans are on the nice end of the spectrum; they proudly say MN stands for Minnesota Nice. The upscale shop employees in general are classy and happy to offer assistance. One salesperson told us, "We can tell when someone is a serious shopper or a browser." If you're wondering if you need to dress up for your trip to MOA, we suggest not going to extremes—remember, you will be doing a lot of walking—but looking nice will help the sales clerks take you seriously.

What Should I Expect from MOA Salespeople?

The most common employee we've dealt with on weekends is the teenager or young adult. Occasionally, we have encountered employees in this age range appearing annoyed with an eye roll or long sigh when we asked them a question while they were on their phone texting or chatting with coworkers or friends visiting. On the other hand, you can tell when a manager is present because these young people will be at your beck and call immediately. Most of the time unengaged youth move on to another place of employment rather quickly, aiding the high turnover often seen at such businesses. This is not to say all young people make bad employees. We have had some excellent customer service at MOA by all ages. During the school year, weekday employees are often more mature, and many are professional salespeople who enjoy working in retail and retaining regular customers. If you encounter poor customer service, never hesitate to contact the store directly.

PART TWO

WHERE *to* STAY

ABOUT *the* HOTEL AREA

BY THE END OF 2016, Bloomington will have more than 40 hotels, offering out-of-town guests more than 9,000 hotel rooms, the thickest concentration of accommodations in the state of Minnesota.

Travelers who show up looking for a hotel without a reservation may be perplexed by the many choices. While there aren't any given "areas" to recommend or avoid, each hotel in the Mall of America (MOA) area, meaning within 2–3 miles, falls into one of four hotel tiers: luxury, business/upscale, moderate, and budget.

LUXURY There are only a handful of top-tier luxury hotels in the immediate MOA vicinity. The new **Hyatt Regency** is rather tempting, and it's only 2 miles from the mall. However, the two hotels attached to the mall, **Radisson Blu** and **JW Marriott,** are equally enticing because access to your room is only a walk away (no coat to haul!). Plus, staff from these hotels will meet guests and deliver shopping bags to your guest room while you continue shopping. Bonus! If you don't mind the higher cost, you won't be sorry with any of these choices.

unofficial **TIP**
When staying at hotels near the airport, be thoughtful during late-night and early-morning hours. Many flight crews stay at these hotels, and we all appreciate a well-rested crew when we fly.

BUSINESS/UPSCALE The next tier of hotels includes what we consider the more business-minded options, meaning guests may or may not visit the mall and may be opting for the hotel as a close-to-airport option (think **Marriott, Embassy Suites, Hilton,** and **Crowne Plaza**). While summers and holidays are crazy regardless of what hotel you choose, you have a little less chance of having neighbors who like to jump on the beds at these establishments. Not that it won't happen, but many of the guests who frequent these choices, such as flight crews and business travelers, are traveling without children. All of these options have regular mall shuttle service and relaxing bar ambiences.

MODERATE Next in line are the most common hotel chains (examples include **Radisson, Best Western Plus, Hyatt Place,** and the several Inn & Suites brands). Many of these are clustered around MOA on the southeast corner of I-494/MN 77 and spill over across 77 to the western area. These options are much more reasonably priced for the average traveler, and they usually offer perks such as free coffee and breakfast. A few of these choices are even a short walk to the mall. Country Inn & Suites, Best Western Plus, and Homewood Suites guests can take the covered pedestrian bridge over Killebrew Drive to the mall.

unofficial **TIP**
Choosing a hotel near Mall of America, meaning within 1–2 miles, pretty much guarantees a shuttle to the airport and the mall. Outside of that range, most hotels will offer an airport shuttle but not regularly scheduled mall service. Mall visitors not driving will want to look at the immediate MOA area.

BUDGET Most budget choices sit on the west side of MN 77, south of I-494, and are easily $30–$70 less than the moderate choices (examples include **Quality Inn, Comfort Inn,** and **La Quinta**). While the no-frills theme is common in this area, many of these locations have had recent renovations or updates.

Other hotel options with varying prices expand through the surrounding suburbs, some of which we include in our hotel profiles below. Bloomington doesn't have many choices on airbnb.com. However, if you're looking for a unique experience, both Minneapolis and Saint Paul have a wide selection of charming abodes to choose from, including rooms in historic mansions. Campers have a handful of choices (see pages 50–52 at the end of this chapter), but note that there is no overnight parking or camping on mall premises.

PROXIMITY TO THE AIRPORT

The airport is located on the north side of I-494 and can be seen from several of the hotels south of 494. North-south Runway 35 runs slightly east of Mall of America. Air noise may be of concern since you can see landing gear from some hotels' rooms, but in our experience, rooms at the hotels surrounding Runway 35 are soundproof. However, hotels under Runway 17, in Eagan, aren't as protected.

GETTING *the* BEST ROOM RATE

IF YOU HAVEN'T FIGURED IT OUT BY NOW, scoring the best hotel room is a game, and there are a lot of players. The hotels around Mall of America are no different. My parents were coming to town for a visit, so I figured that would be a good time to figure out how to find the best deals in the area. I started with Radisson Blu Mall of America. My folks were staying three nights, so I called the hotel directly and requested the rates but was disappointed to find out the hotel was booked up the third night of their stay. The remaining two nights were starting at $291/night. The reservationist was obviously trained to suggest the other property, the Radisson Bloomington (home to Water Park of America) only 2 minutes down the road. My family has stayed at this hotel, and it functions well for a family. For $171/night my parents could stay in a deluxe room with a queen bed and a bunk bed (not a bad idea if the grandkids wanted to stay with them). A quick check online revealed that on Expedia Radisson Blu's starting rate was $264, with a promise to be the lowest price on the Internet. Expedia succeeded because the next lowest price we found was Travelocity at $265. However, Travelocity's $163 rate out beat Expedia's $172 rate at the Radisson Bloomington. My parents chose neither and decided on a more affordable hotel in the southern Twin Cities suburbs. Moral of the story: It pays to shop around. For more on that, keep reading.

HOTEL SHOPPING ON THE INTERNET: WELCOME TO THE WILD WEST

UNMATCHED AS AN EFFICIENT and timely distributor of information, the Internet has become the primary resource for travelers seeking to shop for and book their own air travel, hotels, rental cars, entertainment, and travel packages. It's by far the best direct-to-consumer distribution channel in history.

INTERNET ECONOMICS 101 The evolution of selling travel on the Web has radically altered the way airlines, hotels, cruise lines, rental-car companies, and the like do business. Before the Internet, these entities depended on travel agents or direct contact with customers by phone. Transaction costs were high because companies were obligated to pay commissions and fund labor-intensive in-house reservations departments. With the advent of the Internet, inexpensive e-commerce transactions became possible: Airlines and rental-car companies began using their own websites to effectively cut travel agents out of the sales process. Hotels also developed websites but continued to depend on wholesalers and travel agents as well.

It didn't take long before independent websites sprang up that sold travel products from a wide assortment of suppliers, often at deep discounts. These sites, called online travel agencies (OTAs), include such familiar names as Travelocity, Orbitz, Priceline, Expedia, Hotels.com, and Hotwire. Those mentioned and others like them attract huge numbers of customers shopping for hotels.

OTAS AND THE MERCHANT MODEL In the beginning, hotels paid OTAs about the same commission that they paid travel agents, but then the OTAs began applying the thumbscrews, forcing hotels to make the transition from a simple commission model to what's called a merchant model. Under this model, hotels provide an OTA with a deeply discounted room rate that the OTA then marks up and sells. The difference between the marked-up price and the discounted rate paid to the hotel is the OTA's gross profit. If, for example, a hotel makes $120 rooms available to an OTA at a 33% discount, or $80, and the OTA sells the room at $110, the OTA's gross profit is $30 ($110-$80=$30).

The merchant model, originally devised for wholesalers and tour operators, has been around since long before the Internet. Wholesalers and tour operators, then and now, must commit to a certain volume of business, commit to guaranteed room allotments, pay deposits, and bundle the discounted rates with other travel services so that the actual hotel rate remains hidden within the bundle. This is known as opaque pricing. The merchant model costs the hotel two to three times the normal travel agent commission—considered justifiable because the wholesalers and tour operators also promote the hotel through brochures, websites, trade shows, print ads, and events.

OTAs now demand the equivalent of a wholesale commission or higher but are subject to none of the requirements imposed on wholesalers and tour operators. For instance, they don't have to commit to a specified volume of sales or keep discounted room rates opaque. In return, hotels give up 20%–50% of gross profit and are rewarded by having their rock-bottom rates plastered all over the Internet, with corresponding damage to their image and brand.

What's more, doing business with OTAs is very expensive for hotels. A hotel's cost of a multiday booking on its own website is $10–$12, including site hosting and analytics, marketing costs, and management fees. This is 10–20 times cheaper than the cost of the same booking through an OTA. Let's say a hotel sells a $100 room for six nights on its own website. Again, the booking would cost the hotel around $12, or $2 per night. If an OTA books the same room having secured it from the hotel at a 30% discount, the hotel receives $70 per night from the OTA. Thus the hotel's cost for the OTA booking is $30 per night, or $180 for six nights—15 times as costly as selling the room online with no middleman.

In the hotel industry, occupancy rates are important, but simply getting bodies into beds doesn't guarantee a profit. A more critical metric is revenue per available room (RevPAR). For a hotel full of guests booked through an OTA, RevPAR will be 20%–50% lower than for the same number of guests who booked the hotel directly, either through the hotel's website or by phone.

It's no wonder, then, that hotels and OTAs have a love/hate relationship. Likewise, it's perfectly understandable that hotels want to maximize direct bookings through their own websites and minimize OTA bookings. The problem is that the better-known OTAs draw a lot more Web traffic than a given hotel's (or even hotel chain's) website. So the challenge for the hotel becomes how to shift room-shoppers away from the OTAs and channel them to its website. A number of hotel corporations, including Choice, Hilton, Hyatt, Inter-Continental, Marriott, and Wyndham, have risen to that challenge by forming their own OTA called Room Key (roomkey.com). The participating chains hope that working together will generate enough visitor traffic to make Room Key competitive with the Expedias and Travelocities of the world.

MORE POWER TO THE SHOPPER Understanding the market dynamics we've described gives you a powerful tool for obtaining the best rates for the hotel of your choice. It's why we tell you to shop the Web for the lowest price available and then call your travel agent or the hotel itself to ask if they can beat it. Any savvy reservationist knows that selling you the room directly will both cut the hotel's cost and improve gross margin. If the reservationist can't help you, ask to speak to his or her supervisor. (We've actually had to explain hotel economics to more than a few clueless reservation agents.)

As for travel agents, they have clout based on the volume of business they send to a particular hotel or chain and can usually negotiate a rate even lower than what you've found on the Internet. Even if the agent can't beat the price, he or she can often obtain upgrades, preferred views, free breakfasts, and other deal sweeteners. If you enjoy cyber-shopping, have at it, but hotel shopping on the Internet isn't as quick or convenient as handing the task to your travel agent. When we bump into a great deal on the Web, we call our agent. Often she can beat the deal or improve on it, perhaps with an upgrade. *Reminder:* Except for special arrangements agreed to by you, the fee or commission due to your travel agent will be paid by the hotel.

THE SECRET The key to shopping on the Internet is, well, shopping. When we're really hungry for a deal, we always check out the Bloomington and Eagan CVB websites (blooomingtonmn.org and eaganmn. com/hotels). We scour these sites for unusually juicy hotel deals that meet our criteria (location, quality, price, amenities). If we find a hotel that fills the bill, we check it out at other websites and comparative travel search engines such as Kayak (kayak.com) and Mobissimo (mobissimo.com) to see who has the best rate. (As an aside, Kayak used to be purely a search engine but now sells travel products, raising the issue of whether products not sold by Kayak are equally likely to come up in a search. Mobissimo, on the other hand, only links potential buyers to provider websites.) Your initial shopping effort should take about 15–20 minutes, faster if you can zero in quickly on a particular hotel.

Next, armed with your insider knowledge of hotel economics, call the hotel or have your travel agent call. Start by asking about specials. If there are none, or if the hotel can't beat the best price you've found on the Internet, share your findings and ask if the hotel can do better. Sometimes you'll be asked for proof of the rate you've discovered online—to be prepared for this, go to the site and enter the dates of your stay, plus the rate you've found to make sure it's available. If it is, print the page with this information and have it handy for your travel agent or for when you call the hotel. (Note: Always call the hotel's local number, not its national reservations number.)

ANOTHER WRINKLE Finally, a quick word about a recent trend: bidding sites. On these sites you enter the type of accommodation you desire and your travel dates, and hotels will bid for your reservation. Some sites require that you already have a confirmed booking from a hotel before you can bid. A variation is that you reserve a room at a particular hotel for a set rate. If the rate drops subsequently, you get money back; if the rate goes up, your original rate is locked in.

TripAdvisor's Tingo (tingo.com) and Montreal-based BackBid (backbid.com) both claim to be able to beat rates offered by hotel websites and OTAs.

Simply put, bidding sites work best when hotels are dumping inventory—something that is rare among the better properties. Two-star hotels can always be booked for two-star prices, so nobody bids on the hotels with fewer than three stars.

IS IT WORTH IT? You might be asking yourself if it's worth all this effort to save a few bucks. Saving $10 on a room doesn't sound like a big deal, but if you're staying six nights, that adds up to $60. Earlier we referred to unusually juicy deals, deep discounts predicated by who-knows-what circumstances that add up to big money. They're available every day, and with a little perseverance, you'll find them. Good hunting!

GETTING *a* ROOM THAT MEETS YOUR EXPECTATIONS

THIS DISCUSSION APPLIES to any hotel, anywhere. Hotels and, by extension, hotel guest rooms are usually ranked by stars, ranging from one to five. Some publications and websites use other icons, such as TripAdvisor's little green bull's-eyes, but it still comes down to a one-to-five rating system, with five being best.

However, ratings are just a generalization, an average; in other words, not all rooms in a four-star-rated hotel are necessarily four-star quality. Except for the first two years of a hotel's life, when everything is brand-new, there are differences, sometimes quite substantial, in the quality of available rooms. It's important to specify that we're discussing the quality of the room itself, that is decor, furniture, bedding, and so on, rather than a room being close to an ice machine, elevator, or other variables, though these can be important as well.

Most of us have had the experience of booking a room in, say, a four-star hotel and being assigned a room with chipped furniture, worn carpeting, or any number of other defects that are not consistent with four-star status. The reason is that rooms in properties more than a few years old show wear and tear, some more than others. And while it's deflating to be assigned such a room, there are ways to maximize your chances of getting a room you'll enjoy.

Hotels, of course, want to offer their guests a good experience and are also sensitive to their star ratings. Consequently, they keep tabs on the condition of their rooms and schedule attention for below-average rooms. This attention comes in various forms, from refurbish to remodel.

Refurbishing a room may include upgrading televisions and Wi-Fi; replacing mattresses and/or carpets, other soft goods, and wall coverings; and painting. It may or may not include changing the decor. Depending on the scope of the refurbish, it usually takes one to two weeks. By contrast, remodeling is a big deal and often includes structural reconfigurations, major changes to the bathroom, and new furniture, as well as most of the items involved in a refurbish. Remodels take three to five weeks.

At any moment, in any hotel, there will be rooms that don't require attention, newly refurbished/remodeled rooms, rooms currently undergoing a refurbish or remodel, and rooms scheduled for a refurbish or remodel. To you, newly refurbished/remodeled rooms are most desirable, followed by rooms that are OK as is. Least desirable are rooms awaiting a refurbish or remodel. Rooms undergoing a refurbish or remodel are, of course, out of service, as are (in some hotels) the rooms on the floors above and below, which minimizes noise and disruption for guests. This approach ties up about 10% of a hotel's room inventory. Not unexpectedly, companies with a number of hotels take care of their most upscale properties first, refurbishing or remodeling them more frequently than mid-range or value hotels. Refurbishes and remodels continue all year, irrespective of season, though some accommodation is made for periods/days of peak demand.

In most properties, a range of prices is offered, generally with little explanation, but if you dig, you'll find upcharges for newly remodeled rooms, followed by newly refurbished rooms, with rooms awaiting attention on the lower end of the price range. Booking with the hotel directly (though not through the hotel chain's 800 number) rather than through a third party such as an online seller (Expedia, Travelocity, Hotels.com, etc.) allows you to ask reservationists exactly what you get for certain rates advertised on the Internet and elsewhere. Such due diligence largely prevents getting stuck with a room that doesn't live up to the hotel's star rating.

Beyond the room's intrinsic qualities, you might be interested in a room on a higher floor, or a room facing a certain direction. Make these preferences known when booking, and then follow up with a fax to the hotel. Always mention anything you're celebrating, such as an anniversary or birthday, and sign up, preferably before you book, for the hotel's loyalty program. Hotels rarely guarantee that requests will be honored but will try their best to accommodate you.

At most properties your reservation is documented in the hotel's system, but your specific room is not assigned until you arrive. There has been a lot of press about slipping the desk clerk $20 or so to get an upgrade or to respond to a special request. The researchers of *The Unofficial Guide to Mall of America* have tested this technique many times, and we can tell you that it's not as straightforward as it appears.

First, for small chain and proprietary hotels, there's not much of an upside. The latitude afforded front desk staff varies considerably from hotel to hotel. Second, a front desk clerk is limited by what rooms are available. More rooms will be unassigned and available at 3 p.m. than after 6 p.m. or later when the hotel begins to fill.

The approach that works the best for us is to fold a $20 bill and hand it to the clerk along with your credit card (even if you pre-paid your room, he'll ask for a credit card to cover incidentals). Say something like: "This is really a special trip for me. Anything you can do to make it more special would really be appreciated." Though other travel specialists disagree, we find this works better than asking directly for a room upgrade or something specific. Plus it leaves you some opportunity for tweaking after your room is assigned. For example, you might like the type of room assigned but would prefer a higher floor. Nothing's final yet, so he'll be happy to see if the same room type is available higher up. Sometimes the desk clerk will ask you what you're looking for. Have a reply ready and be reasonable.

Things he *might* have latitude to grant are room upgrades; rooms on floors with the best views; rooms situated out of earshot of traffic, ice machines, or elevators; amenities such as wine or fruit sent to your room; and coupons for the hotel bar or breakfast buffet. If you're hoping for a room upgrade at check-in, book a midvalue room or suite when you make your reservation so there's room to move up.

Remember, you're only risking $20, so temper your expectations and don't get in a huff if you're granted less than you'd hoped for. Be happy, friendly, and upbeat, addressing the clerk by name if he has a nametag. If you've patronized the hotel before, let it be known.

Before approaching the front desk, look for an upbeat person with obvious experience and seniority. Young unseasoned clerks are some-times confused if they haven't confronted the situation before. They also may be anxious about accepting the tip when a supervisor is around. In our experience, offering the $20 the way we describe in no way offends the clerk. He might return your $20, but he'll do so graciously and thank you for the overture.

Using the strategies above will almost always eliminate disappoint-ing surprises, as well as offer the best chances for upgrades and other enhancements.

BOOKING PACKAGES

MOST MALL OF AMERICA HOTELS offer hotel packages, as does the Bloomington Convention and Visitors Bureau (visit blooming tonmn.org). These packages are usually themed and may include shopping, parking (park and fly), American Girl, and Nickelodeon Universe. Familiar themes include seasonal (Halloween, Christmas, etc.); family; romantic; and girlfriend getaway.

My family has taken advantage of some of these packages, and if you plan it right, you can save money. The best packages obviously appeal to your personal preferences. In our experience, the family packages with Nickelodeon Universe all-day wristbands usually pay for themselves and cover the options most desirable for families. More often than not, a Mall of America shopping bag and coupon book accompany the package.

FREE BREAKFASTS

Having worked in the travel spectrum for a while, we understand how travelers appreciate complimentary hotel breakfasts. Embassy Suites has one of the best offerings, with an omelet station, waffles, and other fresh foods. We have stayed in our share of hotels offering hot breakfasts, and this is what we have learned: Regardless of the brand, when the hotel is busy the free breakfast dining room can be a zoo, and despite large seating areas it can be difficult to find a place to sit. If the free breakfast is important to you, hotel employees have told us that the earlier you arrive, the better. There is often a rush right before the buffet ends. Also, it's a nice gesture to tip the staff as a thank you for their hard work.

HOTEL PROFILES

AmericInn Bloomington East—Airport

1200 E. 78th St., Richfield, MN 55423; ☎ 612-869-8600; americinn.com

Rate per night $93. Shuttle Yes. **Valet parking** No. **Indoor pool** Yes. **Fitness center** Yes. **Pet friendly** No. **Wi-Fi** Yes. **Laundry** Yes. **Check in/out** 3 p.m./11 a.m. **Free breakfast** Yes.

THIS AMERICINN IS LOCATED only 1.3 miles from Mall of America, across I-494 at 12th Ave. in the suburb of Richfield. All guest rooms feature flat-panel TVs. A hot tub accompanies the indoor pool. Coffee drinkers appreciate the hotel's AmericInn Perk 24-Hour Coffee Bar.

AmericInn Bloomington West

4201 American Blvd. W., Minneapolis, MN 55437; ☎ 952-835-6643; americinn.com

Rate per night $123. Shuttle Yes. **Valet parking** No. **Indoor pool** Yes. **Fitness center** Yes. **Pet friendly** No. **Wi-Fi** Yes. **Laundry** No, but dry-cleaning service available. **Check in/out** 3 p.m./11 a.m. **Free breakfast** Yes.

Continued on page 40

Mall of America Accommodations

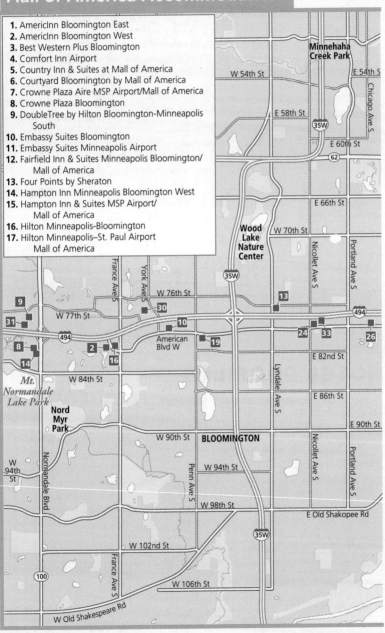

1. AmericInn Bloomington East
2. AmericInn Bloomington West
3. Best Western Plus Bloomington
4. Comfort Inn Airport
5. Country Inn & Suites at Mall of America
6. Courtyard Bloomington by Mall of America
7. Crowne Plaza Aire MSP Airport/Mall of America
8. Crowne Plaza Bloomington
9. DoubleTree by Hilton Bloomington-Minneapolis
   South
10. Embassy Suites Bloomington
11. Embassy Suites Minneapolis Airport
12. Fairfield Inn & Suites Minneapolis Bloomington/
    Mall of America
13. Four Points by Sheraton
14. Hampton Inn Minneapolis Bloomington West
15. Hampton Inn & Suites MSP Airport/
    Mall of America
16. Hilton Minneapolis-Bloomington
17. Hilton Minneapolis–St. Paul Airport
    Mall of America

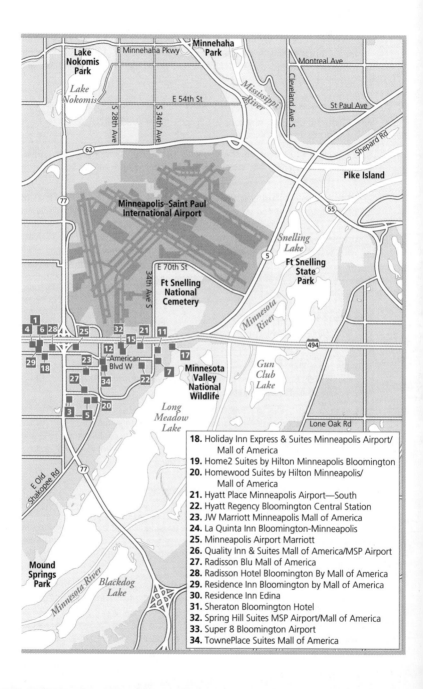

18. Holiday Inn Express & Suites Minneapolis Airport/
Mall of America
19. Home2 Suites by Hilton Minneapolis Bloomington
20. Homewood Suites by Hilton Minneapolis/
Mall of America
21. Hyatt Place Minneapolis Airport—South
22. Hyatt Regency Bloomington Central Station
23. JW Marriott Minneapolis Mall of America
24. La Quinta Inn Bloomington-Minneapolis
25. Minneapolis Airport Marriott
26. Quality Inn & Suites Mall of America/MSP Airport
27. Radisson Blu Mall of America
28. Radisson Hotel Bloomington By Mall of America
29. Residence Inn Bloomington by Mall of America
30. Residence Inn Edina
31. Sheraton Bloomington Hotel
32. Spring Hill Suites MSP Airport/Mall of America
33. Super 8 Bloomington Airport
34. TownePlace Suites Mall of America

Continued from page 37

THIS AMERICINN IS ABOUT 5 MILES from Mall of America and 2.5 miles from the Southdale Mall. A 24-hour Denny's is attached to the hotel. A recent makeover revealed updated furnishings, room decor, flat-panel TVs, and Serta Perfect Sleeper beds.

Best Western Plus Bloomington

1901 Killebrew Dr., Bloomington, MN 55425; ☎ 952-854-8200; bestwesternbloomington.com

Rate per night $209–$219. **Shuttle** Yes. **Valet parking** No. **Indoor pool** Yes. **Fitness center** Yes. **Pet friendly** No. **Wi-Fi** Yes. **Laundry** Yes. **Check in/out** 3 p.m./11 a.m. **Free breakfast** Yes.

LOCATED ACROSS THE STREET FROM MALL OF AMERICA, the western side of the hotel is situated on the off ramp of MN 77, although you can't access it from 77. Sometimes guests are concerned about traffic noise, but this ends up being a nonissue thanks to the hotel's soundproofing efforts. Families with young children will enjoy the pool area, which features a small slide, water buckets, and a mushroom-shaped water feature. RedRossa Italian Grill is a best-kept secret as a local hotel restaurant. The wood-fired Neapolitan pizzas are especially good.

Comfort Inn Airport

1321 E. 78th St., Bloomington, MN 55425; ☎ 952-854-3400; choicehotels.com/minnesota/bloomington/comfort-inn-hotels

Rate per night $129. **Shuttle** Yes. **Valet parking** No. **Indoor pool** Yes. **Fitness center** Yes. **Pet friendly** No. **Wi-Fi** Yes. **Laundry** No, but valet dry cleaning available. **Check in/out** 3 p.m./11 a.m. **Free breakfast** Yes.

LOCATED LESS THAN A MILE FROM MALL OF AMERICA, this Comfort Inn recently received a complete overhaul. Some rooms feature a microwave, refrigerator, and whirlpool tub. Long-term park-and-fly packages are available. Apart from the free breakfast, there isn't a hotel restaurant. However, an Outback Steakhouse, home to the Bloomin' Onion, is adjacent to the hotel.

Country Inn & Suites at Mall of America

2221 Killebrew Dr., Bloomington, MN 55425; ☎ 952-854-5555; countryinns.com

Rate per night $145–$166. **Shuttle** Yes. **Valet parking** No. **Indoor pool** Yes, 2 pools. **Fitness center** Yes. **Pet friendly** No, but they recommend boarding at Four Paws Pet Resort (fourpawsinc.com) only 5 miles from the hotel. **Wi-Fi** Yes. **Laundry** Yes. **Check in/out** 3 p.m./noon. **Free breakfast** Yes.

THIS COUNTRY INN & SUITES LOCATION has recently been beautifully renovated. Until the on-site Radisson Blu and JW Marriott came along, Country Inn & Suites was the closest hotel to Mall of America, and it's still the closest budget choice. IHOP is attached to the hotel, making for a nice breakfast alternative if you choose to bypass the free hotel breakfast. Ideal for groups.

OUR TOP 10 MOA HOTELS

1. RADISSON BLU   Attached to the mall; upscale amenities

2. JW MARRIOTT   Attached to the mall; upscale amenities

3. HYATT REGENCY BLOOMINGTON CENTRAL STATION   Upscale amenities

4. RADISSON HOTEL BLOOMINGTON   Ideal for families; Water Park of America is on-site

5. BEST WESTERN PLUS BLOOMINGTON   Ideal for families; kids love the water features at the pool

6. COUNTRY INN & SUITES   Newly renovated; short walk to MOA

7. MINNEAPOLIS AIRPORT MARRIOTT   Nice amenities; close to MOA

8. HOMEWOOD SUITES   Nice family amenities; short walk to MOA

9. TOWNEPLACE SUITES MALL OF AMERICA   New hotel; short walk to MOA

10. HYATT PLACE   Newly renovated, spacious rooms, and close to MOA

This location has earned the Sports Approved status with Carlson Rezidor Hotel Group for working successfully with sports groups.

Courtyard Bloomington by Mall of America

7800 Bloomington Ave. S., Bloomington, MN 55425; ☎ 952-876-0100; marriott.com

Rate per night $156. **Shuttle** Yes. **Valet parking** No. **Indoor Pool** Yes. **Fitness center** Yes. **Pet friendly** Yes. **Wi-Fi** Yes. **Laundry** Yes. **Check in/out** 3 p.m./noon. **Free breakfast** Yes.

A NICE PERK HERE DURING THE FRIGID WINTER MONTHS is heated underground parking for $10 per night. Jake's full-service restaurant and bar provides breakfast daily, lunch (Monday–Friday), dinner (Monday–Saturday), and room service. Plus, a 24-hour market offers sandwiches, snacks, and beverages, so you can always grab a bite after a long day at the mall.

Crowne Plaza Aire MSP Airport/MOA

3 Appletree Square, Bloomington, MN 55425; ☎ 952-854-9000; crowneplaza.com

Rate per night $150. **Shuttle** Yes. **Valet parking** Yes. **Indoor pool** Yes. **Fitness center** Yes. **Pet friendly** Service animals only. **Wi-Fi** Yes. **Check in/out** 3 p.m./noon. **Free breakfast** No.

CROWNE PLAZA AIRE (formerly Crowne Plaza Hotel) is located east of Mall of America, adjacent to the light rail, nearly bordering the Minnesota Valley National Wildlife Refuge, which is a great place to enjoy hiking and birdwatching. The hotel recently completed an aviation-themed renovation. On-site dining is available at Martel's Restaurant and Lounge and Caribou Coffee Kiosk; both serve breakfast, lunch, and dinner.

Crowne Plaza Bloomington

5401 Green Valley Dr., Bloomington, MN 55437; ☎ 952-831-8000;
crowneplaza.com

Rate per night $132. **Shuttle** Yes. **Valet parking** No. **Indoor pool** Yes. **Fitness center**
Yes. **Pet friendly** No. **Wi-Fi** Yes. **Laundry** Valet only. **Check in/out** 3 p.m./noon. **Free
breakfast** No.

THIS CROWNE PLAZA is a little less than 7 miles from Mall of America. Recent
renovations include a Junior Olympic–size indoor pool, fitness center, and hot
tub. The on-site North Dining Room is open for breakfast, lunch, and dinner
and offers an extensive menu. North Lounge is a nice place to relax and offers
happy-hour specials daily, 4–6 p.m. The free shuttle runs to the airport and
MOA 5 a.m.–11:30 p.m. Complimentary coffee is offered in the lobby.

DoubleTree by Hilton Bloomington-Minneapolis South

7800 Normandale Blvd., Minneapolis, MN 55439; ☎ 952-835-7800;
doubletree3.hilton.com

Rate per night $179. **Shuttle** Yes. **Valet parking** Yes. **Indoor pool** Yes. **Fitness center**
Yes. **Pet friendly** Yes. **Wi-Fi** Yes. **Laundry** Yes and valet service. **Check in/out** 3
p.m./noon. **Free breakfast** No.

ARRIVAL GREETING INCLUDES DoubleTree's signature warm chocolate chip
cookie. The on-site Crescent Kitchen has a farm-to-table concept with
weekly seasonal chef specials. Crescent Kitchen Bar features 16 craft beer
selections on tap and more than 80 small-batch bourbons and scotches.
Happy hour features specials on tap, rail/well drinks, and wine daily, 4–7 p.m.
This location is a short drive west on I-494 and is very popular as a conference location. While the guest rooms may be on the verge of an update
soon, there are various room and suites options, including pool-side balcony
rooms, whirlpool tub suites, and a presidential suite with a king bed.

Embassy Suites Bloomington

2800 American Blvd. W., Bloomington, MN 55431; ☎ 952-884-4811;
embassysuites3.hilton.com

Rate per night $159. **Shuttle** Yes. **Valet parking** No. **Indoor pool** Yes. **Fitness center**
Yes. **Pet friendly** Service animals only. **Wi-Fi** Free standard Wi-Fi. **Laundry** Coin laundry and valet service. **Check in/out** 4 p.m./noon. **Free breakfast** Yes—made to order.

LOCATED ABOUT 5 MILES from Mall of America, this Embassy Suites recently
underwent a renovation, with noticeable atrium and breakfast-area updates.
We are big fans of Embassy Suites. These aren't the least-expensive hotels,
but the evening receptions (free happy hour, but tip your bartenders) and
made-to-order breakfasts (the earlier you arrive the better) are top-notch.

Embassy Suites Minneapolis Airport

7901 34th Ave. S., Bloomington, MN 55425; ☎ 952-854-1000;
embassysuites3.hilton.com

Rate per night $179. Shuttle Yes. Valet parking No. Indoor pool Yes. Fitness center Yes. Pet friendly Service animals only. Wi-Fi Free standard Wi-Fi. Laundry Coin laundry and valet service. Check in/out 4 p.m./11 a.m. Free breakfast Yes—made to order.

THIS EMBASSY SUITES IS LOCATED only 1.5 miles from Mall of America on 34th Ave. South, near the Hiawatha light rail. Three on-site restaurants—Corner Bar, Caribou Coffee Bar, and Woolley's Steakhouse—offer plenty of dining options. Evening reception includes a free happy hour with snacks.

Fairfield Inn & Suites Minneapolis Bloomington

2401 American Blvd. E., Bloomington, MN 55425; ☎ 952-858-8475; marriott.com

Rate per night $129–$149. Shuttle Yes. Valet parking No. Indoor pool Yes. Fitness center Yes. Pet friendly No. Wi-Fi Yes. Laundry Yes. Check in/out 3 p.m./noon. Free breakfast Yes.

LESS THAN A HALF MILE from Mall of America, this hotel is an easy walk to the mall, but expect to cross the busy 24th Avenue at Lindau Lane. In 2016 it received an updated, contemporary new look and added fridges in all guest rooms. Connecting rooms are not available.

Four Points by Sheraton

7745 Lyndale Ave. S., Richfield, MN 55423; ☎ 612-861-1000; fourpointsminneapolisairport.com

Rate per night $156. Shuttle Yes. Valet parking No. Indoor pool Yes. Fitness center Yes. Pet friendly Yes. Wi-Fi Yes. Laundry Valet service. Check in/out 3 p.m./noon. Free breakfast No.

LOCATED ON THE NORTH SIDE of I-494 in Richfield, about 3 miles from MOA, this property offers the Four Points Best Brews Program, a selection of beers on tap often locally sourced. The on-site restaurant, Lyndale Smokehouse, features American barbecue and Mediterranean fare. Room service is available.

Hampton Inn Minneapolis Bloomington West

5400 American Blvd. W., Bloomington, MN 55437; ☎ 952-905-2950; hamptoninn3.hilton.com

Rate per night $149. Shuttle Yes. Valet parking No. Indoor pool Yes. Fitness center Yes. Pet friendly Yes. Wi-Fi Yes. Laundry Yes. Check in/out 3 p.m./noon. Free breakfast Yes.

LOCATED 8 MILES from Mall of America at I-494 and Normandale Blvd., this new location offers all of the perks that usually accompany a Hampton Inn stay.

Hampton Inn & Suites MSP Airport/Mall of America

2860 Metro Dr., Bloomington, MN 55425; ☎ 952-854-7600; hamptoninn3.hilton.com

Rate per night $189. Shuttle Yes. Valet parking No. Indoor pool Yes. Fitness center Yes. Pet friendly Service animals only. Wi-Fi Yes. Laundry Coin laundry and valet service. Check in/out 3 p.m./noon. Free breakfast Yes.

THIS HAMPTON INN & SUITES LOCATION was updated in 2014 with modern furnishings and decor. A 24-hour Pavilion Pantry Market and complimentary beverage area are nice touches. The spacious suites, featuring two queen beds, a sofa bed, and a wet bar, are comfortable for families.

Hilton Minneapolis-Bloomington

3900 American Blvd. W., Bloomington, MN 55437; ☎ 952-893-9500; hilton.com

Rate per night $149. Shuttle Yes. Valet parking No. Indoor pool Yes. Fitness center Yes. Pet friendly Yes, with $50 nonrefundable deposit; 2 pets maximum; 50-pound limit. Wi-Fi Yes. Laundry Yes. Check in/out 3 p.m./noon. Free breakfast No (unless included with a package).

ON-SITE BLOOMINGTON CHOPHOUSE RESTAURANT is noted for its delicious steaks. The Olive Lounge, located right off the lobby, offers American fare for breakfast, lunch, and dinner and is open late for cocktails and appetizers (until midnight Monday–Thursday and 1 a.m. Friday and Saturday).

Hilton Minneapolis–Saint Paul Airport Mall of America

3800 American Blvd. E., Bloomington, MN 55425; ☎ 952-854-2100; hilton.com

Rate per night $129. Shuttle Yes. Valet parking No. Indoor pool Yes. Fitness center Yes. Pet friendly Yes, with nonrefundable $50 deposit. Wi-Fi Yes; complimentary for all Hilton Honors members. Laundry No. Check in/out 4 p.m./11 a.m. Free breakfast No.

THIS HILTON HAS BEEN NEWLY RENOVATED and appeals to both Mall of America visitors and business travelers. Nature lovers will appreciate this hotel's location, as it sits directly across the street from the Minnesota Valley National Wildlife Refuge Visitor Center. Another perk is on-site covered parking. A park-and-fly option is available for air travelers. On-site restaurant Blue Water Grill has been recognized as one of the top seafood restaurants in the Twin Cities. In addition to dinner, breakfast options include buffet or menu items, while lunch offerings include soups, salads, sandwiches, and wraps.

Holiday Inn Express Minneapolis Airport/Mall of America

1601 American Blvd. E., Bloomington, MN 55425; ☎ 952-854-1687; ihg.com/holidayinnexpress

Rate per night $144. Shuttle Yes. Valet parking No. Indoor pool Yes. Fitness center Yes. Pet friendly No. Wi-Fi Yes. Laundry Coin and same-day dry cleaning. Check in/out 4 p.m./11 a.m. Free breakfast Yes.

THIS HOLIDAY INN EXPRESS & SUITES recently received a head-to-toe renovation that includes a new bar, restaurant, and lobby. At press time, half of the guest rooms had been completely revamped with new beds, carpet, paint, and more. Be sure to ask for a renovated room when you book your reservation.

Home2 Suites by Hilton

2270 W. 80-1/2 St., Bloomington, MN 55431; ☎ 952-888-2282; home2suites3.hilton.com

Rate per night $159. **Shuttle** Yes. **Valet parking** No. **Indoor pool** Yes, saline. **Fitness center** Yes. **Pet friendly** Yes, with $100 nonrefundable deposit; 50-pound limit. **Wi-Fi** Yes. **Laundry** Yes. **Check in/out** 3 p.m./noon. **Free breakfast** Yes.

THIS HOME2 SUITES BY HILTON is the first of its type in the Twin Cities area. Located 5.2 miles from Mall of America, it's worth the drive being brand new. One big perk: complimentary breakfast at the Inspired Table, serving waffles, warm artisan sandwiches, and more. Work out while you wash with the cool Spin2 Cycle laundry and fitness room combo.

Homewood Suites by Hilton

2261 Killebrew Dr., Bloomington, MN 55425; ☎ 952-854-0900; homewoodsuites3.hilton.com

Rate per night $199. **Shuttle** Yes. **Valet parking** No. **Indoor pool** Yes. **Fitness center** Yes. **Pet friendly** Yes, with $100 nonrefundable deposit; 50-pound limit. **Wi-Fi** Yes. **Laundry** Yes. **Check in/out** 3 p.m./noon. **Free breakfast** Yes.

FIND TRADITIONAL ONE- AND TWO-BEDROOM SUITES with kitchens and dining tables. Homewood Suites is one of the few hotels accessible via the pedestrian bridge crossing Killebrew Drive. Chevys Mexican restaurant is located directly in front of the hotel, and IHOP and TGI Fridays are just a short walk across the parking lot.

Hyatt Place Minneapolis Airport—South

7800 International Dr., Bloomington, MN 55425; ☎ 952-854-0700; minneapolisairport.place.hyatt.com

Rate per night $166. **Shuttle** Yes. **Valet parking** No. **Indoor pool** Yes. **Fitness center** Yes. **Pet friendly** Yes, $75 nonrefundable deposit. **Wi-Fi** Yes. **Laundry** Laundry and dry-cleaning services. **Check in/out** 3 p.m./noon. **Free breakfast** Yes.

WE HAVE YET TO MEET A HYATT PLACE hotel we didn't like between the free breakfasts at the Kitchen Skillet (with breakfast sandwiches) and the spacious, divided suites. A beer, wine, and coffee bar (serving Starbucks espresso roast) is in the lobby. The on-site Gallery Menu offers 24/7 service of burgers, sandwiches, and appetizers. This Hyatt Place was recently remodeled with new furniture, carpet, and more, so expect a fresh look when you go.

Hyatt Regency Bloomington Central Station

3200 E. 81st St., Bloomington, MN, 55425; ☎ 952-922-1234; bloomington.regency.hyatt.com

Rate per night $219. **Shuttle** Yes. **Valet parking** Yes. **Indoor pool** Yes. **Fitness center** Yes. **Pet friendly** Service animals only. **Wi-Fi** Yes. **Laundry** Laundry and dry-cleaning services. **Check in/out** 3 p.m./noon. **Free breakfast** No.

BLOOMINGTON CENTRAL STATION is a transit-oriented, mixed-use urban village and home to this brand-new (opened 2016) Hyatt Regency. Located near the Metro Blue (Hiawatha) Line, guests can take a bus and transfer from the light rail to the Minneapolis–Saint Paul Airport or Mall of America. However, we recommend sticking with the free hotel shuttle. Guests have three dining options: Urbana Craeft Kitchen serves locally sourced breakfast, lunch, and dinner. Bar Urbana has local tap microbrews, cocktails, wine, and light fare and burgers. The Market provides easy grab-and-go snacks and sandwiches.

JW Marriott Minneapolis Mall of America

2141 Lindau Lane, Bloomington, MN; ☎ 612-615-0100; marriott.com

Rate per night $172. **Shuttle** Yes, to airport. **Valet parking** Yes, $25/day. **Indoor pool** Yes. **Fitness center** Yes. **Pet friendly** No. **Wi-Fi** Yes, complimentary in lobby and public areas but $11.95–$14.95/day in guest rooms. **Laundry** Valet dry cleaning only. **Check in/out** 3 p.m./noon. **Free breakfast** No.

JW MARRIOTT, KNOWN FOR ITS LUXURY HOTELS in premier destinations, found Mall of America worthy of hosting the first property in the state of Minnesota. The hotel offers direct access to MOA. The 321 rooms and 21 suites are situated on 15 floors. A French-American restaurant with an outdoor patio, bar, fitness center, pool, executive lounge, and underground parking round out the hotel amenities. The JW Marriott entrance is located on the east side. When entering from MOA you must walk through the main restaurant located near the MOA Front Door entrance on the north side.

La Quinta Inn Bloomington-Minneapolis

7815 Nicollet Ave. S., Bloomington, MN 55420; ☎ 952-881-7311; lq.com

Rate per night $72. **Shuttle** Yes. **Valet parking** No. **Indoor pool** No. **Fitness center** Yes. **Pet friendly** Yes. **Wi-Fi** Yes. **Laundry** Yes. **Check in/out** 3 p.m./noon. **Free breakfast** Yes.

ONLY 2 MILES FROM MALL OF AMERICA and situated next to Culver's fast-food restaurant, this La Quinta is a good choice for budget-conscious families. All rooms are accessible indoors and feature pillow-top mattresses.

Minneapolis Airport Marriott

2020 American Blvd. E., Bloomington, MN 55425; ☎ 952-854-7441; marriott.com

Rate per night $230. **Shuttle** Yes. **Valet parking** No. **Indoor pool** No. **Fitness center** Yes. **Pet friendly** No. **Wi-Fi** Yes. **Laundry** Yes. **Check in/out** 4 p.m./11 a.m. **Free breakfast** No.

THIS MARRIOTT HAS ALL OF THE NICETIES expected from the brand: bathrobes, water in the room, and newspapers in the lobby. The on-site Bistro 79 is open for breakfast, lunch, and dinner. The hotel is within walking distance of the mall, but we recommend taking the hotel shuttle during inclement weather or when you have arms full of shopping bags.

Mystic Lake Casino Hotel

2400 Mystic Lake Blvd., Prior Lake, MN 55372; ☎ 952-445-9000; mysticlake.com

Rate per night $189. **Shuttle** Yes. **Valet parking** Yes. **Indoor pool** Yes. **Fitness center** Guest pass to Dakotah Sport and Fitness Center. **Pet friendly** No. **Wi-Fi** Yes. **Laundry** Laundry and dry-cleaning services. **Check in/out** 3 p.m./11 a.m. **Free breakfast** No.

AS THE LARGEST CASINO RESORT IN THE AREA, Mystic Lake Casino is a destination in itself, with a spa, championship golf course, shows, a state-of-the-art bingo hall, 100 Blackjack tables, and more than 4,000 slot machines. Mystic Casino has 12 restaurants and bars on-site, including a buffet. The hotel has 586 rooms, and by the end of 2016, all rooms will be updated with new carpeting, wall coverings, bathroom tile and fixtures, furniture, and bedding. New in-room amenities will include Keurig coffee makers, refrigerators, and 49-inch HDTVs. Depending upon the time of day and traffic, Mystic Casino is 20–30 minutes away from Mall of America. Regularly scheduled shuttles pick up and drop off at MOA and the nearby Twin Cities Premium Outlets in Eagan (a few minutes south of MOA).

Quality Inn & Suites

814 American Blvd. E., Bloomington, MN 55420; ☎ 952-854-5558; choicehotels.com

Rate per night $115. **Shuttle** Yes. **Valet parking** No. **Indoor pool** Yes. **Fitness center** Yes. **Pet friendly** No. **Wi-Fi** Yes. **Laundry** Valet service only. **Check in/out** 3 p.m./11 a.m. **Free breakfast** Yes.

THIS DECENT BUDGET HOTEL is only a mile and a half from Mall of America. Some rooms have balconies, which can be a nice plus in warm weather. Free newspapers are provided on weekdays. The breakfast area and front lobby were recently renovated, and rumor has it that more updates are in the works.

Radisson Blu Mall of America

2100 Killebrew Dr., Bloomington, MN 55425; ☎ 952-881-5258; radissonblu.com

Rate per night $160–$207. **Shuttle** Yes. **Valet parking** Yes. **Indoor pool** Yes. **Fitness center** Yes. **Pet friendly** Yes. **Wi-Fi** Yes. **Laundry** 3-hour express service available for a fee. **Check in/out** 3 p.m./11 a.m. **Free breakfast** No.

RADISSON BLU IS LOCATED on the southern side of Mall of America and was the first hotel connected to the mall. Access to the hotel is easy from Level 2 of the mall. The hotel makes a good first impression with a luxurious lobby and a swanky open meeting space decorated with whimsical chairs and artwork. The on-site FireLake Grill is one of the most exquisite restaurants in the mall, with creative farm-to-table American cuisine and a more informal cocktail bar. Families will want to opt for the Family Fun Package with Marty the Moose, which includes passport activities to engage the children.

Radisson Hotel Bloomington by Mall of America (Water Park of America)

1700 E. American Blvd., Bloomington, MN 55425; ☎ 952-854-8700; radisson.com

Rate per night $159–$175. **Shuttle** Yes. **Valet parking** No. **Indoor pool** Paid-entry water park. **Fitness center** Yes. **Pet friendly** No. **Wi-Fi** Yes. **Laundry** Yes. **Check in/out** 4 p.m./11 a.m. **Free breakfast** No.

NOTE: SOME VISITORS (WHO HAVEN'T DONE THEIR HOMEWORK) think this hotel is inside or part of Mall of America. It isn't. The upscale Radisson Blu (see above) is attached to Mall of America. However, this Radisson is a little more affordable, and it is less than 2 miles from MOA; we highly recommend this location. This hotel's claim to fame is being home to Water Park of America, where it's always a balmy 85 degrees. Some rooms are equipped with bunk bed coves holding one to two bunk beds (four stacked twin beds), so families with more than two kids will be comfortable here. If the water park is on your agenda for an entire day, you don't have to leave the building.

We suggest you visit the Radisson Hotel Bloomington deals page for hotel-water park combo packages: waterparkofamerica.com/radisson-bloomington-hotel-deals.

Water Park of America has body and tube slides; a lazy river; the Lake Superior wave pool; activity pools with hoops, nets, and balancing logs; a Flow Ride Simulator; a 10-story-tall raft ride that travels more than a mile; and two restaurants and a café. Hotel guests can opt for a paid package admission and access the water between 9 and 11 a.m., before the public. The 5,800-square-foot Northern Lights Arcade is located between the hotel lobby and Water Park of America and has more than 100 games. Players can earn credits and win prizes. For more information on Water Park of America, see pages 5–6 in our Introduction.

Residence Inn Bloomington by Mall of America

7850 Bloomington Ave. S., Bloomington, MN 55425; ☎ 952-876-0900; marriott.com

Rate per night $159. **Shuttle** Yes. **Valet parking** No. **Indoor pool** Yes. **Fitness center** Yes. **Pet friendly** Yes. **Wi-Fi** Yes. **Laundry** Yes. **Check in/out** 3 p.m./noon. **Free breakfast** Yes.

THIS RESIDENCE INN IS HIGHLY REGARDED as a nice extended-stay hotel with studio, one-bedroom, and two-bedroom suite options. Suites include a full-size refrigerator, microwave, dishwasher, cookware, and dinnerware. All suites have been recently renovated and include new pillow-top mattresses, triple sheeting, and plush pillows. If you'd like to save money by cooking and dining in during your trip, this property is a great option.

Residence Inn Edina

3400 Edinborough Way, Edina, MN 55435; ☎ 952-893-9300 marriott.com

Rate per night $139–$149. **Shuttle** Yes. **Valet parking** No. **Indoor pool** Yes. **Fitness center** Yes. **Pet friendly** Yes, with $75 nonrefundable deposit. **Wi-Fi** Yes. **Laundry** Yes. **Check in/out** 3 p.m./noon. **Free breakfast** Yes.

LOCATED ABOUT 5 MILES FROM MALL OF AMERICA, this Residence Inn location is adjacent to the Edinborough Park, an indoor rec center with a two-story kid's playground and tot area ($7.50/child), swimming pool, running track, and fitness area. Hertz rental-car service has an office on-site. The hotel's studio, one-, and two-bedroom suites are equipped with full kitchens.

Sheraton Bloomington Hotel

5601 W. 78th St., Minneapolis, MN 55439; ☎ 952-835-1900; sheratonbloomingtonhotel.com

Rate per night $119. **Shuttle** Yes. **Valet parking** No. **Indoor pool** No. **Fitness center** Yes. **Pet friendly** Yes. **Wi-Fi** Free for SPG members or $9.95/day. **Laundry** No. **Check in/out** 3 p.m./noon. **Free breakfast** No.

LOCATED ABOUT 7 MILES FROM MALL OF AMERICA, this Sheraton's recent $15-million renovation includes new guest rooms, a fitness center, interactive meeting space, an updated lobby, and a new restaurant. This hotel had a pool before the renovation, but it was not included in the update. The Sheraton caters primarily to business travelers but still sees MOA guests.

Springhill Suites

2870 Metro Dr., Bloomington, MN 55425; ☎ 952-854-0300; springhillsuites.marriott.com

Rate per night $149–$169. **Shuttle** Yes. **Valet parking** No, but $15/day covered self-parking available. **Indoor pool** Yes. **Fitness center** Yes. **Pet friendly** Service animals only. **Wi-Fi** Yes. **Laundry** Yes. **Check in/out** 3 p.m./noon. **Free breakfast** Yes.

LOCATED LESS THAN A MILE FROM MALL OF AMERICA, Springhill Suites is a convenient and nice suite option. The two-bedroom suites have pullout sofas. The partially separated living and sleeping areas work well for families. Suite features include flat-panel TVs, mini-fridges, microwaves, and coffeemakers.

Super 8 Bloomington Airport

7800 2nd Ave. S., Bloomington, MN 55420; ☎ 952-888-8800; super8.com

Rate per night $81. **Shuttle** Yes. **Valet parking** No. **Indoor pool** No. **Fitness center** Yes. **Pet friendly** Yes; maximum 2 pets; $15 plus tax per pet per day. **Wi-Fi** Yes. **Laundry** Yes. **Check in/out** 2 p.m./11 a.m. **Free breakfast** Yes.

THIS SUPER 8 IS LOCATED right off I-494 (Nicolette Exit) and is less than 2 miles from Mall of America. There isn't a pool, but guests can enjoy a hot tub and sauna. Air travelers can print their free boarding pass in the business center.

TownePlace Suites Mall of America

2500 Lindau Lane, Bloomington, MN 55425; ☎ 952-540-4000; marriott.com

Rate per night $179–$209. **Shuttle** Yes. **Valet parking** No. **Indoor pool** Yes. **Fitness center** Yes. **Pet friendly** Yes. **Wi-Fi** Yes. **Laundry** Yes. **Check in/out** 4 p.m./noon. **Free breakfast** Yes.

THIS NEW $15 MILLION PROPERTY opened in July 2015. It is an extended-stay hotel with 118 rooms. Studio options include a king or two queens with sofa bed; one-bedroom suites also have sofa beds. Amenities include typical extended-stay options of fully equipped kitchens, free breakfast, high-speed Internet, and a convenience store near the front desk.

TownePlace Suites MSP Airport

3615 Crestridge Dr., Eagan, MN 55122; ☎ 651-994-4600; marriott.com

Rate per night $134. **Shuttle** Yes. **Valet parking** No. **Indoor pool** No, but there is an outdoor pool. **Fitness center** Yes. **Pet friendly** Yes. **Wi-Fi** Yes. **Laundry** Yes and valet dry cleaning. **Check in/out** 3 p.m./noon. **Free breakfast** Yes.

THIS MARRIOTT PROPERTY is in the nearby suburb of Eagan. The area has several restaurants, including Wendy's and Chili's, and across the main street is Pilot Knob, a shopping center with more food and shopping, including a Walmart. This hotel offers a park-and-fly option for Minneapolis–Saint Paul International Airport. It's a nice extended-stay option with kitchenettes.

COMING IN 2016

THE $25-MILLION AC HOTEL BY MARRIOTT will be finished by the end of 2016. Located at Lindau Lane and 24th Ave. South, the 148-room, five-story upscale AC Marriott MOA will have a parking garage, a restaurant, and a coffee shop.

COMING IN 2017

A 160-ROOM CAMBRIA HOTEL & SUITES is planned for the intersection of 28th Ave. South and American Blvd.

RV CAMPING

RVERS HOPING TO SET UP CAMP in a Mall of America parking lot are out of luck. First, all oversize vehicles must park in the Lindau Lot, north of MOA, off Lindau Lane. Second, there is no overnight parking at MOA in any lot. Vehicles will be towed. Call MOA security at ☎ 952-883-8888 for more information. The good news is there are several campgrounds in the area.

Dakotah Meadows RV Park

2341 Park Place, Prior Lake, MN 55372; ☎ 952-445-8800; dakotahmeadows.com

---

Camping season Year-round (**water** is turned off during winter). **Rates** Off-season: $29/night, $141/week; peak season: $39/night, $211/week. **RV space** Yes. **Tent space** Yes. **Sanitary dump station** Yes. **Water** Yes (turned off in winter). **Electric** Yes. **Camp store** Yes. **Laundry** Yes. **Restrooms** Yes. **Showers** Yes. **Children's play area** Yes. **Pool** No. **Wi-Fi** Yes. **Check in/out** 2 p.m./noon.

WE CONSIDER DAKOTAH MEADOWS Campground (at Prior Lake) an upscale campground with gorgeous facilities. It's loaded with amenities, including an RV wash, weather shelter, and on-site store. A shuttle runs from the campground to the nearby Mystic Lake Casino Hotel, but the big draw for us is that there is a shuttle running round-trip between Mystic Lake and Mall of America for guests ages 18 and over with either a Club Mystic Card, valid driver's license, or valid state ID. RVers without another form of transportation will certainly want to consider this campground. In addition, Tipis are available for $25/night.

Fish Lake Acres Campground

3000 210th St. E., Prior Lake, MN 55372; ☎ 952-492-3393;
flac.bcpnet.net/FLAC.htm

Camping season May–mid-October. **Rates** $24–$28/night, $144–$168/week. **RV space** Yes. **Tent space** Yes. **Sanitary dump station** Yes. **Water** Yes. **Electric** Yes. **Camp store** Yes. **Laundry** No. **Restrooms** Yes. **Showers** Yes. **Children's play area** Yes. **Pool** Yes. **Wi-Fi** No. **Check in/out** Before gates close at 10 p.m./noon.

FISH LAKE ACRES CAMPGROUND (at Prior Lake) is on the rustic side, meaning you won't find a lot of amenities and the buildings are dated. However, we were impressed with the pretty half mile of lakeshore, and there are plenty of trees for shade. We noticed a cement boat launch and a sandy beach where families were playing. You should arrive loaded with everything you need because there is not a store on-site. Fish Lake has 93 sites with water and electricity and 50 basic sites, so you shouldn't have any trouble finding a site. Some online reports indicate that noise can be a problem between guests getting rowdy in the wee hours and the neighboring gun range.

Lebanon Hills Regional Park Campground

12100 Johnny Cake Ridge Road, Apple Valley, MN 55124; ☎ 651-480-7773;
www.co.dakota.mn.us/parks/parksTrails/LebanonHills/Pages/lebanon-hills-campground.aspx

Camping season late April–early October (dates vary by year). **Rates** Tent sites $20, pull-through $37, full hookup $31, **electric** only $25; $8 nonrefundable reservation fee per site. **RV space** Yes. **Tent space** Yes. **Sanitary dump station** Yes ($8). **Water** Yes (turned off when temperatures drop below freezing). **Electric** Yes. **Camp store** Yes. **Laundry** Yes. **Restrooms** Yes. **Showers** Yes. **Children's play area** Yes. **Pool** No. **Wi-Fi** Yes, available in West Camping Loop only. **Check in/out** 1 p.m./noon.

CAMPERS LOOKING FOR A "REAL" OUTDOORSY, woodsy experience will absolutely want to check out Lebanon Hills Campground. This 2,000-acre regional park has miles of trails and lakes. Outdoor rental equipment is available at the main visitor center off Cliff Road. The campground is a favorite because it is well kept. Camping reservations must be made 7–365 days in advance; no same-day reservations. Fridays and summer holidays require a 2–3-night minimum stay, and there's a 14-day maximum stay within a 30-day period.

Minneapolis Southwest KOA

3315 W. 166th St., Jordan, MN 55352; ☎ 952-492-6440;
koa.com/campgrounds/minneapolis-southwest

Camping season May 1–October 11. **Rates** Vary depending upon space/time of year: tent site $27, RV site $35, cabins $55. **RV space** Yes. **Tent space** Yes. **Sanitary dump station** Yes. **Water** Yes. **Electric** Yes. **Camp store** Yes. **Laundry** No. **Restrooms** Yes. **Showers** Yes. **Children's play area** Yes. **Pool** Yes. **Wi-Fi** Yes. **Check in/out** 2 p.m./noon.

IN OUR OPINION, you can never go wrong with a KOA Kampground. And yes, KOA fans will be happy to know there is a location in the Twin Cities, about 30 minutes from Mall of America. It's not located in the MOA parking lot, but it might just be worth the drive. Besides all of the typical KOA camping options of tent sites, RV sites (90-foot max length), and air-conditioned cabin rentals, the campground also features an indoor pool and free Wi-Fi. Mini-golf and bike rentals are available for a fee. What makes this campground special are the Saturday night hay rides.

Town and Country Campground

12630 Boone Ave., Savage, MN 55378; ☎ 952-445-1756; townandcountrycampground.com

Camping season Year-round. **Rates** Basic tent site $30, **electric** and **water** $40, full hookup $44; **rates** may increase on holiday weekends. **RV space** Yes. **Tent space** Yes. **Sanitary dump station** Yes. **Water** Yes. **Electric** Yes. **Camp store** Yes. **Laundry** Yes. **Restrooms** Yes. **Showers** Yes. **Children's play area** Yes. **Pool** Yes and hot tub. **Wi-Fi** Yes. **Check in/out** 2 p.m./11 a.m.

TOWN AND COUNTRY CAMPGROUND is a favorite with families. When we visited, kids were happily splashing in the pool and playing on the playground. Kids also enjoy the newly remodeled game room. Grounds are clean, well-kept, and organized. Pets are allowed with 3 dogs max per site and a fee of $1 per day per dog. Campers can choose among 48 full hookup sites, 35 electric and water sites, and 16 tent sites.

PART THREE

ARRIVING *and* GETTING ORIENTED

▌ GETTING THERE

MALL OF AMERICA (MOA) is probably one of the most accessible suburban malls in the United States as far as modes of transportation are concerned. Besides being located off a major Minnesota highway (MN 77), the Metro Blue Line light rail shoots down from Minneapolis and stops at the Minneapolis–Saint Paul International Airport, then continues on to MOA. This explains why you will see shoppers hauling their rolling luggage around the mall. Often, these people are on a long enough layover to spend some time at the mall. After a bout of shopping, back to the light rail they go to catch their flights.

Getting to MOA is a breeze: The Twin Cities have a nice public transit system (visit metrotransit.org), taxis are a phone call away, and Uber and Lyft drivers are a tap away. If you are staying at a local hotel, free shuttle service should be available to MOA and the Minneapolis–Saint Paul International Airport. A handful of hotels are within walking distance of the mall, and two luxury hotels, JW Marriott and Radisson Blu, are attached to the mall. While you can't reach the mall by boat, Saint Paul is a port city for American Cruise Lines' *Queen of the Mississippi,* and Viking River Cruises intends to make Saint Paul an official port city and run from there to New Orleans by the end of 2017.

ARRIVING BY PLANE

MINNEAPOLIS–SAINT PAUL INTERNATIONAL AIRPORT (MSP) is the largest airport in Minnesota and serves roughly 155 nonstop markets, including 126 domestic and 29 international markets. In 2015, the airport saw more than 36 million passengers. MSP has two terminals: Terminal 1–Lindbergh (2.8 million square feet) and the much smaller Terminal 2–Humphrey (595,699 square feet).

MSP is the hub airport for Sun Country Airlines, Delta Air Lines, and Delta Connections Compass Airlines and Endeavor Air. Sun Country runs scheduled and charter services and serves Terminal 2–Humphrey to destinations in the United States, Mexico, Caribbean, and Costa Rica. It often has fares that beat out competition. To give you an idea, we did a search for September rates. Usually fall is considered off-season in the tourism industry because kids are back in school. We plugged in a round-trip flight from Dallas. Rates on Sun Country were $84 one-way, or $166 round-trip. Delta also has a hub in Minnesota, so we plugged in the same days and found one-way fare to be $267, making a round-trip $534. As you can see, there is no comparison. Here's the caveat: Sun Country is a Minnesota hometown airline, and most locals don't leave here in the summer. Why would they? The weather is nice and everyone seems to own a cabin somewhere in the state or across the St. Croix River in Wisconsin. Therefore, you may not find Sun Country flights during the summer. Regardless, it's worth comparing fares.

Despite the severe winter, MSP has it under control and is efficient at handling storms of any sort. It's rare for the airport to close. However, de-icing is common in the winter, and occasionally planes can pile up for their turn at being sprayed, so you may encounter delays.

When it's time to go home, as with any airport, we recommend arriving 2 hours before departure. Morning and weekend security lines can get long. Sometimes airlines will change not only gates but also terminals, instigating a long walk. For more information on MSP, visit mspairport.com.

Getting to Mall of America from the Airport

LIGHT RAIL Metro Transit offers free light-rail service between the airport terminals, as well as access to 17 destinations with a paid fare. Fare from MSP to MOA is $1.75–$2.25, depending on time of day. Ticket machines are located at the rail stations. Tram Level is located on the level below baggage claim and can be reached via escalator, elevator, or stairs. Follow the signs to the tram and hop aboard to the Transit Center. Signs to the light-rail stations are well marked. The Terminal 1–Lindbergh light-rail station is located between the Blue and Red parking ramps below the Transit Center. The Terminal 2–Humphrey light-rail station is situated on the north side of the Orange parking ramp, which can be reached via the skyway. Simply take the elevator or escalator from the Level 1 ticket counters to the Orange ramp skyway. Again, signs for the light rail are well marked. Once in the station, take the escalators or elevators down one level to the station platform. You can wait indoors, but if you are departing, and it's early in the morning, expect a large crowd of employees and flight crews heading to work. During peak hours (Monday–Friday,

6–9 a.m. and 3–6:30 p.m.) the trains run every 10 minutes, and as traffic slows down the frequency is closer to 10–15 minutes. The ride to MOA from the airport is about 12 minutes. For more information on light-rail service, as well as bus transportation, see the "Metro Transit" section later in this chapter on pages 58–59.

GROUND TRANSPORTATION SuperShuttle, the same blue van found in most major cities, offers shared van service from MSP to MOA. The fee starts at $17, and each additional passenger costs $9 (up to 10 passengers); a fuel surcharge of $1.50 is also added. If you have the cash and would prefer direct, private service, exclusive nonstop van service is available for $65 per person, with no discount for additional passengers. For more information and online reservations, visit supershuttle.com.

Taxi service is available at both terminals. If arriving at Terminal 1–Lindbergh, from the Tram Level (Level T), go up one level to the taxi starter booth, where staff will assist you. If arriving at Terminal 2–Humphrey, head to the Ground Transport Center, located on the ground level of the Purple parking ramp across from the terminal building. Taxi fare from the airport to MOA is about $15.

Lyft ($10–$18 from MSP to MOA) and Uber ($12–$39, depending on your needs, from MSP to MOA) currently drop off at the airport. Pickup formerly had issues. For one thing, taxi drivers were up in arms that these new services are dipping into their fares—close to 2,000 per day—but the drivers were also bypassing the official pickup line. Recently, airport officials addressed the issue. In April 2016, Uber and Lyft pickups were approved but with an additional $6 pickup fee, and drivers are only allowed to pick up in the limo lot/lane.

If you decide to rent a car for your visit, you'll find plenty of options at the airport. For more information on car rentals, see pages 59–60 later in this chapter.

ARRIVING BY CAR

Driving to Minnesota

All roads lead to Mall of America. There's a reason for that. MOA is located off Interstate 494, which connects to all major arteries running through the Twin Cities. Interstate 35 runs north–south, but beware: The highway splits into two separate interstates through the Twin Cities. I-35 West cuts through Minneapolis, while I-35 East shoots through Saint Paul. The two reconvene in the southern suburb of Burnsville, north of the one ski hill in the area, Buck Hill.

*un**official* **TIP**
Avoid I-494 during rush hour, as it gets especially backed up during these times. Of course, the mall is not open during the morning rush, so this should be a nonissue.

DRIVING IN FROM THE SOUTH We recommend taking I-35 East to MN 77 North (Cedar). You will take the exit for Killebrew Drive and see MOA on your left.

Mall of America Surrounding Area

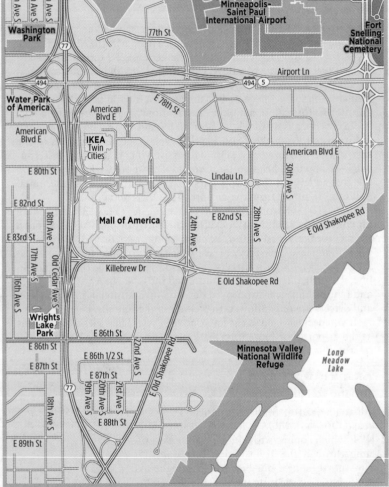

DRIVING IN FROM THE NORTH You can take either I-35 West or I-35 East to MOA. Both eventually lead to I-494.

DRIVING IN FROM THE EAST If you're coming from Wisconsin and beyond (for example, Chicago, Milwaukee, or Green Bay), you will eventually merge on to I-94 and then on to I-494.

DRIVING IN FROM THE WEST Driving from Fargo is an easy shot on I-94 to I-494.

Driving Directions to Mall of America

Over the last few years, the City of Bloomington has wrapped up several massive road construction projects, making life better for locals and visitors alike. However, more updates are in the works, as the city is expected to add three more light rails, as well as other enhancements by 2025. These improvements include changes to MOA and impact shoppers by helping the flow of traffic, providing smoother rides, and making the area safer for mall pedestrians. In the meantime, as detours and congestion ebb and flow, accessing MOA is pretty easy since it's situated off two main Twin Cities arteries, the I-494 corridor and MN 77 (Cedar). For now, here are the best routes to MOA.

ARRIVING ON I-494 FROM THE WEST Take MN 77 South to Killebrew Drive or 81st Street/Lindau Lane east (exits are unnumbered).

ARRIVING ON I-494 FROM THE EAST Take Exit 2A/24th Avenue South. Once on 24th Avenue, stay in the far right lane for direct access to East Parking via the East Ramp Entrance. Another option, and sometimes a better choice, is to take a right on Lindau Lane, before Sears, then a left at the first light. Follow signage to the parking ramp. A third option is to continue on until you hit Killebrew Drive. Turn right, then make another right into the East Ramp South Entrance, or continue on to Southwest Court for West Parking access. *Note:* Metro Transit light-rail trains cross 24th Avenue, before Killebrew Drive, so be prepared for a possible stop by the light-rail crossing gates. Flashing lights warn drivers when the rail is in motion.

*uno*fficial **TIP**
Warning: Drivers heading west on I-494 should be especially attentive since the low-flying jets taking off from or landing at the airport often fascinate and distract drivers.

ARRIVING ON MN 77 FROM THE SOUTH The merge onto Killebrew Drive can be tricky. The reason: If you're planning to park in West Parking, drivers must creatively cross two lanes of traffic very quickly in order to get into the MOA turn lane for Southwest Court. This can set drivers into panic mode because you're unexpectedly competing with swiftly moving vehicles exiting MN 77 arriving from the north. If you're a nervous driver, skip the Killebrew Drive exit and continue to the less-stressful exit at 81st St./Lindau Lane, which offers easy access into the West Parking North Entrance by Nordstrom and East Parking North Entrance by Sears.

ARRIVING ON MN 77 FROM THE NORTH Coming in from the north, it's a breeze pulling into the Southwest Court turn lane. After turning, turn either left for the West Parking South Entrance or right for East

Parking South Entrance (past Radisson Blu). Incoming traffic does not stop. Another option is to continue on Killebrew Drive past Radisson Blu and make a left onto the East Ramp South Entrance, or continue on to 24th Avenue, turn left, then left again into the East Parking East Entrance (not recommended on weekends as there is usually a bottleneck here).

Escape Plan

While planning your arrival is helpful, it may prove even more beneficial to plan your escape. *Here's a secret:* Depart from the south side of MOA. You have instant access to northbound and southbound MN 77. Northbound 77 allows you to hop on I-494 East or West. Taking this route means you will avoid the traffic congestion and several stoplights along 24th Avenue.

GETTING AROUND

METRO TRANSIT LIGHT RAIL AND BUSES

METRO TRANSIT LIGHT RAIL stops at Minneapolis–Saint Paul Airport, Mall of America, and other Twin Cities destinations. Trains depart about every 10 minutes during most hours on weekdays and every 15–30 minutes on evenings and weekends. Visit metrotransit.org for a full map and stops and pay attention because sometimes a bus line takes over where the light rail leaves off.

Currently, the light rail will take you into Minneapolis. While the Green Line connects Minneapolis and Saint Paul, unfortunately, there is no direct tram route into Saint Paul from Bloomington or any suburb, but there are bus routes that dominate the entire Twin Cities and surrounding areas.

If MOA is a good portion of your visit but you plan to catch a Minnesota Twins baseball game or go into downtown Minneapolis, there is a good chance you won't need a rental car because the Blue Line (light rail) departs from the MOA Transit Center and will take you to Target Field. Other stops include Nicollet Mall in downtown Minneapolis, Fort Snelling, and Minnehaha Park (with a pretty waterfall, as well as bike rentals and a restaurant).

If you want to catch a Minnesota Wild (NHL) game in Saint Paul, express bus transportation from MOA to downtown Saint Paul is available via Route 54, with limited-stop service. The bus also stops at both Minneapolis–Saint Paul Airport terminals. Service runs every 30 minutes, 7 days a week. Fare from MOA to Union Depot in Saint Paul is $1.75. *Note:* Wi-Fi was being tested on select buses at press time.

Ticket machines are located at all rail stations. Adult fare is $2.25 during peak hours (6–9 a.m. and 3–6:30 p.m.) and $1.75 all other hours. Discounts are offered to seniors, children (ages 6–12), and people with disabilities. Children ages 5 and under ride free (limit 3 per fare-paying adult). A Day Pass ($6) covers unlimited rides for 24 hours on all buses and Metro lines. Passes are valid immediately if purchased in person, but if you purchase online, these passes need to be initialized on a bus or at a Metro Transit Service Center. The Event 6-Hour pass ($1.50–$4) covers unlimited rides for 6 hours on all buses and Metro lines. These can be purchased in advance online for Twins, Vikings, and Gophers games and other special events.

The light rail doesn't break down very often, but we have experienced delays and maintenance issues. If something does happen, you will want to make sure you have plenty of time to reach your destination, especially if you're traveling to the airport to make your flight. Check metrotransit.org for train times.

RENTAL CARS

TO RENT OR NOT TO RENT, that is the question. If you are flying into Minnesota and MOA is your only destination, we can say with 100% certainty to skip the rental car. It's more hassle than it's worth because the airport is only 1.5 miles from the mall, and some hotels are even closer to the airport. Every hotel offers a shuttle service to the mall and airport. Some hotels are within walking distance of the mall, and others are within walking distance of the Metro system.

AIRPORT CAR-RENTAL COMPANIES		
Advantage 800-777-5500 advantage.com	Alamo 800-327-9633 alamo.com	Avis 800-831-2847 avis.com
Budget 800-527-0700 budget.com	Dollar 800-800-4000 dollar.com	Enterprise 800-325-8007 enterprise.com
Hertz 800-654-3131 hertz.com	National 800-227-7368 nationalcar.com	Thrifty 800-847-4389 thrifty.com
OFF-AIRPORT CAR-RENTAL COMPANIES		
Payless 800-729-5377 paylesscar.com	Sixt 952-345-4017 sixt.com	

However, if you want to see more of the Twin Cities, there are plenty of rental-car companies from which to choose. The Minneapolis–Saint Paul International Airport has a nice selection. We have rented from there several times, and, in our experience, the process has been fast, the service courteous, and the pick-up and drop-off experience seamless. The trickiest part can be finding the on-site car-rental counters in Terminal 1–Lindbergh. As in most large airports, it's a bit of a trek from the plane to the rental cars. Here's the easiest breakdown:

- Follow signs to the baggage claim.
- Go down one level to the Ground Transportation Center.
- Follow signs to the airport tram.
- After exiting the tram, take the elevators or escalators to the Blue and Red parking ramps.
- Take the elevator or escalator to the second or third floor.
- Counters are clearly marked.

At Terminal 2–Humphrey, finding the on-site rental-car counters is a much easier experience, as they are located in the Ground Transportation Center on the ground level. Look for the Purple parking ramp directly across from Terminal 2.

There are two off-airport car-rental companies. Shuttle buses provide service to the off-airport car rental companies from the Terminal 1–Lindbergh Transit Center found between the Blue and Red parking ramps. If you are arriving from the Humphrey Terminal, ride the tram to the Transit Center, then take an escalator or elevator up one level.

TAXIS

ONE-WAY COST FOR TAXI SERVICE is about $15 from MOA to Minneapolis–Saint Paul International Airport and about $30 from MOA to downtown Minneapolis or Saint Paul. Of course, fare may be drastically different depending on route, traffic, and weather.

TAXI OPERATORS		
10/10 Taxi 952-936-0010 1010taxi.com	**Airtaxi** 952-831-5168	**Arrow Taxi** 952-486-7715 arrowtaxi.net
Limo Car Service MN 952-994-1994 limocarservicemn.com	**Red Wing Taxi** 651-385-8294 redwingtaxi.com	**ReliaCar Transportation** 952-926-8294 reliacar.us
Taxi Services Inc. 612-888-8888 taxiservicesinc.com	**Twin Cities Airport Taxi** 952-545-5555 twincitiestaxi.com	**Viking Airport Taxi** 952-995-0110 vikingairporttaxi.com

MALL *of* AMERICA LAYOUT

ORIGINALLY THE FOUR SIDES THAT MAKE UP Mall of America's rectangular shape (North Garden, East Broadway, South Avenue, and West Market) had their own unique ambience. North Garden was the "green" strip with plants, trellises, and bridges and formerly promoted as a "walk in the park." East Broadway, the location of the event-gathering Rotunda, was the hip area with more glitz and glam. South Avenue

Mall of America Overview

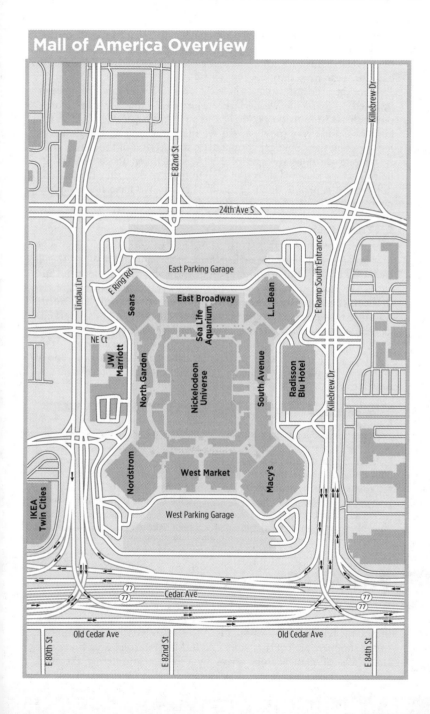

offered a hint of upscale sophistication, while the West Market provided a much-needed wider space with natural sunlight vaguely seeping in from minimal skylights overhead. The space was supposed to be reminiscent of a European train station.

Over time the atmospheres in each corridor have changed and been updated. In 2014 the West Market welcomed a much brighter corridor with a 450-foot-long skylight and a sleeker, modern ambience. It's gorgeous, and every time we visit we thank the shopping mall fairies for spritzing their magical goodness on this section of the mall.

Despite the massive size of MOA, something about the layout helps visitors' sense of direction kick in quicker than they think. That doesn't mean people don't get lost. They do. We have helped many people by pointing them in the right direction.

ENTRANCES

THE ORIGINAL FOUR-SIDED MOA has an entrance on each side that leads directly into the mall: North, East, South, and West. Ahead each of these corridors continues on to entrances to Nickelodeon Universe. The East Entrance seems to be the busiest because it leads directly to the Rotunda, where events, shows, and concerts are held. The North Entrance formerly led directly outside to where taxis and buses parked, as well as to overflow parking. Now, Phase II has extended over that area, now known as the Front Door. You will see the big colorful MOA America star logo marking the circular driveway, JW Marriott, and a wall of windows where Culinary on North, the Level 3 food court, is now located.

THE ROTUNDA

Shoppers from the 1980s generation will likely recall the shopping mall scene in *Bill & Ted's Excellent Adventure* where Saint Joan of Arc ends up leading a fitness class. If the movie took place today at Mall of America, the exercise class would have been held in the Rotunda. This is where all of the action happens, including concerts, events, competitions, and other unique happenings. HGTV has set up an oversize ginger bread house, Caribou Coffee once set up a five-story-tall Pinterest board, and in 2014 a new world record was launched for the most people simultaneously tying their shoes in honor of World Diabetes Week.

PARKING

MY HUSBAND SAYS THE BEST PARKING place at Mall of America is a vacant one. Then again, we usually frequent the mall, as a family, during the busiest time—weekends. As a one-stop destination, four out of ten shoppers are tourists, and a 2006 Mall Intercept Study revealed that 74% of mall visitors arrive by vehicle. Considering the mall welcomes more than 42 million visitors annually, you'll likely agree it's a good idea to have a parking plan. Before we begin, know this: MOA has two main parking structures offering direct access to the mall: East and West Parking, each with several entrances.

VALET PARKING

WHILE THE PARKING STRUCTURES ARE AN OBVIOUS CHOICE, Radisson Blu always offers valet parking, and Macy's and Nordstrom sometimes offer valet parking over busy times, meaning weekends and holidays. A new feature with the introduction of MOA's Phase II is valet parking at what is now known as the Front Door. For $10, shoppers can leave their cars with a valet at any of the four planned valet points, Radisson Blu and three others. Here's the best part: Guests can have their cars delivered to any of the four locations by texting or using the new Mall of America app. Simply download the app, go to the Parking tab, and click on Retrieve from Valet. Users will see the text number plugged into their phone for easy valet communication.

THE SCOOP ON SCORING A PARKING PLACE

TWENTY THOUSAND PARKING SPACES—that's how many cars MOA can welcome. With 12,550 parking spaces split between the two ramps, along with the new parking lot and overflow parking farther north of the building offering plenty of additional spaces, you'd think parking wouldn't be a problem. Think again. Parking at MOA, especially on weekends, holidays, and during massive events, gives new meaning to the phrase, "hunting season."

The good news: Parking at MOA is free. The not-so-good news: The parking ramps of MOA can be compared to the throes of a Minnesota winter: dark, dreary, and accompanied with the hopeless feeling that you may never see the light of day again. Okay, it's not that bad, but on dreary days the structures are dark despite being outdoors, and the signage is rather minimal. While there is some lighting, the signs hanging overhead are not illuminated and can make for difficult navigation, especially for first-timers.

East and West Parking are similar in most ways and can easily be confused. East Parking is on the same side as Sears and the former Bloomingdale's, which now houses L.L. Bean, Forever 21, and the Crayola Experience, while West Parking is shared between Macy's and Nordstrom. Both sides offer access to the middle of the mall with a direct path into Nickelodeon Universe. If you have specific stores in mind, it's best to visit the online MOA shopping directory at mallofamerica.com/shopping/directory; it not only gives locations and hours but also which parking ramp to choose.

Both parking ramps have a large outer ramp that takes drivers up to P5 with continued access to the lower levels. The ramp then peaks at P5, descending back down to ground level. To reach P6 and P7, drivers must find the inner ramp, centrally located within the structure, that allows drivers access to P3–P7. Lower levels P1 and P2 can be accessed via an inner ramp found directly under the far east and west main ramps (not in the center of the garages as expected). There are no signs leading you to these ramps, but they are marked once you are in eyesight.

Crazy mall days, like Black Friday, bring out mall security and parking attendants to direct traffic. Lighted "open" or "full" signs will disclose each level's availability. On days where high traffic is expected, factor in parking time (30–60 minutes) as part of your day at the mall. If you are staying at a local hotel, it's best to opt for the free hotel shuttle, or better yet, stay at an on-premise hotel, walk, or take the light rail.

If you've ever been to Las Vegas, you've likely experienced the "things appear closer than they are" phenomena. Well, at MOA it's a similar idea. It's not difficult to cruise through the ramps in search of a parking place near a certain entrance only to realize after you park that your car is actually closer to another mall entrance.

The best time to park at MOA is in the morning at retail opening (10 a.m.). However, don't be surprised to find many of the cherished front-row parking places already occupied long before the official opening. There are two reasons: the public parking spaces are shared with mall employees, and the main mall door opens at 7 a.m. for Mall Stars (aka: MOA walkers).

The opposite of up-close spaces are found in the parking structure's perimeter, which usually offers the most available spaces; however, the edges are open, which means the front of your car might get dusted with snow during the winter or a light mist from a rain shower. Unless the wind is wild, you won't be exposed to the elements getting in and out of the car in one of these spaces. While Fitbit users may appreciate the extra steps by parking far away, distance does matter in the winter when the temperatures dip well below zero (see pages 16–17 for advice how to dress for MOA and toting winter gear into the mall), not to mention you may be carrying two heavy handfuls of shopping bags at the end of the day.

As far as parking levels go, P1 and P2 on both sides fill up first due to their easy mall access. Heading to P3 and P4 means you will likely

---

RIDING ON TWO WHEELS

There is no designated bicycle area, but cyclists can secure their bikes down in the transit area. Don't forget to bring a bike lock. For those cruising in on their Harley Davidson (there is a store in MOA: W344, 952-854-1225) or Gold Wing, there is no designated parking area for motorcycles. You're in competition with the automobiles. We notice most riders park on the edges of the lot away from the congestion.

find a space much quicker, followed by P5 and P6. The roof-top parking (P7) is last to be filled for several reasons. There is no roof or overhead coverage (bring a snow brush and ice scraper in the winter), and shoppers must hike down several flights of stairs or take the elevator down, which can take eons if the mall is busy. When it's time to leave, good luck. There are no exit signs on P7. The best advice is to drive south (that means the Minneapolis skyline behind you if visibility is good) to the end and look for the down ramp.

If you want a direct drive-and-park scenario on an average day, we recommend taking the ramp up to Parking Level 3 or 4 (Level 4 if you have a stroller since the floor offers direct access to the mall via a flat skyway).

Regarding moving traffic within the ramps, each lane has two-way traffic, but be forewarned, there isn't a stop sign in sight and main entrance/exit traffic will not stop. The lanes are very narrow. If it looks like an auto is about to depart and the vehicle in front of you decides to wait and claim that spot, expect to wait because the aisles are too narrow to pass. Do your best not to lean on the horn despite severe temptation.

What qualifies as a decent parking place relies on several things, mainly weather, your mall plans, and accessibility needs. Consider that each parking side has three main entrance options: two corners where the anchor stores are located (Macy's, Nordstrom, Sears, and the former Bloomingdale's) and a main mall entrance in the middle. One of the benefits of parking on a higher level, rather than the first floor, is the easy access to the enclosed skyways leading into the mall. Parking on the first floor is fine, but if it's raining or there's a blustery snowstorm, you have to cross what's called the ring road surrounding MOA.

If you need to avoid steps because of a stroller, wheelchair, electric cart, or any other reason, P1 and P4 are for you. P1 provides flat ground access and plenty of handicapped parking spaces marked with the universal blue and white wheelchair signs. P4 offers the same in regard to reserved parking spaces and has a flat surface through the skyway. The remaining floors' (2 and 3) mall access requires ascending or descending stairs.

If you're not afraid of steps and you park on the outskirts of P5–P7 (away from the main elevator and stairwell), there are four other stairwells (covered on P7) situated in the middle of the parking structures that pass through all lower levels.

It's pretty obvious where the mall entrances are, as signs with arrows lead shoppers to the closest entrance. Regardless of where you park, find the closest pedestrian walkway (these are well marked) for the safest route into the mall because drivers are likely looking for open spaces rather than people.

unofficial TIP
Text your parking level's state name to 952-373-0816 to receive your parking location.

KNOW THY PARKING PLACE

ONE WAY TO RUIN YOUR MOA EXPERIENCE is to not pay attention to where you park. In fact, observing shoppers trying to find their cars would make for an entertaining reality show. Parking boils down to four important factors: side, level, row, and section. Getting confused between East and West Parking happens often. The first thing mall security will ask: Did you park in East or West Parking?

HOW TO BREAK DOWN PARKING			
SIDE	LEVEL	PARKING ROW	PARKING SECTION
East or West Parking	P1, P2, P3, P4, P5, P6, P7	1-17	Letter A-F

MOA has kindly made remembering parking levels easy by designating each parking level a state accompanied by a regionally affiliated image: New York (P5 East) Statue of Liberty, Texas (P1 West) cowboy boot, Arizona (P4 West) cactus, Florida (P4 East) crocodile, and so on. The signs are generously peppered throughout the parking structure on posts, the elevator areas, and inside the elevator next to each level's numbered button. Another clue our friend and long-time Minnesota resident Linda Kramer pointed out: eastern states are in East Parking and western states are, you guessed it, in West Parking.

West Parking

WEST PARKING LEVELS		
Level 1: Texas Level 2: California Level 3: Hawaii	Level 4: Arizona Level 5: Nevada	Level 6: Colorado Level 7: Alaska

GETTING INTO THE MALL FROM WEST PARKING Here's a breakdown of MOA entrances from West Parking:

- **P1 WEST:** Ground level direct outdoor access
- **P2 WEST:** 10 steps up
- **P3 WEST:** 10 steps down—Skyway
- **P4 WEST:** Direct access via Skyway
- **P5-P7 WEST:** Elevator or stairwells down to skyways or P1

Both Macy's and Nordstrom parking have one working elevator each (P1–P7), while the center entrance has two working elevators (P1–P7). Know which skyway level you wish to take (P2 and P3 or P4) because there is no indication that a skyway is even an option. Some first-time shoppers will automatically go to the starred ground level (P1) for mall entry.

East Parking

EAST PARKING LEVELS		
Level 1: Maine Level 2: Georgia Level 3: Indiana	Level 4: Florida Level 5: New York	Level 6: Tennessee Level 7: Pennsylvania

GETTING INTO THE MALL FROM EAST PARKING Both the Southeast Entrance and Sears have one working elevator (P1–P7), while the center entrance has two working elevators (P1–P7). Skyway levels are the same as West Parking (P2 and P3 or P4), but Level 2 skyway is not accessible since Bloomingdale's closed. If you park on the southeast end you will have to either walk up or down the stairs or walk to the main East Entrance.

Note: From P7 of East Parking, plane spotters can enjoy views of aircraft taking off and landing on MSP International Airport's 17/35 runway. In the evening, look west from either East or West Parking for splendid sunset and Minneapolis skyline views.

SOCIAL MEDIA LOVE
If you're wondering which parking ramp makes for easier parking, the truth is it simply depends on the weekend. However, insider scoop is offered via @MallofAmerica on twitter. Employees behind the scenes offer live updates on where and when parking is available. Shoppers can follow the mall's twitter handle and search the hashtag #moaparking with tweets like this:
@mallofamerica: East Ramp is now opening up. Parking is now available in both ramps. #moaparking
@mallofamerica: Best option for parking is currently the West Ramp. #moaparking
@mallofamerica: Parking is currently available in both the East and West Parking Ramps #moaparking
You might even score free dating advice like this:
@kittlesruff: Every first date should have to find parking @mallofamerica on a busy day. Really learn a lot about character #moaparking

OUTDOOR PARKING

ALL FOUR ORIGINAL MALL CORNERS and the anchor stores have a slice of outdoor parking. These outdoor lots fill up quickly, even during inclement weather, because of the easy department store access. On the north side of the mall, across Lindau Lane but south of American Boulevard, is the huge overflow parking lot called the Lindau Lot, with ample parking spaces. This area is said to eventually be built on as the mall builds out. In the meantime, it's an option during peak seasons. Shoppers can walk or rely on the free shuttle that runs regularly to and from the mall on weekends.

Lindau Lot is where all vehicles with trailers, RVs, campers, moving rental trucks, school and charter buses, semi-trucks, and box trucks can park. The ramps simply can't accommodate oversize vehicles. Before entering the ramps, warning signs announce vehicles are limited to 7 feet. Take this rule to heart. In 2011 the driver of a U-Haul underestimated the truck's height and hit a concrete and steel support beam in West Parking, causing the beam to fall and crush the vehicle's cab.

MOA does not allow overnight parking in any of its lots, including the park-and-ride spaces in the East Parking underground garage for the Hiawatha Light. This is to discourage airport passengers from leaving their cars for extended times. Unattended vehicles will be towed at the owner's expense.

WHERE CAN I FIND . . .

A Map of the Mall

Printed Mall of America maps are available at every Guest Services counter. Be forewarned that stores and attractions turn over regularly, so often the maps are outdated but will be updated during the next printing. If you're not sure whether a store is still open, stationary maps are found throughout the mall.

Elevators and Escalators

A pair of elevators is located in the middle of the east and south mall corridors, directly in front of the entrances to Nickelodeon Universe. Single elevators are located directly in front of the West Entrance and at the intersection of North Court and Central Parkway (on Level 3 it's nestled to the left of the new Shake Shack). The south and east elevators are by far the most crowded elevators in the mall, particularly the south location because it is a portal to the third-floor food court, where most mall eateries are located.

Escalators are located at the Macy's Court, at the Nordstrom Court, adjacent to the south elevators (near LEGO), across the Rotunda (east), and on the west side (mid-mall). The elevator on the north side is hidden on the right side of the Culinary on North Food Court, while a set of escalators is nestled in the back right corner of the food court. Each department store has escalators and elevators.

ATMs

There is not a bank in the mall, but there are many ATMs:

• 2 in Nickelodeon Universe	• 4 in East Entrances on all levels
• 1 near Hooters on Level 4	• 1 in North Entrance on Level 1

- 1 in Culinary on North inside Food Court Level 3

- 1 in South Entrance on Level 1	- 1 in South Food Court on Level 3
- 1 in West Entrance on Level 1	

Currency Exchange

The Minneapolis–Saint Paul International Airport has Travelex currency exchange offices in Terminal 1–Lindbergh between doors 5 and 6 in the ticketing lobby and at the entrance to Concourse G. In Terminal 2–Humphrey, Travelex is located in the ticketing lobby and a currency exchange ATM is located near gate H6.

At MOA an Xchange of America (E218, ☎ 888-796-2962, xchangeofamerica.com) has a booth near the Level 2 West Entrance.

Help in an Emergency

Any shoppers who may need some type of emergency assistance (think flat tires, lost cars, or dead batteries) will find yellow "Call for Help" signs with paging systems near all parking ramp elevators and stairwells. These connect shoppers with the mall's dispatch center. In addition to the mall's call boxes, pay phones have direct lines to the dispatch centers or you can opt for the direct line by calling ☎ 952-883-8888. Dispatch center employees monitor numerous security cameras located throughout the parking ramps and surface lots 24 hours a day.

A Place to Meet

In our experience, the best places to meet are at any of the many coffee shops on Level 1. Our favorites include **Barnes and Noble** and **Starbucks** near the Rotunda, **Nordstrom's eBar,** and **Caribou Coffee** in the center of Nickelodeon. Each of these places obviously offers refreshments and places to sit while you wait.

All-Day Lockers

Locker options at MOA have electronic key codes, so no need to worry about losing a key, but do hang on to the slip that prints your code. The code is good for the entire day. Lockers are found on Levels 1, 2, and 3 on the east and west sides and on Level 1 on the north and south sides. In Nickelodeon Universe, a patch of lockers are located underneath the Ferris wheel. Lockers come in four sizes: regular ($6), large ($8), extra large ($11), and jumbo ($13). For travelers coming from the airport with several bags, the jumbo-size lockers are large enough to hold luggage.

Wheelchairs, ECVs, and Shopping Carts

Wheelchairs and shopping carts are available to all guests for a fee. Electronic carts are $30 per day (no deposit required), wheelchairs are $5 per day, and shopping carts are $7 per day. All rentals require a refundable

$5 deposit. If the rental is not returned or returned damaged, full value will be charged to the guest's credit card. See pages 97–98 in Part Five: Mall of America with Kids for information on stroller rentals.

A Place to Charge My Cell Phone

For the longest time there were no designated places to charge phones or any other electronic devices. We've asked many mall employees, and they all say the same thing with a shrug, "Look for random outlets throughout the mall." But times are changing. The new food court, Culinary on North, has charging stations for mobile devices.

Verizon Destination Store (E264, ☎ 952-853-0022) welcomes customers to charge phones in the store, but you must have a charger on hand. While you wait you will likely be tempted to play with the latest consumer technology demos.

Apple (S132, ☎ 952-229-5630) will allow you to replenish your iPhone battery by unplugging an iPad charger for you to use. You won't want to walk away, however, as other customers may think it's a demo and start surfing your iPhone.

Pet Boarding and Day Care

Some hotels in the area accept pets, but a better alternative to leaving your pet in a hotel or car is opting for boarding or doggy day care. There are several in the area. Day prices vary from $15 to $25, and overnight boarding prices range from $25 to $60, depending upon animal, size, and lodging choice. Check out the following locations:

LUCKY DOG PET LODGE (1067 American Blvd. E. Bloomington, MN 55420; ☎ 952-767-2040; luckydogpetlodge.com) is the closest option to MOA. Accepts dogs only.

NOW BOARDING (6002 28th Ave. S., Minneapolis, MN; ☎ 612-454-4850) is located north of the airport. Accepts cats, dogs, and critters.

FOUR PAWS PET RESORT (4020 Old Sibley Memorial Hwy., Eagan, MN 55122; ☎ 651-882-2211) offers day and overnight care. Accepts dogs and cats. We can recommend Four Paws, as we had a pleasant two-week dog-boarding experience there.

PEANUT'S PLACE (1904 Shawnee Road, Eagan, MN 55122; ☎ 651-686-1056; ppdogdaycare.com) Accepts dogs only. Cage-free environment. Must complete an interview/screening process in person or by phone before being accepted.

WAGGING TAILS PET RESORT (3275 Sun Drive, Eagan, MN 55121; ☎ 651-483-3647; waggingtailspetresort.com). Accepts dogs.

THE CAT'S MEOW GROOMING & SUITES (8579 Lyndale Ave. S., Bloomington, MN 55420; ☎ 952-582-4429). Accepts cats.

Lost and Found

Go directly to Guest Services (☎ 952-883-8932) or fill out the online form for missing items. Be as detailed and keyword-focused as possible: item, brand, color, other details. Example: Ladies, navy blue, London Fog trench coat; size medium; sunglasses in pocket. Items are only held for two weeks and then donated to charity.

Extra Luggage

If you find yourself in need of extra luggage, we recommend **Macy's, Sears, JS Trunk** (a division of Samsonite), or **Tumi.**

INTERVIEW *with a* PERSONAL SHOPPER

CARLY GATZLAFF, FASHION STYLIST and owner of À La Mode Wardrobe Consulting, knows Mall of America, as well as other Twin Cities malls. She explains what she does and offers some of her insider tips for visiting MOA.

Q: Tell us about your business.

A: The main services we provide are closet analysis (helping clients work with what they currently have) and personal shopping (typically at malls, occasionally special ordering/bringing things to clients). We do public speaking, print work, photo shoots, and editorial writing.

Q: How can/do you help shoppers?

A: We help shoppers by navigating them to the items they need in their wardrobe. Starting with an initial consult, we hone in on our clients style and style hang-ups. We then personalize a shopping trip for them, styling outfits that fit their budget and lifestyle. Basically, we take the stress out of shopping. Our clients are led on a three-hour fashion adventure, in a no-pressure situation in which they can relax and walk away with a new wardrobe they love.

Q: What do you like about Mall of America?

A: There is so much variety. Many of the chain stores are the biggest around, so they carry interesting items you can't always find at other malls.

Q: Is there anything you would improve?

A: If you are having to shop on weekends, everything. Crowds are huge, stores are picked over/messy, and parking is tough. On a weekday, especially in the morning, no . . . love the mall and think everything about it is fabulous.

Q: Where do you recommend shoppers "on a mission" park?

A: West Parking, Level 2, California, outside Nordstrom. Typically, you'll find tons of parking, and Nordstrom opens 5–10 minutes before 10 a.m., so you can walk through the tunnel there, get a head start, and be on the same floor as the nicest bathroom in the mall (women's lounge of Nordstrom is on the second floor).

Q: What is your favorite wing of the mall and why?

A: Definitely the West Market. So many of the stores I love, easy parking, great way to get in, get what you need, and get out!

Q: What stores do you find to have the best clearance sections?

A: Overall, MOA is not a great mall for clearance/bargain shopping, as it is a very shopped mall, so good items go quickly. The only real exception to this is J. Crew, which has an entire clearance room, and it's humongous! Nordstrom rack always has good bargains, especially during their "clear the rack" sales.

Q: What stores do you recommend for shoppers on a budget?

A: LOFT at MOA is fabulous about having sales, and their staff is amazingly helpful (you feel like you are in a boutique, but at a much lower price point). The DSW is the best I have ever been in; many items offered are not even on the DSW website. Old Navy is a bit overwhelming at MOA but has lots of great items very similar to those at Gap and Banana Republic (its sister stores), so it's great for fashionable finds without a big price tag. H&M, Nordstrom Rack, and Forever 21 are great but can be overwhelming and difficult to shop, so not for the faint of heart.

Q: What stores do you recommend for shoppers who don't need to worry about a budget?

A: Nordstrom is definitely a one-stop shop for everything and has a great range of super-high-end, all the way to great store brands at a reasonable price. Club Monaco, often overlooked, is great for fashion-forward, high-quality pieces. Burberry has a phenomenal selection of jackets, and it is rare to see so many in one place and be able to compare (which makes spending all of the money a bit easier, as you know you have seen all the choices and made the best one for you).

Q: How do you compare weekdays and weekends?

A: If you can shop on a weekday, you will have a much better experience. Many of the staff at MOA stores during the week are full-time employees, know their products, and are amazing at their jobs. Crowds are much smaller, stores are cleaner and better stocked, parking is generally easy, and you get to experience the mall and not be overwhelmed by it.

Avoid weekends if at all possible—crowds are huge and very over-whelming. Most of the staff is more weekend-only (if you can find any help) so not as knowledgeable. Items are much more picked over. If you thrive on people and crowds, are going more for the people-watching, and are not on a timeline, however, weekends are definitely an experience.

Q: Any tips on navigating Mall of America?

A: Plan ahead on what stores you want to hit, so you end up getting everywhere you want in the wing (as you sometimes miss stores that are on different floors). Utilize Nickelodeon Universe to cut through. If you are hoping to quickly get from one wing to the other, cut through the middle, so you are not always having to do full-circle laps. Escalators can be tough to come by, so remember all of the anchor stores have them, so be sure to utilize them if you are shopping in an anchor store and trying to transition to a different level. The same with elevators: the ones in the middle of the mall wings are super busy, but Macy's has an elevator that is rarely used if you need one.

For more information, visit alamodewc.com or e-mail Carly at info@alamodewc.com.

PRECAUTIONS *for* DESTINATION TRAVELERS

WITH ANY SHOPPING EXPERIENCE, it's best to know what you are getting into before you make a purchase. For example, **CordaRoys** (E348, ☎ 952-854-0335) has a cool selection of foam-filled chairs and sofas that convert to beds. Shipping is possible, but you can take certain sizes with you on the plane. Before you do, compare shipping prices and the airline checked-bag and weight prices.

Mall of America is one place you don't want to have to make a return, if only because of the size. We strongly suggest trying on clothes in the dressing rooms before you purchase. While this should go with-out saying, don't forget to review your receipt before departing the store to ensure you were charged properly, and keep your receipts well organized in case you do need to exchange or return. Finally, review and keep warranties in a safe place when you return home.

PART FOUR

DINING

DINING *at* MALL *of* AMERICA

FOODIES FIGURE OUT PRETTY QUICKLY THAT, with the exception of a handful of restaurants, most of the dining choices in Mall of America (MOA) are chain restaurants. While locals might gripe, the idea works well. Most malls in America are filled with familiar restaurants, and it makes for an easier dining experience for weary shoppers. It seems that the familiarity of chain restaurants keeps customers coming back, even at MOA. The locally inspired restaurants, such as **Twin City Grill** (N130, ☎ 952-854-0200); **Tucci Benucch** (W114, ☎ 952-853-0200); and **Magic Pan Crepe Stand** (W114) all have fantastic reputations and food. Visit the Lettuce Entertain You restaurants in the Twin Cities Area website (leyemn.com/#booklet) for a coupon book on these three restaurants and others in the Twin Cities.

RESTAURANT CATEGORIES

FOOD SERVICE COMES IN ALL FORMS and price ranges at MOA. You can snag some decent and affordable lunches, such as a $6.99 California roll from **Tiger Sushi** or $6 burger and fries from **Johnny Rockets.** And there's always the dollar-ish menu at **Burger King.** Full-service restaurants can be a nice choice if you need to unwind and relax without having to battle for a food court seat.

As for food locations, you can expect to find them scattered throughout the mall. The east entrances have quite a few snack offer-

unofficial **TIP**
Watch your belongings: Thieves know that crowded places are great places to pickpocket or steal purses, and the MOA food court's tight tables have been known to be a playing field for swiping merchandise and purses hung on chairs. The thief walks by and lifts items from unsuspecting hungry people.

ings, like pretzels, pizza, and ice cream. **Nestlé Toll House** has two places both on the east entrance (E283, 952-853-0272) and west entrance (W152, 952-767-7760) near the Nickelodeon Universe entrance. **Magic Pan Crepe Stand** (W114) is on the first floor near the west entrance, while **Freshens** (W328, 952-854-9434), featuring crepes and smoothies, is near the third floor entrance.

There are two food courts, both on Level 3: the **South Street Dining Food Court** and the new **Culinary on North Food Court,** part of the latest Phase II renovation. As of this writing, restaurants are still rolling out. Peppered along the south side of Level 3 are several full-service options, including the new **Rainforest Cafe** (moved from the first floor in 2016, S306, ☎ 952-854-7500); **Bubba Gump Shrimp Co.** (S396, ☎ 952-853-6600); **Margaritaville** (E344); **Benihana** (S358, ☎ 952-594-6205); **Buffalo Wild Wings** (S312, ☎ 952-346-3740); **Crave** (S368, ☎ 952-854-5000); and **Tony Roma's** (S346, ☎ 952-854-7940). Sadly, two of our favorite restaurants, Famous Dave's and Kokomo Island Café, closed in 2015. Those two restaurants were replaced with the new **Zio Italian** (S320, ☎ 952-855-7700) and **Burger Burger** (S321, ☎ 952-855-7800).

RESTAURANTS WITH A NICKELODEON UNIVERSE VIEW
AMERICAN GIRL BISTRO (C5160-1, ☎ 877-247-5223)
CANTINA #1 (E406, ☎ 952-854-6500)
CRAVE (S368, ☎ 952-854-5000)
HARD ROCK CAFE (C5115, ☎ 952-853-7000)
SOUTH STREET DINING FOOD COURT (Level 3)

RESTAURANTS WITH GLUTEN-FREE MENUS AND ALLERGY AWARENESS

MANY MOA RESTAURANTS have become sensitive to the food allergies and sensitivities of customers. While there aren't specific peanut-free menus, we have found several gluten-free menus.

As for peanut allergies, we talked to a couple of local mothers who have children with food allergies. Missy Voronyak, a local mother who also covers food allergies on her blog MarketingMama.com, says her go-to places at MOA are **Rainforest Cafe, Hard Rock Cafe, Chipotle,** and **Crave.** She also reminds parents to do their research, talk to managers in advance of ordering, and always make sure to have emergency medication with them.

"**Cold Stone** is good for a treat," says Linda Kramer, another local mom. "They open a new tub of ice cream and then take it in the back and mix it in a separate container instead of on the slab where everything else is mixed." She also points out that **American Girl** is another good choice that offers customers a reminder on its menu to notify the restaurant of allergies: "Before placing your order, please inform your server if anyone in your party has a food allergy."

Disclaimer: We do not guarantee that the aforementioned restaurants will cater to your allergies or food needs. Please take precautions before eating out at MOA or anywhere else if food allergies or sensitivities affect you or your family. Do your homework by calling restaurants beforehand and asking many questions upon arrival.

As for gluten-free specific menus, visit these restaurants:

- Bubba Gump Shrimp Co. (S396, ☎ 952-853-6600)
- Cadillac Ranch (S352, ☎ 952-854-1004)
- Chipotle (S322, ☎ 952-252-3800)
- Crave (S368, ☎ 952-854-5000)
- Ruby Tuesday (N234, ☎ 952-854-8282)
- Tucci Benucch (S358, ☎ 952-594-6205)
- Twin City Grill (N130, ☎ 952-854-0200)

HAPPY HOURS

COMPLIMENTS TO MOA RESTAURANTS for their nice selection of happy hours. We're talking $3–$5 appetizers and the typical happy hour beverages. While we could recommend our favorites, it depends on what atmosphere you prefer. If the kids are with you and you need somewhere lively that doesn't mind the tots, **Bubba Gump Shrimp Co.** (S396, ☎ 952-853-6600); **Tony Roma's** (S346, ☎ 952-854-7940); **Ruby Tuesday** (N234, ☎ 952-854-8282); **Cantina #1** (E406, ☎ 952-854-6500); and **Hard Rock Cafe** (C5115A, ☎ 952-853-7000), right off Nickelodeon Universe, are a nice fit. If chilling out and watching a game is your scene, then settle in at **Buffalo Wild Wings** (S312, ☎ 952-346-3740); **Cadillac Ranch** (S352, ☎ 952-854-1004); or **Hooters** (E404, ☎ 952-854-3110). For a quieter scene, try **Tucci Benucch** (W114, ☎ 952-853-0200); **Crave** (S368, ☎ 952-854-5000); **Fire-Lake Grill House & Cocktail Bar** (Radisson Blu, S2000, ☎ 952-881-5258); and the new **Cedar + Stone, Urban Table** (JW Marriott, C1000, ☎ 612-615-0100). **The Lounge @ House of Comedy** (E408-1, ☎ 952-858-8558) is ideal if you're looking for some fun entertainment. For a complete list, see our chart on pages 78–79.

NEWS FOR JAVA JUNKIES (AND TEA LOVERS)

CAFFEINE ADDICTS WILL BE HAPPY to know that there is no lack of coffee shops in MOA. Locally founded **Caribou Coffee** has five locations, including one in the center of Nickelodeon Universe (C5102). Another Caribou Coffee is located around the corner from the third-floor South Street Dining Food Court (S226). Down a level is a shop located off the bridge leading to Radisson Blu (N232). The other two are both on the northwest side (N224 and N194). Wi-Fi is available at S226, N232, and N194.

HAPPY HOURS

BENIHANA (S358, ☎ 952-594-6205) • Monday–Friday, 3–6 p.m.
• Appetizers and sushi, $3–$6; sake, beer, and premium well drinks, $3–$5; wine and specialty cocktails, $6

BUBBA GUMP SHRIMP CO. (S396, ☎ 952-853-6600) • Monday–Friday, 3–5 p.m.; Sunday–Thursday, 9 p.m.–close • Appetizers, $3–$5; 16-ounce well drinks, $4; domestic draft, $3

BUFFALO WILD WINGS (S312, ☎ 952-346-3740) • Monday–Friday, 3:30–6:30 p.m. and 10 p.m.–midnight • Select appetizers, $3; Jack and Coke, Captain and Coke, Absolut mixers, and domestic draft, $3

CADILLAC RANCH (S352, ☎ 952-854-1004) • Monday–Friday, 3–7 p.m.; daily, 9 p.m.–midnight • Select appetizers, $3–$5 (bar and patio only); 3–7 p.m.: beer, wine, liquor, and martini list (bar only), $3–$5; 9 p.m.–midnight: drink specials vary

CANTINA #1 (E406, ☎ 952-854-6500) • Monday, 3–6 p.m. and 9–10 p.m.; Tuesday–Friday, 3–6 p.m. and 9 p.m.–midnight • Appetizers, start at $5.99; beer, well drinks, and house margaritas, $3–$5

CANTINA LAREDO (W300, ☎ 952-406-8311) • Monday–Friday, 4–7 p.m.; Saturday, 11 a.m.–5 p.m. • Bar plates, 50% off; domestic/import beer, well drinks, house wine, and Casa Rita, $2–$5

CEDAR + STONE, URBAN TABLE (C1000, JW Marriott; ☎ 612-615-0100) • Daily, 3–6 p.m. • Appetizers, $7; wine by the glass, $3 off; draft and well cocktails, $5

CRAVE (S368, ☎ 952-854-5000) • Monday–Thursday, 2–6 p.m.; Friday, 2–5 p.m. • Select appetizers, $4; beer, wine, and cocktails, $4–$5

FIRELAKE GRILL HOUSE & COCKTAIL BAR (Radisson Blu, S2000; ☎ 952-881-5258) • Daily, 11 a.m.–5 p.m. (bar only) • Burger and beer or lunch trio with house wine, $12

If you want a real treat, the **Paciugo Gelato & Caffè** (W392) menu offers a to-die-for hot drink called a Gelatte, a latte steamed with your choice of gelato.

Seattle-based **Starbucks** has two locations, one directly off the Rotunda (E164 and W276).

Sears is home to **Coffee & Tea LTD** (Level 1), a coffee roaster and tea importer located in Minneapolis.

Nordstrom eBar (Level 1), located just outside of Nordstrom, offers a ton of seating in the court. In addition to coffee, it offers pastries and snacks.

HAPPY HOURS *(continued)*

HARD ROCK CAFE (C5115, ☎ 952-853-7000) • Sunday–Thursday, 4–6 p.m.
• Appetizers (excludes jumbo combo), 50% off; beer, wine, and hurricanes, $3–$5

HOOTERS (E404, ☎ 952-854-3110) • Monday–Friday, 9 p.m.–close
• Appetizers, $3–$5; domestic beer, well drinks, and top-shelf tequila, vodka, or whiskey drinks, $3–$5

THE LOUNGE @ HOUSE OF COMEDY (E408, ☎ 952-858-8558)
• Tuesday, all day; Wednesday–Friday and Sunday, 4–6 p.m.; Saturday, 3:30–6 p.m. • Select appetizers, $2 off; draft beer, wine, and well drinks, $4

MASU SUSHI & ROBATA (S344, ☎ 952-896-6278) • Monday–Friday, 3–6 p.m. • Sushi, *izakaya,* robata, and noodle specials, $2–$11; house sake, select draft beer, select wine, and Shochu Gummi Sours, $2–$5

RUBY TUESDAY (N234, ☎ 952-854-8282) • Monday–Friday, 4–6 p.m. and 9 p.m.–close (bar only) • Dips, $2 off; beer and wine, $1 off; well drinks, $5

SKY DECK SPORTS GRILLE & LANES (E401, ☎ 952-500-8700) • Sunday–Thursday, 3–6 p.m. and 9 p.m.–midnight • Appetizers, $2 off; drinks, $1 off

TONY ROMA'S (S346, ☎ 952-854-7940) • Monday–Friday, 3–6 p.m.
• Appetizers, $6; draft/bottle beer, wine, and well drinks, $3–$6

TUCCI BENUCCH (W114, ☎ 952-853-0200) • Daily, 2–6:30 p.m. (bar and patio only) • Select appetizers, draft beer, and select wine, $3.99–$5.99

TWIN CITY GRILL (N130, ☎ 952-854-0200) • Monday–Friday, 3–6 p.m.
• Appetizers, 50% off; select beer, wine, and cocktails, $3–$5; Thursday, 50% off wines

ZIO ITALIAN (S320, ☎ 952-855-7700) • Monday–Thursday, 3–6 p.m.; Friday, 3–5 p.m. • Appetizers, start at $3; select domestic and craft beers and select cocktails, $4–$6

Barnes and Noble Café (E118) is located in the large bookstore off the Rotunda. There is almost always ample sitting room in this option as well.

Sencha Tea Bar (formerly The Tea Garden; N392) has refreshing tea beverages but also coolers, shakes, chais, and tea lattes.

Teavana (W128) is a favorite for deliciously flavored teas. Choose from 100 types.

David's Tea (E114) offers 150 loose teas to take home, as well as a tea bar with tea and tea lattes to enjoy in the moment.

Chatime Tea (S343) has a menu of 70 freshly prepared drinks.

FREE SAMPLES: *Try Before You Buy*

The European tradition of offering tastes is alive and well in Mall of America. Chocolates, cheeses, Scotch, popcorn, and even gelato are a few treats you can taste before purchasing. Most of these stores are specialty shops, so the employees enjoy talking about the craft behind the concoctions they're sharing.

THIRD FLOOR

DOC POPCORN (E306, ☎ 952-854-9844) is the king of snacks, and a sample is almost always offered on the counter. However, you can ask for a sample of any flavor available that day.

NORTHWOODS CANDY EMPORIUM (N312, ☎ 952-373-4959) is full of all the good stuff, including nostalgic candy you thought was long-gone. Sample a variety of fudges.

PACIUGO GELATO AND CAFFÈ (W392, ☎ 952-814-3528) provides samples from its gelato case.

PEPPER PALACE (E360, ☎ 952-456-2714) has rows of shelves filled with pickled items, jellies and jams, and an array of gift ideas. Taste tests here include the barbecue sauces, hot wing sauces, salsas, and horseradish. Use a new spoon or fresh chip for each sample. Tasters must be ages 18 and up unless a parent is present.

RUBY THAI KITCHEN (S379, ☎ 952-854-5309) sits on the edge of the food court along the main southern corridor. Watch for employees with stretched-out arms offering chicken samples on a toothpick. The samples are tasty and may have you returning for a meal.

RYBICKI CHEESE (W382, ☎ 952-854-3330) has a constant offering of cheese samples. The must-try and -buy are the squeaky cheese curds. Tip: They squeak when they're fresh.

SECOND FLOOR

LINDT MASTER SWISS CHOCOLATIER (S284, ☎ 952-854-1917) has barrels of the delightful Swiss chocolates and truffles. Employees will happily pass you a sample of these delectable sweet treats.

SEE'S CANDIES (N284, ☎ 952-854-5772) offers an assortment of candy, depending on the day. The sweetly dressed clerks are some of the friendliest and most helpful in the mall. Join the rewards program.

VOMFASS (E280, ☎ 952-426-3222) is divided into two stores: One features oils and vinegars; the other has spirits and wine. You could spend the day tasting offerings from barrels filled with flavored oils, vinegars, and maple syrups. Tip: Let the employees do their job and help you with the samples. The knobs can be tricky, and the staff are trained professionals. As for sampling the liquor, have your ID ready. Tasters must be age 21 and up.

FREE SAMPLES: *Try Before You Buy (continued)*
FIRST FLOOR

DAVID'S TEA (E114, ☎ 952-854-5405) always brews a couple of samples adjacent to the tea bar. Knowledgeable staff are happy to give a report on that day's tea sample.

GODIVA CHOCOLATIER (W126, ☎ 952-858-9306) dessert trays offer bits of seasonal or traditional offerings. Join the rewards program.

PEEPS & COMPANY (Nickelodeon Universe, ☎ 952-854-5130), on the west side of Nickelodeon Universe, is a top pick for any kid. You can't miss the big yellow Peep on top. Free samples are constantly flowing. Try a variety of flavored Peeps, the full spectrum of Hot Tamales, and various chocolates.

TEAVANA (W128, ☎ 952-853-9880) is a favorite, with deliciously flavored teas. Employees greet guests at the entrance with enticing teas.

Fast-Food Dining
SOUTH STREET DINING FOOD COURT

- **A&W All American Food** (S376) Classic burgers, hot dogs, root beer, and more

- **Asian Chao/Maki of Japan** (S385) Freshly made Asian dishes and sushi

- **Baja Sol Tortilla Grill** (S392) Typical Mexican fare: tacos, burritos, and enchiladas

- **Bruegger's Bagels** (S338) Bagels and sandwiches

- **Burger Burger** (S321) Hormone- and antibiotic-free burgers

- **Chipotle** (S322) Mexican grill: burritos, tacos, salads, and bowls

- **Cold Stone** (S382) Customized ice cream

- **Cupcake** (W384) Locally sourced ingredients and locally roasted coffee

- **Freshëns Yogurt** (S336) Frozen yogurt with toppings and smoothies

- **Freshii** (S319) Salads, wraps, rice bowls, burritos, soups, and frozen yogurt

- **Great American Cookies** (S336A) Variety of soft cookies

- **Great Steak** (S388) Philly cheesesteaks

- **Johnny Rockets** (S370) Classic Americana-themed burger joint offering inexpensive burgers, fries, and shakes

- **Long John Silver's** (S378) Fast-food fish joint

- **Noodles & Company** (S342) Asian, American, and Mediterranean noodle dishes and salads

- **Paciugo Gelato and Caffè** (W392) Gelato and coffee

- **Panda Express** (S374) American Chinese food

- **Pita Pit** (S372) Pita sandwiches with meat and veggies

- **Pizza Studio** (S340) Create your own pizza

- **Ruby Thai Kitchen** (S379) Thai dishes

- **Sbarro** (S390) Best known as "the mall pizza place" but serves other traditional Italian fare

- **Subway** (E244) Custom-made sub sandwiches

CULINARY ON NORTH FOOD COURT

- **A&W All American Food** (N352) Classic burgers, hot dogs, root beer, and more

- **Auntie Anne's** (N366) Warm pretzels, pretzel dogs, dips, and drinks

- **Burger King** (C360) Fast-food burgers

- **Disco Fries** (C332) Fries topped with cheese, gravy, meatballs, and more

- **Doc Popcorn** (E306) Buttered and flavored popcorn and lemonade

- **Freshëns** (W328) Crêpes, salads, rice bowls, and smoothies

- **Great Steak** (C368) Philly cheesesteaks

- **Jamba Juice** (E317) Healthy juice options

- **Little Tokyo** (C380B) Fast Japanese cuisine

- **Meatball Spot** (C380A) Meatball dishes, salads, sandwiches, and flatbreads

- **Meltshop** (C322) Sandwiches, salads, and shakes

- **Naf Naf Grill** (C326) Middle Eastern pitas, salads, shawarma, and falafel

- **Panda Express** (C370) American Chinese food

- **Piada Italian Street Food** (N326) Hand-rolled Italian piadas (warm wraps)

- **Qdoba** (C364) Mexican grill: burritos, tacos, salads, nachos, and quesadillas

- **Shake Shack** (N332) Burgers, hot dogs, frozen custard, beer, and wine

ELSEWHERE IN THE MALL

- **Auntie Anne's** (E242) Warm pretzels, pretzel dogs, dips, and drinks

- **Cinnabon** (E180) Cinnamon rolls

- **Dairy Queen/Orange Julius** (E282) Burgers, chicken sandwiches, and ice-cream desserts; fruit smoothies

- **Grub** (C5140, Nickelodeon Universe) Dippin' Dots, ICEEs, pizza, and more

- **Häagen-Dazs** (E130) Ice cream

- **Magic Pan Crepe Stand** (W114) Dessert and lunch crêpes

- **Nestlé Toll House Café** (W152 and E283) Cookies, brownies, coffee, ice cream, and smoothies

- **Orange Julius** (W130) Fruit smoothies

- **Pinkberry** (Level 1, Macy's) Tart frozen yogurt

- **Villa Italian Kitchen** (E216) Pizza, stromboli, and pastas

- **Wetzel's Pretzels** (W1805) Pretzels with interesting flavors, such as jalapeño or cinnamon

FULL-SERVICE RESTAURANTS IN MALL OF AMERICA: MINI-PROFILES

TO HELP YOU FIND PALATABLE FOOD that suits your tastes, we provide thumbnail profiles of the mall's full-service restaurants, listed alphabetically. Cost (entrées only) is categorized as **inexpensive** (less than $13), **moderate** ($13–$23), or **expensive** ($24 and up). The restaurants are rated for quality, value, and portion size. Value ratings range from A to F, as follows:

A	Exceptional value; a real bargain	**D**	Somewhat overpriced
B	Good value	**F**	Extremely overpriced
C	Fair value; you get exactly what you pay for		

American Girl Bistro

C5160-1, ☎ 877-247-5223, americangirl.com, inexpensive

American   QUALITY Excellent   VALUE B   PORTION Medium

RESERVATIONS Recommended for weekends, holidays, and special events.
SELECTIONS Pastas, pizzas, burgers, salads, and fruit fondue.
COMMENTS American Girl Bistro provides an ambience that caters to girls and their dolls, making for a special experience. The food is tasty and very good. Afternoon Tea and Craft (Monday–Friday, 2–4:30 p.m.) is $13.50/person, excluding tax and gratuity.

Benihana

S358, ☎ 952-594-6205, benihana.com, moderate–expensive

Japanese   QUALITY Excellent   VALUE B   PORTION Medium

RESERVATIONS Recommended weekends and holidays.
SELECTIONS Teppanyaki, sushi, and sashimi, as well as chicken and shrimp dishes.
COMMENTS Sign up online for the Chef's Table to receive birthday specials.

Bubba Gump Shrimp Co.

S396, ☎ 952-853-6600, bubbagump.com, inexpensive–moderate

| Seafood | QUALITY Good | VALUE B | PORTION Medium-large |

RESERVATIONS Recommended nights and weekends.
SELECTIONS Boiled, fried, baked, or steamed shrimp; fried chicken, baby back ribs, mac and cheese, and salads.
COMMENTS Communicate with the staff with a STOP, FORREST, STOP sign.

Buffalo Wild Wings

S312, ☎ 952-346-3740, buffalowildwings.com, inexpensive

| American | QUALITY Good | VALUE B | PORTION Medium-large |

RESERVATIONS Not accepted; please notify if a large party is coming.
SELECTIONS Wings, burgers, sandwiches, ribs, wraps, and salads.
COMMENTS Lots of TVs to watch "the game."

Cadillac Ranch

S352, ☎ 952-854-1004, cadillacranchgroup.com, inexpensive

| American | QUALITY Good | VALUE B | PORTION Medium-large |

RESERVATIONS Not accepted.
SELECTIONS Pizza flatbreads, tacos, wings, steak, pastas, and salads.
COMMENTS Some beers on the menu are from Minnesota-based Granite City Food & Brewery. Must be age 18 and up to ride the mechanical bull.

Cantina #1

E406, ☎ 952-854-6500, cantina1.com, inexpensive–moderate

| Mexican | QUALITY Fair | VALUE C | PORTION Medium-large |

RESERVATIONS Accepted.
SELECTIONS Fish tacos, fajitas, Tex-Mex, and seafood.
COMMENTS The food can be hit or miss. Chips and salsa are not free: $2.45. Some booths have views of Nickelodeon Universe. Entertainment includes karaoke on Wednesday and Thursday and a DJ on Friday and Saturday nights. A favorite for happy hour. If you are a Mexican food or Tex-Mex aficionado, you will be disappointed. We've never had bad food here but have heard that the experience and food varies depending on the day and time of visit.

Cantina Laredo

W300, ☎ 952-406-8311, cantinalaredo.com, moderate–expensive

| Mexican | QUALITY Good | VALUE B | PORTION Medium |

RESERVATIONS Accepted; using opentable.com is recommended.
SELECTIONS Fish tacos, empanadas, flautas, ceviche.
COMMENTS Hand-squeezed lime juice margaritas. Opened in 2015. If you are a Mexican food or Tex-Mex aficionado, you will be disappointed. We've never had bad food here, but the experience and food can vary depending on the day and time of visit.

Cedar + Stone, Urban Table

JW Marriott, C1000, ☎ 612-615-0100, tinyurl.com/cedarstone, expensive

| American | QUALITY Excellent | VALUE A | PORTION Medium |

RESERVATIONS Recommended evenings, weekends, and holidays.

SELECTIONS Soups, salads, walleye, pork belly, steak, Gouda mac and cheese, garlic chips, and sautéed kale.

COMMENTS Chef-crafted dishes. Prices are standard for a luxury dining experience. The room is plush and cozy with good acoustics. Minnesota/Great Lakes specialties include several walleye (close relative of the European pike perch) preparations, steaks grilled over a wood fire, and a signature scallops and pork belly dish.

Crave

S368, ☎ 952-854-5000, craveamerica.com, moderate–expensive

| American | QUALITY Excellent | VALUE C | PORTION Small–medium or small |

RESERVATIONS Recommended evenings, weekends, and holidays.

SELECTIONS Sushi, seafood, steaks, pastas, sandwiches, chicken, and burgers.

COMMENTS The food at Crave is some of the best and freshest in the mall. If you're famished, this may *not* be the restaurant for you. Crave does a thriving takeout business, which is something to consider in lieu of room service at your hotel.

Dick's Last Resort

S402, ☎ 612-276-6995, dickslastresort.com, moderate

| American | QUALITY Fair | VALUE C | PORTION Medium, |

RESERVATIONS Large groups of more than 12 only.

SELECTIONS Ribs, catfish, fish-and-chips, variety of salads and burgers.

COMMENTS Dick's is a boisterous pub with a down south vibe and dozens of spelling errors on the menu. Guests who have never been to Dick's need to be warned that the staff is dripping with sarcasm and humor. If you can't take a joke, stay away. Looking for a laugh? You're sure to have fun.

FireLake Grill House & Cocktail Bar

Radisson Blu, S2000, ☎ 952-881-5258, firelakerestaurant.com, expensive

| American | QUALITY Excellent | VALUE A | PORTION Medium |

RESERVATIONS Recommended weekends, evenings, and holidays.

SELECTIONS Seasonally fresh, meats, fish, seafood, and creative appetizers.

COMMENTS Locally sourced dishes. One of the best restaurants at the mall, Fire-Lake serves Minnesota regional dishes and a variety of game dishes featuring bison, quail, venison (sausage), wild turkey, and, from the lake, walleye. Many meats, including chicken, prime rib, leg of lamb, and pork ribs, are rotisserie roasted. We recommend the Charcuterie Platter and Corn Bread Skillet as starters. Half the room is well appointed and swank, while the other half is publike. Can be noisy, depending on where you sit. Honeybee colonies sit atop the hotel for restaurant use.

Hard Rock Cafe

C5115, ☎ 952-853-7000, hardrock.com, moderate

American	QUALITY Good	VALUE B–C	PORTION Medium–large

RESERVATIONS Not accepted directly but available on opentable.com.

SELECTIONS Appetizers such as nachos, wings, and potato skins; salads; burgers; fajitas; and more.

COMMENTS Hard Rock Cafe shot glass and T-shirt collectors will be happy to find this new location (opened in 2014). Menu is standard and comparable to all the other Hard Rock Cafes in the world. Considering Prince called Minneapolis home, the "Purple Rain" star's collection of memorabilia is worth a peek. The restaurant patio is "outside" in Nickelodeon Universe.

Hooters

E404, ☎ 952-854-3110, hooters.com, inexpensive

American	QUALITY Good	VALUE C	PORTION Medium

RESERVATIONS Not accepted.

SELECTIONS Wings, beer, and cute Hooters girls.

COMMENTS If you've been to one Hooters, you've been to them all. Newly renovated patio in interior corridor.

The Lounge @ House of Comedy

E408, ☎ 952-858-8558, houseofcomedy.net, moderate

American	QUALITY Good	VALUE B	PORTION Medium

RESERVATIONS Not accepted; however, prepurchased tickets are recommended for shows.

SELECTIONS Appetizers of cheese curds, poutine, and "State Fare" snacks (such as doughnut holes and mac-and-cheese bites). Main dishes include flatbreads, salads, and sandwiches, as well as turkey, chicken, or beef burgers.

COMMENTS Adjacent to Rick Bronson's House of Comedy.

Margaritaville

E344, margaritavillemallofamerica.com, moderate

Florida-Caribbean	QUALITY Good	VALUE C	PORTION Medium

RESERVATIONS Priority seating is available.

SELECTIONS Caribbean, Florida fusion, and American items.

COMMENTS Jimmy Buffett covers are popular (no surprise) as is island music and light rock. If you eat dinner here, you'll probably want to find another vantage point when the band cranks up on the main stage. There's usually an acoustic guitarist strumming from 5 p.m. daily. If you are already inside the restaurant eating dinner before the cover charge kicks in, you won't be kicked out when the band kicks off.

Masu Sushi & Robata

S344, ☎ 952-896-6278, masusushiandrobata.com, inexpensive

Japanese	QUALITY Good	VALUE B	PORTION Medium

RESERVATIONS Recommended for lunch, evenings, and weekends.
SELECTIONS Beef udon, miso soup, shrimp tempura with veggies, seaweed salad.
COMMENTS A nice option for causal Japanese food. Expect good food, friendly service, and a nice variety.

Nordstrom Marketplace Café

Level 3, Nordstrom, ☎ 952-883-2121, restaurants.nordstrom.com, inexpensive–moderate

American	QUALITY Excellent	VALUE A	PORTION Small-medium

RESERVATIONS Not accepted.
SELECTIONS Sandwiches, salads, and pastas.
COMMENTS Try the lemon ricotta cookie for dessert.

Rainforest Cafe

S306, ☎ 952-854-7500, rainforestcafe.com, inexpensive–moderate

American	QUALITY Good	VALUE C	PORTION Medium

RESERVATIONS Recommended for weekends and holidays.
SELECTIONS Soups, salads, seafood, pastas, wraps, burgers, fajitas, chicken, and ribs.
COMMENTS In 2016 it relocated to the third floor across from sister restaurant Bubba Gump Shrimp Co. The dining room is designed to look like a jungle, complete with animatronic elephants, bats, and monkeys. There's occasional thunder and even some rainfall.

Ruby Tuesday

N234, ☎ 952-854-8282, rubytuesday.com, moderate

American	QUALITY Good	VALUE B–C	PORTION Medium

RESERVATIONS Recommended for weekends and holidays.
SELECTIONS Seafood, chicken, steak, and sandwiches.
COMMENTS The only salad bar in the mall. Kids eat free Tuesday evenings.

Sky Deck Sports Grille & Lanes

E401, ☎ 952-500-8700, skydecklanes.com, inexpensive

American	QUALITY Fair	VALUE C	PORTION Medium

RESERVATIONS Not accepted, but a group planner is available for larger parties.
SELECTIONS Burgers, salads, sandwiches, and pasta appetizers.
COMMENTS Typical sports bar food.

Tiger Sushi

N100, ☎ 952-876-9410, tigersushiusa.com, moderate

Japanese	QUALITY Excellent	VALUE B–C	PORTION Medium

RESERVATIONS Accepted.
SELECTIONS Sushi, sashimi, soups, salads, appetizers, sake, beer, and wine.
COMMENTS A hip, little sushi bar. Good sushi.

Tony Roma's

S346, ☎ 952-854-7940, tonyromas.com, inexpensive–moderate

| American | QUALITY Fair-good | VALUE B | PORTION Medium-large |

RESERVATIONS Recommended on weekends and holidays.
SELECTIONS Appetizers, steak, chicken, seafood, salads, and sandwiches.
COMMENTS Family steak house best known for ribs.

Tucci Benucch

W114, ☎ 952-853-0200, tucci-benucch.com, moderate

| Italian | QUALITY Excellent | VALUE A | PORTION Medium-large |

RESERVATIONS Recommended for lunch, dinner, weekends, and holidays.
SELECTIONS Pasta, pizza, and salads.
COMMENTS Cozy Italian restaurant, locally owned. A nice, quiet escape from the mall madness.

Twin City Grill

N130, ☎ 952-854-0200, twincitygrillrestaurant.com, moderate–expensive

| American | QUALITY Excellent | VALUE A | PORTION Medium-large |

RESERVATIONS Recommended for evenings, weekends, and holidays.
SELECTIONS Burgers, steak, and salads.
COMMENTS A top mall choice. Friendly ambience and delicious menu. Try the burgers.

Zio Italian

S320, ☎ 952-855-7700, zioitalian.com, inexpensive–moderate

| Italian | QUALITY Good | VALUE B-C | PORTION Medium-large |

RESERVATIONS Recommended on weekends and holidays.
SELECTIONS Handmade pasta, pizzas, and salads.
COMMENTS The complimentary warm bread and olive oil before the meal is a nice touch, and the mellow ambience and dim lighting make for a great place to unwind during the afternoon between the lunch and dinner rush.

GOOD TIMES FOR GROWN-UPS

Grown-ups looking for a lively time are best off going straight to Level 4. Restaurants and bars include **Dick's Last Resort** (S402, ☎ 612-276-6995); **Hooters** (E404, ☎ 952-854-3110); **Cantina #1** (E406, ☎ 952-854-6500); **Sky Deck Sports Grille & Lanes** (E402, ☎ 952-500-8700); **Rick Bronson's House of Comedy and Lounge** (E400, ☎ 952-858-8558); and **Theatres at Mall of America** (S401, ☎ 952-858-8558).

Those looking for a quieter atmosphere will appreciate the elegant setting of **FireLake Grill House & Cocktail Bar** (Radisson Blu, S2000, ☎ 952-881-5258). In the mall **Tucci Benucch** (W114, ☎ 952-853-0200); **Crave** (S368, ☎ 952-854-5000); and **Twin City Grill** (N130, ☎ 952-854-0200) are good choices for a casual but relaxing experience without hoopla.

FULL-SERVICE MOA RESTAURANTS BY CUISINE

CUISINE	LOCATION	QUALITY	VALUE
AMERICAN			
American Girl Bistro	C5160-1	Excellent	B
Buffalo Wild Wings	S312	Good	B
Cadillac Ranch	S352	Good	B
Cedar + Stone, Urban Table	JW Marriott, C1000	Excellent	A
Crave	S368	Excellent	C
Dick's Last Resort	S402	Fair	C
FireLake Grill House & Cocktail Bar	Radisson Blu, S2000	Excellent	A
Hard Rock Cafe	C5115	Good	B-C
Hooters	E404	Good	C
The Lounge @ House of Comedy	E408	Good	B
Nordstrom Marketplace Café	Level 3, Nordstrom	Excellent	A
Rainforest Cafe	S306	Good	C
Ruby Tuesday	N234	Good	B-C
Sky Deck Sports Grille & Lanes	E401	Fair	C
Tony Roma's	S346	Fair-good	B
Twin City Grill	N130	Excellent	A
FLORIDA-CARIBBEAN			
Margaritaville	E344	Good	C
ITALIAN			
Tucci Benucch	W114	Excellent	A
Zio Italian	S320	Good	B-C
JAPANESE			
Benihana	S358	Excellent	B
Masu Sushi & Robata	S344	Good	B
Tiger Sushi	N100	Excellent	B-C
MEXICAN			
Cantina #1	E406	Good	C
Cantina Laredo	W300	Good	B
SEAFOOD			
Bubba Gump Shrimp Co.	S396	Good	B

DINING *Outside*
MALL *of* **AMERICA**

UNOFFICIAL GUIDE RESEARCHERS TAKE THEIR FOOD SERIOUSLY, and while Mall of America has a nice selection of choices, you will most likely be familiar with most of the eateries because many are national chain restaurants. Guests staying in one of the three hotels across Killebrew Drive, south of MOA, will take comfort in knowing that an **IHOP** and **T.G.I. Friday's** are clustered together alongside Country Inn & Suites and are within easy walking distance of the other hotels. The same goes for **RedRossa Italian Grille,** which is inside Best Western Plus, while **Chevys Fresh Mex** is adjacent to Homewood Suites. These options are used to crowds and deliver fast and courteous service. Beyond MOA's pocket of Bloomington, I-494 is lined with many restaurants, some of which are also chain restaurants, while other eateries are found in surrounding suburbs. Here are a variety of options we recommend outside the mall.

WHERE TO EAT OUTSIDE MOA

AMERICAN

KINCAIDS 8400 Normandale Lake Blvd., Bloomington, MN 55437; ☎ 952-921-2255; kincaids.com; expensive. Steaks and seafood.

LUCKY'S PUB 1800 American Blvd. W, Bloomington, MN 55431; ☎ 952-405-2213; luckys13pub.com; moderate. Generous portions of burgers, sandwiches, salads.

Q. CUMBERS 7465 France Ave. S, Minneapolis, MN 5435; ☎ 952-831-0235; qcumbers.com; moderate. Salad bar buffet, plus small section of rotating hot comfort foods (chicken, beef, potatoes, pasta).

CHINESE

MANDARIN KITCHEN 8766 Lyndale Ave. S, Minneapolis, MN 55420; ☎ 952-884-5356; moderate. Traditional Chinese dishes of seafood, pork, chicken, beef, and dim sum.

GREEK

ANSARI'S MEDITERRANEAN GRILL & LOUNGE 1960 Rahncliff Court, Eagan, MN 55122; ☎ 651-452-0999; ansarisgrill.com; moderate. Authentic Mediterranean dishes and platters: Gyros, hummus, dolma, and tabbouleh salad.

GYRO'S GRILL 1710 E. Old Shakopee Road, Bloomington, MN 55425; ☎ 952-888-2121; ordergyrosgrill.com; inexpensive. No-frills place to grab a gyro or Greek salad.

ITALIAN

REDROSSA ITALIAN GRILLE 1901 Killebrew Drive, Bloomington, MN 55425; ☎ 952-814-2910; redrossa.com; moderate. Traditional Italian pasta dishes, wood-fired pizza, salads, hot sandwiches.

MEXICAN

ANDALE TAQUERIA 7700 Nicollet Ave. S, Richfield, MN 55423; ☎ 612-259-8868; andaletaqueriaymercado.com; inexpensive. Great tacos and burritos.

CHEVYS FRESH MEX 2251 Killebrew Drive, Bloomington, MN 55425; ☎ 952-814-9555; chevys.com; moderate. A good Mexican chain.

PART FIVE

MALL *of* AMERICA *with* KIDS

A **BIT** *of* **PREPARATION**

SHOPPING MALLS GENERALLY aren't the most family-friendly places, at least for more than a couple of hours. Padded play areas, the food court, gumball machines, and a handful of quarter rides (or more like dollar rides these days) are usually the limit to kid fun at the average shopping mall, and that's the reason a trip to the mall can be met with an eye roll from school-age kids and end with a toddler's tantrum shrieks bouncing off the marble floors.

But wait . . . what's that? Lights beam down as music plays in the background. In glides the Mall of America (MOA), waving her hand in slow, beauty queen fashion. Behind her parades a long line of shiny attractions: a theme park, an aquarium, miniature golf, a mirror maze, the LEGO store, American Girl, Disney Store, Build-A-Bear Workshop . . . and the list goes on. It's a parent's dream come true: shopping *and* days worth of fun for the kids!

Then you show up and reality hits. Those quarter rides turn into $6 rides, the gumball machine is now a $5 serving of Dippin' Dots, the fourth-grader is pouting that you won't let her get her ears pierced at Claire's, and the toddler is stomping her feet because the Dora meet and greet was replaced with SpongeBob. All the while you're panicking that the Godiva samples will be gone and Nordstrom Rack will be empty by the time you finally start shopping. (We promise that Nordstrom Rack [W324] will have plenty of selections left.)

Fear not. MOA truly is a family travel destination, and it is what you make of it. After hours and hours of roller coaster rides, miles of shopping, and some fierce parking maneuvers, it comes down to this: The best way to tackle MOA with kids is with a plan.

The loud noises, overstimulation, and confusion of such a massive structure can be overwhelming to all involved. Luckily, keeping the family's spirits up, avoiding hunger pains, and maintaining a shopping and attraction rhythm is easier at MOA than it is while visiting an outdoor theme park because overheating, sunburn, and dehydration are unlikely. And no matter where you are in the mall, a restroom, resting place, and bottle of water are all a short distance away. The key to a successful day: knowing exactly what it is that you want to do. Shop? Play? Eat?

As we mentioned in Part One: Planning Your Visit, the first app you should add is the free **Mall of America app.** Parents will appreciate the list of happenings under Events, stroller and locker information, and discounts under Deals.

If you're traveling with toddlers, plan to wear them out (keep reading for more on kid activities) and then tackle your shopping list as they nap in the stroller. If your kids are older, rest time can mean a quick drink or bite to eat, like a slice of pizza or refreshing ICEE at Nickelodeon Universe's **Grub** (C5140, West Entrance) with its 12-flavor Mix-It-Up Station, or perhaps a bubble tea at **Chatime Tea** (S343). As for the young non-nappers, we appreciate the quiet ambience of the children's section at **Barnes & Noble** (E118). Sometimes the rest is more for the adults than the kids.

Maintaining a well-orchestrated day is possible, but there are a few things you need to know. Stroller-pushers and others who can't use stairs or escalators, this is for you: Elevator waits can be horrendous during weekends, on holidays, and on days with large events. During the week, especially summer months, you could be battling a number of MOA-goers, including those from tour buses, kid camps, and massive events—and don't forget the fans there to see the latest reality TV stars or up-and-coming boy band. Throw in a broken escalator, and you can forget changing floors. Therefore, you will want to avoid the up-down-up-down as much as possible. Mapping out your shops, attractions, and dining beforehand and crossing them off floor by floor will save precious time. We recommend starting at the top and working your way down. That way you're going against the flow on elevators and escalators because most shoppers work their way up

unofficial **TIP**
Let your spouse, friend, or mom take the kids on their own adventure while you shop. Or if you're alone, try this: "We will go on the rides/visit the Peeps store/ hit the mirror maze after I go to (fill in the blank)." Trust us. It can work.

as the day progresses. If you can, plan to time your floor change near lunchtime. Both food courts are on Level 3, as are most of the full-service dining options. The South Street Dining Food Court is above the LEGO store, and the new Culinary on North Food Court is on the same side as the Ferris wheel in Nickelodeon Universe. The Magic Pan Crepe Stand (W114) on Level 1 is a perfect place to grab a bite to eat. See Part Four: Dining for the scoop on all food and drink selections. After lunch, plan your next phase, whether it is more shopping, an attraction, or an event, and then keep the cycle.

MATERNITY SHOPPING

SPEAKING FROM EXPERIENCE, it can be challenging to find maternity wear, but moms-to-be will be pleasantly surprised to discover that a number of stores have maternity sections and specialty stores for the pregnant market. **Macy's** (Level 2) has a cozy section featuring Motherhood Maternity, as well as a nice selection on the clearance racks, from pajamas to professional wear. **Old Navy** (E138) offers an affordable selection of up-to-date maternity wear, as does **H&M** (W117), but be forewarned that the selection can be hit or miss. **Destination Maternity** (S258) is a favorite, thanks to its friendly customer service and comfy couches. **Long Tall Sally** (W282) has a limited selection, but the leggings come highly recommended for expectant ladies of height. Sadly, **Gap** stopped carrying maternity selections at MOA in spring 2016.

VISITING MALL *of* AMERICA *with* INFANTS *and* TODDLERS

BABY-CHANGING FACILITIES

EVERY PUBLIC RESTROOM in Mall of America (MOA) has a built-in changing table somewhere near the sinks (see Part Three: Arriving and Getting Oriented for information on mall restrooms). If you're low on wipes, be forewarned that there are no paper towels to use as backups in MOA restrooms, only high-powered hand dryers. While you could use toilet paper, running water over toilet paper is never a good idea, especially when it's the cheap, commercial-grade variety. The hand dryers are very, very loud and can startle little ears if your infant is sound sensitive. Naturally, the dryers are located adjacent to the changing tables. Better options include the Macy's (Level 1) or Nordstrom (Levels 2 and 3) ladies' lounges.

Parents with babies already have the "what to pack" list memorized. But there are those rare occasions when you don't bring enough diapers or wipes along. The big question here is where can you buy diapers and wipes at MOA? Sadly, there is no baby supply store in the mall. In our experience **Holiday Station** (W123) does keep diapers stocked, but in larger sizes (sizes 3–4). You will also find training pants for older tots, as well as baby wipes.

Worst-case scenario, you may have to hit up another parent toting an overflowing diaper bag and hope they have more than enough diapers and/or wipes to share. Therefore, bring more than you need, as you may end up being the Good Samaritan helping another parent out.

If you need to stock up on diapers, wipes, formula, or any other baby necessities, **Walmart** (700 American Blvd. E, Bloomington; ☎ 952-854-5600) is only 2 miles from MOA. Three miles north on MN 77 is a **SuperTarget** (6445 Richfield Pkwy., Richfield; ☎ 612-252-0473), and **Babies-R-Us** (900 W. 78th St., Richfield; ☎ 612-861-2249) is less than 4 miles away. **IKEA** (8000 Ikea Way, Bloomington; ☎ 888-888-4532) is a very short jaunt north of MOA and has a baby care area, baby food (free with a meal), microwaves, shopping strollers, and play areas (see page 100 about babysitting).

If you don't want to haul the diaper bag around MOA, all-day electronic lockers are available on Levels 1, 2, and 3 on the east and west sides; on Level 1, north and south sides; and in Nickelodeon Universe underneath the Ferris wheel. Lockers come in four sizes: regular ($6), large ($8), extra-large ($11), and jumbo ($13), and all have easy access to restrooms.

As for warming baby bottles, I recommend bringing a travel bottle warmer. Otherwise, restaurants can always provide diners with warm water for mixing formula.

WHERE TO REST AND NURSE

NURSING IS PERSONAL. Some mothers are comfortable nursing anytime, anywhere, while other mothers (or their babies) prefer a quiet, private location. After much personal experience and talking to many, many local parents, there is one consensus: Mall of America lacks private designated nursing locations. The only stores with any type of comfortable place to relax with a baby—while not people-watching or vice versa—are **Nordstrom** (ladies' lounges on Levels 2 and 3) and **Macy's** (ladies' lounge on Level 1). Both stores offer changing tables. Some websites will suggest Carter's Baby nursing room, but a remodel a few years ago phased out that perk.

If you can adjust to nursing in more public places with your breast and the baby's head covered with a shawl or some such, nursing will not be a problem at all. Also, please know that the normalizing breastfeeding movement is in full swing. We have seen many mothers openly breast-feeding on mall benches without covers.

A mom from Georgia wrote to us, and we totally agree with her:

Many women have no problem nursing uncovered, and they have the right to do so in public without being criticized. Even women who want to cover up may have a baby who won't cooperate and flings off the cover. I understand that peace and quiet help, but babies will eat almost anywhere, and mothers shouldn't feel pressured to sneak off when a baby is hungry.

Destination Maternity (S258) welcomes mothers to use its dressing rooms for privacy or to use the comfortable store seats (expectant mothers will appreciate this resting place too). Of course, you are in a mall, so any quiet store with dressing rooms (especially those specializing in women's or children's apparel) could be an option, depending on how busy the store is and how accommodating the staff is (not that you need to tell them what you're doing). Culinary on North, the new food court, has the added perk of a family restroom complete with double sinks, a changing table, and one chair for nursing. Adjacent to the room is a private restroom with an adult-size toilet sitting directly across from a tot-size toilet. We're disappointed that there isn't a larger space for mothers and their babies to nurse comfortably.

Other than that, benches and couches offer resting areas throughout the mall, but they're hardly secluded, and sometimes people (such as grandparents or bored husbands) are stretched out sleeping. As for mall restrooms, we don't recommend them for nursing: There are no places to sit, and most are busy and frequently have long lines. Our pick is Nordstrom.

STROLLERS

BRINGING YOUR OWN STROLLER IS RECOMMENDED—nap-age kids are used to some shut-eye in the comforts of their own stroller. If that's not possible, single and double strollers are available for rent at all four Guest Services desks (☎ 952-883-8800) at the East, West, North, and South Entrances on Level 1 (single stroller, $7/day; double stroller, $9/day; plus refundable $5 deposit). Single strollers are also available in skyways leading from the parking ramp to the mall via stroller vending machines. Credit cards accepted include Visa, MasterCard, American Express, and Discover. At Guest Services you have a choice of a single push stroller or a fire truck with a steering wheel, while double strollers are the standard side by side. You must have a credit card to rent, and strollers can't be abandoned.

If the stroller is damaged or not returned, the full stroller value will be charged to your credit card. If you are shopping with an infant, bring your personal stroller because the mall does not rent car seat–accommodating strollers of any kind.

Stroller-parking signs are found throughout Mall of America (MOA), and nearly every full-service restaurant has a stroller parking spot. As always, don't forget to remove merchandise, as well as irreplaceable or expensive belongings, when leaving a stroller alone. No store or eatery will take responsibility for lost or stolen articles.

Parents with plans to see and do more besides MOA can rent a stroller and other baby gear from local companies. **Rockabyerentals .com** (☎ 877-388-2229) has a single stroller option, Baby Jogger Q-Series ($8/day; $48/week), and a double stroller option, Maclaren

Twin Traveller ($9/day; $54/week). Other baby gear, including car seats, swings, cribs, baby monitors, high chairs, and more, are available. A minimum rental of $30 is required, and a $10 delivery fee applies in the immediate Minneapolis–Saint Paul area, $20 if outside the area.

The national company **Rentthebabygear.com** has a variety of baby gear rentals, but it's quite a bit more costly and doesn't offer any daily rates. Stroller choices include the Baby Jogger City Mini Single Stroller ($65/week) and Baby Jogger City Mini Double Stroller ($90/week; discounts for multiple weeks). There is a $10 delivery fee.

Note: MOA makes it clear that strollers are not allowed on escalators, but you will see frustrated parents give up on elevator waits and take strollers up the escalators. A better alternative is to use the quieter department store elevators. If you're desperate and going between Levels 1 and 2 on the south side, the Radisson Blu is located outside the South Entrance. There are two access routes into the mall on this side. Level 1 is exposed to the elements, and you do have to cross the street. Level 2 offers direct access into the mall via a covered walkway. There are a handful of steps alongside a ramp option. You can think of this avenue as sightseeing because the Radisson Blu lobby is certainly worth a peek. Stroller-toting parents visiting Sea Life (E120) can take the hidden elevator on the right past Guest Services when walking toward the Rotunda.

WHEN KIDS GET LOST

CROWDS OF PEOPLE, combined with large spaces and various stores, make shopping malls an easy place to lose kids. Mall of America (MOA) is no different. We once witnessed a mother spinning in the middle of the mall screaming, "My baby! Where's my baby?" We offered to help, but the mother was so distraught that she kept running around screaming. Fortunately, the child was found moments later in the store in which the mother had been shopping. We were glad to see the happy ending, as we know that horrible stomach-dropping feeling of a missing child.

A Bloomington police officer working the mall said that losing track of kids most often occurs when the mall is at its busiest, but parents shouldn't worry. Guest Services and MOA Security work together to swiftly reunite parent and child. If a child gets lost, he/she will be taken to a safe holding area to wait for the parent. At Nickelodeon Universe, children will be held at Guest Services in the center of the park on the north side, across from the carousel.

If your child gets lost, first contact MOA Security (☎ 952-883-8888). If you don't have a phone, you can go directly to Guest Services (all main entrances; ☎ 952-883-8800) to ask for assistance. The mall does not have a paging system, but MOA has more than 100 highly trained security officers who receive the information internally and work proficiently and professionally to reunite child and parent.

HOW MOST CHILDREN GET LOST

1. **THEME PARK ENTRANCE/EXIT.** Nickelodeon Universe has four entrances from the main mall, which easily disorients even adult shoppers until they spend some time getting familiar with the mall. Lost children may be tempted to enter or exit the park in search of a parent.

2. **NICKELODEON UNIVERSE RIDES.** Children exiting rides can easily miss their parents and vice versa.

3. **FOOD COURTS.** Both food courts are huge. Some eateries have self-help soda machines, and when a child runs up for a refill or extra napkins, it's easy to forget where the rest of the family is sitting.

4. **CLOTHING RACKS.** This is the most classic of lost kids' stories because oftentimes the child isn't lost but hiding.

5. **RESTROOMS.** While Mall of America (MOA) restrooms have only one entry/exit point, using the facilities separately can cause confusion. Even if a child calls your name (or you call theirs), you may not hear each other because of the noisy hand dryers and flushing toilets.

6. **MASSIVE CROWDS.** Beside the normal shopping crowds, MOA's Rotunda (east) events draw thousands of people, making it hard to keep track of small children. When the crowd disperses, the challenge increases tenfold.

TIPS FOR KEEPING TRACK OF YOUR BROOD

TAKE A PHOTO OF YOUR KIDS at the beginning of the day, so you can remember exactly what they are wearing and show security personnel what your child looks like.

Talk to your kids about what to do if you get separated. If they are old enough, agree on a meeting place. Nickelodeon Universe entrances are ideal meeting places because of the large landmarks: under the Ferris wheel (north entrance), the big green slime splash chair (east entrance), Peeps store (west entrance), and LEGO store (south entrance). When going on Nickelodeon Universe rides, agree to a meeting place (we suggest the ride exit) after each ride.

Point out the uniformed security officers and store employees to your children, so they know whom they can approach if they are lost.

Tag your toddler. Occasionally stores will hand out free balloons to young shoppers. **Old Navy** (E138, ☎ 952-853-0100) and **Nordstrom** (1000 NW Court, ☎ 952-883-2121) have been known to do this. Tie the balloon to your child, so you can keep easy track of him or her. Fun for him/her is sanity for you. If you have a stroller, tying a balloon to the handle can help older kids (who shun the balloon idea) keep an eye on you.

Put your cell number somewhere on your child. Temporary tattoos have become a hit in recent years. **SafetyTat.com** has an array of temporary tattoos designed for parents to write phone numbers, allergies, or other pertinent information. We've been known to stuff business cards (with a cell number) in our older kids' pockets to hand to someone if help is needed.

BABYSITTING *and* CAMPS

AFTER READING ABOUT LOST KIDS, the idea of babysitting doesn't sound too bad, does it? Unfortunately, there aren't any kid camps or babysitting options on Mall of America (MOA) premises. **IKEA** (8000 Ikea Way, Bloomington; ☎ 888-888-4532) across the way does have free, supervised Småland, but parents must stay in the store. Children must be potty-trained and 37"–54" tall. If your children are school-age and you are visiting MOA in the summer, local schools, community centers, and gyms offer camps and classes. Most camps are in short proximity to the mall, and they vary from day (morning, afternoon, or all day) to weekly and monthly camps. This option gives you time to shop while the children are safely entertained.

Some suggestions:

Bloomington bloomingtonmn.gov	**Eagan** cityofeagan.com
Edina edinamn.gov	**Lakeville** ci.lakeville.mn.us
Lifetime Fitness lifetimefitness.com	**YMCA** ymcatwincities.org

KIDS' ACTIVITIES

kids MALL OF AMERICA (MOA) has plenty of children's apparel stores and a handful of toy stores. Smart marketers have realized that the best way to draw the parent crowd is to provide entertainment for the youngsters. Also see Part Seven: Nickelodeon Universe, Part Eight: Other Attractions, and Part Nine: Group Activities.

Books are best (we know that for a fact), and **Barnes & Noble** (E118, ☎ 952-854-1455) scored one of the best locations in the mall. The huge store is located on Level 1, right off the Rotunda, where large events, concerts, and group activities—including Toddler Tuesday—are held. The store includes a Barnes & Novel Café and an interactive children's section with a stage for story time. Story time is often coordinated with Toddler Tuesday (starting at 11 a.m.) and is also offered other times. Check the store's calendar on its website to see what events are coming up, so you can plan your day.

The wonderful world of Disney—including the **Disney Store** (S118, ☎ 952-854-9119) at MOA—never lets parents down. In addition to all the Disney-themed clothes and toys lining the shelves, a big screen plays Disney favorites, and a table with coloring sheets is always awaiting the next great artist. Princesses may try on their next ball gown in the castle, which has a three-way mirror inside.

As a store that has *kids* in its name, it's no surprise that the **Creative Kidstuff** (E148, ☎ 612-524-6630) floor is teeming with hands-on toys for tots to play with while parents shop. We're talking dollhouses, baby dolls with strollers, games, and other interactive toys.

The **American Girl** store (C5160, ☎ 877-247-5223) is what girly-girl dreams are made of. The two-story store has three entrances: Nickelodeon Universe, Level 1 Rotunda, and Level 2 Rotunda. Complimentary personal shoppers are available, but an appointment is recommended. The store itself is a treat. Special events range from free to a heftier $28–$38 (per person) date with mom or dad. This location has a Doll Hair Salon, complete with stylists, and an American Girl Bistro with a view of the theme park.

The newly remodeled and more efficient **Build-A-Bear Workshop** (E172, ☎ 952-854-1164) is around the corner from American Girl. Fans can expect the traditional warm and cuddly environment that Build-A-Bear offers. The original process followed eight stuffed animal–making stations: Choose Me, Hear Me, Stuff Me, Stitch Me, Fluff Me, Dress Me, Name Me, and Take Me Home. Today, the experience is an all-in-one experience with two 7-foot-tall stuffing machines, each with a spinning bear on top. If you've never partaken in this experience, expect the accessories to add up in price quickly. The $12 bear can easily end up costing $50–$60.

Lotus Beads and Jewelry (N368, ☎ 952-854-9951) is a make-your-own jewelry shop that appeals to adults but is also a fun activity for older kids. School-age children to teens have fun creating their own ensembles. Consultants are on hand to assist with your creations.

If you're worried that there's not going to be something for your kid, let it go.

Ella, age 6:

The Mall of America is like a magic world because it is fun.

Anna, age 10, on the LEGO store:

It's cool how they made all the big things on top of the LEGO store.

Emma Grace, age 12, on the American Girl store:

I like the dolls' high chairs and how they give you little tiny food for the dolls.

Ben, age 15, on MOA in general:

No matter how many times we go, I always enjoy it. It always has a fun atmosphere.

Jonah, age 13, is a fan of the rides in Nickelodeon Universe and the trivia at Buffalo Wild Wings.

TODDLER TUESDAYS

AT MALL OF AMERICA (MOA), every Tuesday, 10 a.m.–noon, is Toddler Tuesday. Depending on the events featured, Toddler Tuesday draws hundreds of tots and their caretakers. Most of the adult attendees are moms, but dads, grandparents, and nannies attend too. The theme and events change weekly but often include arts and crafts, story time, movies, character meet and greets, and giveaways. While the scheduled hours end at noon, the toddler-friendly joy continues well into the afternoon with deep discounts and special offers. Normally, Toddler Tuesday is held in the Rotunda, but if another event is being set up, it may move down to any of the other courts throughout the mall.

Nickelodeon Universe joins the fun by offering the Nickelodeon Universe Toddler Tuesday Rides Deal: a 5-hour toddler wristband for $11.95 plus tax. The toddler wristband is valid for unlimited age-appropriate rides. Unlike the unlimited bracelets that can be prepurchased, these may be used only on the day of purchase. Rides include La Aventura de Azul, Back at the Barnyard Hayride, Backyardigans Swing-Along, Big Rigs, Blue's Skidoo, Bubble Guppies Guppy Bubbler, Carousel, El Circulo del Cielo, Crazy Cars, Diego's Rescue Rider, Ghost Blasters, Log Chute, Pineapple Poppers, Rugrats Reptarmobiles, Swiper's Sweeper, and Wonder Pet's Flyboat. Parents ride for free if a chaperone is required.

Occasionally there are meet and greets with famous cartoon characters—we've "met" Dora, Cat in the Hat, and Backyardigans recently. These sessions usually start at 10 a.m. If the character is a must-see for your child, plan to arrive at 9:30 a.m., grab a cup of coffee from Starbucks, and then get in line. Get there early for character appearances because the wait can be very long and tedious. You may see some moms running late, doing the out-of-my-way elbow jab as they aim to secure their place in line. MOA employees working the event will set up queues, and if you miss the cutoff, you may be waiting a while (about 30 minutes) as the character takes a break.

unofficial **TIP**

Warning: Opting for "one more ride" can easily morph into many more rides. If that's the case, buy the unlimited ride bracelet (see Part Seven: Nickelodeon Universe).

Between the free entertainment and socializing time for parents, these special days are an ideal way to spend a morning with your tot. Toddler Tuesday brochures are available online and at any Guest Services desk on Level 1.

PLAY PLACES

AS FAMILY-FRIENDLY AS MALL OF AMERICA (MOA) is, parents of babies and young children will discover one typical indoor mall staple missing: a padded play area. We can't help but wonder if this is to keep parents in stores or in the theme park to spend money. **LEGO** (S164, ☎ 952-858-8949) does have several kid-size tables of various heights, with buckets in the middle filled with LEGO blocks. Older siblings can play here, but this area can be dangerous for babies and toddlers because LEGOs can be a choking hazard for little ones who want to put anything and everything in their mouths (as you know). But there isn't any place that parents or guardians can sit back and relax while kids go wild. With that said, MOA still has plenty to offer families.

When the kids are on the verge of bouncing off the walls, invest a few dollars and let the kiddos literally bounce off the Pineapple Poppers (must be 36"–58" tall) walls in **Nickelodeon Universe** (west side). The downside with this choice is that you have to pay (3 points worth), and it's only 3 minutes! Plus, you may have to wait in line.

unofficial **TIP**
Warning: Those greedy little claw machines are strategically placed near the arcades. They will take your kids hard-earned chore money faster than Brain-Surge spins on one turn. Run. If your children don't believe you, have them call my son. He'll tell you.

In fall 2015 **Minnesota Children's Museum** opened a temporary pop-up play exhibit space in MOA while awaiting the expansion and remodeling of the downtown Saint Paul–based museum. The MOA's 4,440-square-foot temporary museum is full of interactive exhibits and a great tease for the permanent location. Cost: $7.95/person; members, free. The MOA location plans to close April 2017.

FREE FLICKS AT THEATRES AT MALL OF AMERICA

FREE FAMILY FLICKS ARE HELD at the **Theatres at Mall of America** (S401, ☎ 952-883-8901) every Saturday morning at 10 a.m. on a first-come, first-serve basis. Free Sensory Flicks, ideal for families affected by autism or other developmental disabilities, are provided at the same time. The Sensory Flicks have lower sound, a lighted theater, and additional concessions staff. Attendees in this setting will not be hushed if they dance, sing, or move around in response to the film.

CHARACTERS

A COUPLE OF CHARACTERS ROAM the mall from time to time—mainly Sharky from **Sea Life Aquarium** (E120, ☎ 952-853-0612) and

Shrimp Louie from **Bubba Gump Shrimp Co.** (S369, ☎ 952-853-6600). Nickelodeon characters often appear inside **Nickelodeon Universe** (C5100, ☎ 952-883-8800).

VIDEO GAMES

FOR THE TRADITIONAL ARCADE SCENE, **Namco Arcade & Midway** (northeast corner of Nickelodeon Universe) takes tokens only: 3 tokens/$1; 18 tokens/$5; 40 tokens/$10, and 90 tokens/$20.

Gameworks in Sky Deck Sports Grille & Lanes (E401, ☎ 952-500-8700) allows guests to use game cards. Each card requires a $2 activation fee, but that includes 14 extra credits ($3.50 value). When you Super Charge your card for an additional $2, you receive bonus credits:

- 20 credits/$5
- 40 credits/$10
- 100 credits/$20 (120 credits if Super Charged)
- 140 credits/$25 (190 credits if Super Charged)
- 200 credits/$35 (260 credits if Super Charged)

As for free experiences, **Microsoft** (S162, ☎ 952-487-7372); **Apple** (S132, ☎ 952-854-4870); **Best Buy** (W340, ☎ 952-853-1359); and the two **Game Stop** locations (E284, ☎ 952-814-0082 and N378, ☎ 952-854-6191) allow consumers to sample the latest technology and games.

▌ DINING *with* YOUNG CHILDREN

RESTAURANT STAFF are used to working with all types of people, including grumpy and fidgety children, though some restaurants are louder and busier, which helps kids blend in. **FireLake Grill House** (Radisson Blu, S2000; ☎ 952-881-5258) and the Italian **Tucci Benucch** (W114, ☎ 952-853-0200) have calmer ambiences compared to **Buffalo Wild Wings** (S312, ☎ 952-346-3740) or **Benihana** (S358, ☎ 952-594-6205).

The one thing Mall of America (MOA) restaurants are *not* lacking is children's menus. Usually accompanied by crayons and activity pages, kids' menus are offered in every full-service restaurant and accompanied by lidded, tot-size drinks and usually desserts. Nearly every restaurant has stroller parking, high chairs, and booster seats, and some even offer slings for infant carriers.

unofficial **TIP**
Photo op: In front of Bubba Gump, patrons can sit on the *Forrest Gump* bench and "wear" his shoes (bolted to the ground).

The tropical adventure–themed **Rainforest Cafe** (S306, ☎ 952-854-7500) is certainly a family-friendly full-service restaurant. It opened in January 2016 next to another family-welcoming choice, **Bubba Gump Shrimp Co.** (S396, ☎ 952-853-6600), the lively *Forrest Gump*–inspired seafood joint.

Ruby Tuesday (N234, ☎ 952-854-8282) is your traditional burger fare and salad bar place. **Cadillac Ranch** (S352, ☎ 952-854-1004) has big TVs, a rock-and-roll theme, and a mechanical bull (minimum age: 18). **Cantina #1** (E406, ☎ 952-854-6500) and **Cantina Laredo** (W300, ☎ 952-406-8311) are the only full-service Mexican restaurants in the mall. At Cantina #1 ask for a seat by the window overlooking Nickelodeon Universe. **Dick's Last Resort** chain (S402, ☎ 612-276-6995) is snark at its finest, and the MOA location is no different. The Rugrats menu covers the picky palate. **Tony Roma's** (S346, ☎ 952-854-7940) offers typical kid fare such as burgers, grilled cheese, and Kraft mac and cheese. **Masu Sushi & Robata** (S344, ☎ 952-896-6278) has chopstick cheaters available for little hands who want to eat like the big people.

If you prefer quick-service sit-down options, several are ideal for "I'm hungry now" kids. **Noodles & Company** (S342, ☎ 952-854-5538); **Chipotle** (S322, ☎ 952-252-3800); and **Pizza Studio** (S340, ☎ 952-229-4441) come up as favorites. The fast service of the food court is ideal for a quick eat, and many places offer kid portions.

If you're planning on a full-service meal, try to get to the restaurant of your choice shy of the lunchtime rush, or call ahead to see if reservations are an option. We've noticed that reservations vary depending on mall busyness. If the food court is on your agenda, try to get there before the rush. If you find yourself spinning for a table because the food court is rocking, a divide and conquer tactic is the best bet if you're shopping with other adults because lines will likely be a good 10- to 20-minute wait.

For more on food and drink choices and gluten-free menus, see Part Four: Dining.

SPECIALTY DINING

LOOKING FOR A GIRLY-GIRL AMBIENCE for brunch, lunch, dinner, or afternoon tea and a view overlooking the theme park? **American Girl Bistro** (C5160-1, ☎ 877-247-5223) is your place. Doll-size Treat Seats (with a doll-size cup and saucer) are available for girls toting their American Girl dolls. Reservations are recommended. Lunch and dinner are $15 per person. The children's menu (age 4 and younger) is $7.50 per person. Afternoon Tea and Craft (Monday–Friday, 2–4:30 p.m.) is $13.50 per person. All prices exclude tax and gratuity. Personal shoppers are available to help girls and their families have the perfect shopping experience.

KIDS EAT FREE

EVERY TUESDAY, at the participating Mall of America restaurants listed on the next page, kids under age 6 eat free for lunch and dinner when parents order meals.

• A&W All American Food (S376) • American Girl Bistro (C5160-1)
• Bruegger's Bagels (S338) • Cadillac Ranch (S352)
• Cantina #1 (E406) • Cantina Laredo (W300)
• Chipotle (quesadilla or single taco) (S322)
• Crave (kids also eat free on Sundays) (S368)
• Dick's Last Resort (S402) • Freshii (S319) • Hard Rock Cafe (C5115A)
• Paciugo Gelato and Caffè (W392) • Piada Italian Street Food (N326)
• Pita Pit (S372) • Sky Deck Sports Grille & Lanes (E401) • Subway (E244)
• Tony Roma's (S346) • Tucci Benucch (W114) • Twin City Grill (N130)
• Villa Italian Kitchen (E216) • Zio Italian (S320)

The SCOOP *on* BIG KIDS

LONG GONE IS THE 1980S TEEN HANGOUT SCENE—at least at
Mall of America (MOA). MOA has a security-enforced parental escort
policy that goes into effect Friday–Saturday and select holidays. While
guests under age 16 are certainly welcomed on weekend evenings, they
must be accompanied by an adult 21 years or older 4–10 p.m. One
adult may be responsible for up to 10 kids, but there's one more
important factor: All visitors under age 21 should be prepared to flash
one of the following photo IDs during the parental escort hours:

• United States Driver's License • United States State-Issued ID
• Resident Alien Card • Passport • United States Military ID
• Mexican Consulate ID • Canadian ID

Please note that school IDs (college or high school) are not accepted.
Teenage employees of MOA are exempt from the escort policy but
must be prepared to show their MOA employee identification card.

HOLIDAYS

NEW YEAR'S EVE

MALL OF AMERICA'S NEW YEAR'S EVE PARTY deliberately
appeals to families. While Nickelodeon Universe stays open late for
festivities, there are two New Year countdowns—one family countdown
at 10 p.m. and the official countdown at midnight. The night features
music, dancing, and character meet and greets.

EASTER

THE EASTER BUNNY, presented by Peeps, makes a special spring appearance every year. Kids can meet the Easter Bunny at designated times leading up to Easter, and parents can order memento photos.

HALLOWEEN

MINNESOTA TRICK-OR-TREATERS do their best to incorporate layers of warmth into their Halloween costumes. But that's not the case for the ghosts and goblins scouring the Mall of America (MOA) for sweets on Halloween when MOA welcomes thousands of treat-seekers. The comfortable temp comes in handy year after year during the annual Howl-O-Ween event hosted by MOA and participating retailers.

Nickelodeon Universe gets in on the fun during the annual Black-out: Glow Crazy! The theme park turns spooky with unlit rides, black lighting, and fog effects, while a live DJ turns up the creepy factor with a variety of tunes. Traditionally, free treat bags are distributed and wristbands are discounted.

What's the scoop on trick-or-treating at MOA? Some parents have griped about long lines and "only one piece of candy," but others have had a better experience.

Frank, a dad from Lakeville, Minnesota, said:

We had a blast. Tons of kids, and the parents can pick up a coffee at Starbucks and have dinner there with the kiddos.

PROS	CONS
• Indoors means no need to dress warmly. Leave the coats in the car or rent a locker.	• Long lines for candy: 75-100 people deep (including parents) at popular stores like Disney.
• Safe. No streets to cross or cars to worry about.	• Only a third of the MOA stores participate.
• Restaurants mean food and drinks for the family.	• Stores will run out of candy.
• Entertainment for the little ones.	• 15-minute wait for goody bag in MOA Rotunda.
• Goody bags from the mall (read mention in cons).	
• Easy access to restrooms.	
• Best for toddlers, preschoolers, and children in wheelchairs due to accessibility.	

CHRISTMAS

SANTA CLAUS ARRIVES AT MOA in mid-October and is greeted with a special arrival ceremony. MOA's website and social media pages announce the special date a few weeks before. The event typically includes music, dancers, and treats.

Before you make plans to visit the jolly man in red, there is something you should know. MOA is especially magical because Santa is found in two locations. And while both Santas are sure to never, ever be in the same place at the same time, an employee told us that locations vary from year to year. The most recent locations have been in opposite mall corners: the Sears and Macy's Courts.

Besides the fact that both beards are white and real, their appearances, clothes, demeanor, and styles are rather different. Plus, one takes reservations and books up well in advance.

The "Sears" Santa is promoted on KOOL 108—the Twin Cities Christmas Station—and no appointment is necessary. This Santa has a long, white beard and dresses in the traditional red-and-white suit and hat. Photo packages and holiday merchandise are available for purchase.

The "Macy's" Santa takes reservations and is hosted by MOA's year-round **Professor Bellows Specialty Photography** (N374, ☎ 952-853-9804), which specializes in old-fashioned and event photography. This Santa has been with MOA for more than 20 years. When he's not working at the mall, he's meandering throughout the Twin Cities and is known as SID (Santa in Disguise). Local children recognize him year-round, and his home is said to have a special Christmas room filled with letters, ornaments, and gifts offered to him from his young fans.

The "Macy's" Santa is wonderful with children, especially first-timers. The staff has all kinds of tricks up their sleeves, from working a baby into a photo to calming an apprehensive toddler. This Santa opts for a flannel shirt and suspenders in place of a suit. In fact, he never wears the same shirt twice during the season, so if you visit more than once, you will have variety. DVDs of the visit are available for purchase, and portraits are printed on-site.

PART SIX

The STORES

MALL OF AMERICA (MOA) stores come in all shapes, sizes, and price ranges. Most names will be familiar to the usual shopper, as most brands are found in malls across the United States, but some options are Minnesota-specific. As we mentioned previously, starting on the top floors and working your way down is the best way to avoid crowds during daytime hours, especially on weekends. The checkout lines at **Nordstrom Rack** (W324) can get ridiculous as the day goes by (easily a half-hour wait on weekends), so we recommend visiting that store first. Other upscale shops on the lower floors see a lot of traffic but don't gather the same crowds that midrange stores see, so don't hesitate to save those options for later in the day. During dinner hours and later in the evening are great times to hit stores that may have been overlooked.

LANDMARK STORES

THREE OF THE FOUR ORIGINAL ANCHORS in Mall of America have stayed consistent since opening: **Macy's** (southwest corner), **Nordstrom** (northwest corner), and **Sears** (northeast corner). Bloomingdale's closed in 2012. The space has since been filled by **Forever 21** on Level 1 and in the basement, **L.L.Bean** also on Level 1, and the new **Crayola Experience** on Level 3, filling out 60,000 square feet of space, which makes it one of the mall's largest attractions.

MEET MINNESOTA

MANY OF THE STORES AT MALL OF AMERICA will be familiar to you if you're already a mall shopper. But there are a handful of shops you won't find in any other state (insert long "Ooooooh!" here). To start, Minnesota sports fans will appreciate **Goldy's Locker Room** (W366, ☎ 952-858-9585), which presents all things sporty Minnesota, including sportswear and souvenirs from Minnesota teams Gophers, Vikings, Twins, Timberwolves, and Wild. The store is named for Goldy Gopher, the mascot for the University of Minnesota. **Hockey Minnesota by Goldy's Locker Room** (E160, ☎ 952-854-9484) exudes one of Minnesota's nicknames, State of Hockey.

I Love Minnesota (W372, ☎ 952-854-9100); **Love from Minnesota** (W380, ☎ 952-854-7319); and **Minnesot-ah!** (E157, ☎ 952-858-8531) are all under the same ownership and are the go-to stores for Minnesota-themed souvenirs, gifts, and apparel. You betcha!

Finally, **Explore Minnesota Tourism** is found at East 1. Don't forget to give them a shout-out on social media by tagging your posts and pictures with #OnlyinMN.

BEST OF . . .

WHAT'S ON YOUR SHOPPING LIST? Whatever it is, there is a very good chance you will find it at Mall of America, as well as plenty of price and brand comparison options. There are a few exceptions. Book lovers will find only one bookstore: top-hitter **Barnes and Noble.** As for large household appliances (refrigerators, washers, dryers, lawn mowers, and so on), **Sears** is your place. While **Best Buy** normally has a wide variety of home appliances, the MOA location features mostly technology and entertainment goods. The most overwhelming shopping experience is clothing and shoes. Not only are there many choices, but also some stores have multiple locations. Here are some suggestions to help get your shopping day started.

ELECTRONICS
- Microsoft • AT&T • Sprint • Apple • Best Buy

HOUSEWARES
- Williams-Sonoma • Macy's • Cut Above Home • Marshall's • Anthropologie

LUGGAGE
- House of Samsonite • Tumi • Macy's • Victorinox Swiss Army • Nordstrom

OUTDOORS APPAREL
- L.L.Bean • The North Face • Fjällräven • Columbia • Eddie Bauer • Carhartt

TOYS
- JM Cremp's • Creative Kidstuff • Games by James • Air Traffic Kits & Games
- Go Games! Go Toys!

STORE PROFILES

WE HAVE PROFILED ALL MALL OF AMERICA stores below. While most of the categories included in our profiles are self-explanatory, several items are rated on a scale of 1–10 with specific guidelines.

- **Inventory** Limited to extensive scale of 1–10, with 10 being most extensive
- **Average cost of goods** Scale of 1–10, with 10 being most expensive
- **Value** 1 (incredible bargain) to 10 (vastly overpriced)
- **Sales and discounts** 1 (never) to 10 (almost constantly)

 A

Abercrombie & Fitch

N200, ☎ 952-851-0911, abercrombie.com

Store size Large. **Target market** Teens and 20s, upscale, male/female. **Inventory description** Upscale attire for young consumers looking to present the all-American, preppy look. **Inventory** 8. **Average cost of goods** 9. **Value** 10. **Sales and discounts** 6.

COMMENTS The trendy clothes may be overpriced, but they look great on the right body type (not for everyone).

abercrombie kids

W209, ☎ 952-854-2671, abercrombie.com

Store size Small. **Target market** Kids, upscale, male/female. **Inventory description** Playful, trendy clothes for tiny fashionistas. **Inventory** 6. **Average cost of goods** 9. **Value** 10. **Sales and discounts** 2.

COMMENTS If money is no object, you can guarantee your kids are going to look adorable in these fashions.

aerie by American Eagle Outfitters

E200, ☎ 952-854-4178, ae.com/aerie

Store size Medium. **Target market** 20s–30s, mid-range, female. **Inventory description** Practical but pretty underwear, sleepwear, workout attire for ladies. **Inventory** 8. **Average cost of goods** 4. **Value** 4. **Sales and discounts** 3.

COMMENTS The store offers a nice selection of good-quality clothing at a reasonable price.

Aéropostale

N267, ☎ 952-854-9446, aeropostale.com

Store size Large. **Target market** Teens–40s, budget to mid-range, male/female. **Inventory description** Affordable and fashionable attire. **Inventory** 9. **Average cost of goods** 2. **Value** 2. **Sales and discounts** 8.

COMMENTS You'll find trendy clothing at decent prices.

The Afternoon

E285, ☎ 952-854-7554, theafternoon.com

Store size Small. **Target market** All ages, budget to mid-range, male/female. **Inventory description** Glassware, jewelry, books, cards. **Inventory** 8. **Average cost of goods** 3. **Value** 2. **Sales and discounts** 3.

COMMENTS Fun gifts for that friend who is hard to shop for.

A'GACI

E248, ☎ 952-854-1649, agacistore.com

Store size Medium. **Target market** Teens, mid-range, female. **Inventory description** Ladies attire. **Inventory** 6. **Average cost of goods** 4. **Value** 5. **Sales and discounts** 8.

COMMENTS This is a fun store for young ladies looking for trendy styles; regular shoppers won't want to miss signing up for My A'GACI Rewards.

Air Traffic Kites & Games

N343, ☎ 952-858-9599, airtraffictoys.com

Store size Small. **Target market** Kids+, mid-range, male/female. **Inventory description** Interactive toys for indoors and outdoors. **Inventory** 10. **Average cost of goods** 4. **Value** 3. **Sales and discounts** 4.

COMMENTS As the name implies, kites and games fill store shelves, along with a great selection of planes, boomerangs, disc golf supplies, juggling equipment, classic Rubik's Cubes, and an assortment of other toys. Expect to drag your children kicking and screaming out of here.

ALDO

N188, ☎ 952-854-6118, aldoshoes.com

Store size Small. **Target market** 20s+, mid-range, male/female. **Inventory description** Fashionable upscale men's and women's footwear. **Inventory** 10. **Average cost of goods** 4. **Value** 3. **Sales and discounts** 7.

COMMENTS ALDO's affordable prices make it easy to keep up with the latest trends without spending a fortune. Sales and end-of-season clearance racks offer tempting prices.

ALDO Accessories

N114, ☎ 952-854-9578, aldoshoes.com

Store size Small. **Target market** 20s+, budget to mid-range, male/female. **Inventory description** Accessories-only version of the upscale shoe brand ALDO; carries sunglasses, jewelry, handbags, belts, and watches. **Inventory** 2. **Average cost of goods** 3. **Value** 3. **Sales and discounts** 8.

COMMENTS Shop here for nice merchandise at reasonable prices.

Almost Famous Body Piercing

E350, ☎ 952-854-8000, almostfamouspiercing.com

Store size Small. **Target market** 20s+, mid-range, male/female. **Inventory description** Full-body piercings. **Inventory** 10. **Average cost of goods** 6. **Value** 4. **Sales and discounts** 2.

COMMENTS This professional place for piercings is highly regarded.

Alpaca Connection

E367, ☎ 952-883-0828, alpacaconnection.com

Store size Large. **Target market** All ages, mid-range, male/female. **Inventory description** Products made from 100% Alpaca. **Inventory** 10. **Average cost of goods** 6. **Value** 4. **Sales and discounts** 4.

COMMENTS Look here for unique merchandise, such as Peruvian pima cotton blouses, fur rugs, handbags, beadwork, and more.

American Apparel

N186, ☎ 952-814-1100, americanapparel.net

Store size Small. **Target market** Teens–20s, mid-range to upscale, male/female. **Inventory description** Iconic clothing, **Inventory** 7. **Average cost of goods** 5–8. **Value** 6. **Sales and discounts** 5.

COMMENTS These cool clothes are proudly made in the USA. Don't miss the student discount.

American Eagle Outfitters

Location #1 S120, ☎ 952-851-9011; Location #2 N248, ☎ 952-854-4788; ae.com

Store size Location #1, medium; Location #2, large. **Target market** Teens–20s, mid-range, male/female. **Inventory description** Jeans and casual wear. **Inventory** Location #1, 7; Location #2, 9. **Average cost of goods** 6. **Value** 3. **Sales and discounts** 4.

COMMENTS This affordable and modest line is geared toward teenagers and college-age kids. Watch for buy-one-get-one-free sales.

American Girl

C5160-1 (look for the dollhouse), ☎ 877-247-5223, americangirl.com

Store size Large. **Target market** Kids, upscale, female. **Inventory description** Specialty dolls and accessories; doll hair salon and bistro. **Inventory** 10. **Average cost of goods** 8. **Value** 8. **Sales and discounts** 1–2.

COMMENTS This two-story store sells the upscale 19-inch American Girl dolls ($100+), clothing, accessories, and gifts. The first floor has a doll salon, and the second floor has the American Girl Bistro (C5160-1, ☎ 877-247-5223), where shoppers can enjoy brunch, lunch, dinner, or celebrate birthdays with their dolls. A kids menu is available. Prices can be high, but AG is all about girl power. Author's thought: The American Girl experience is not for a weak budget. However, the history these dolls tell is well worth the investment if your girls get into the stories and learn about past eras. As for the store, the service is superb. Every girl is made to feel special and that her thoughts matter. Personal shoppers are available to assist with all of your American Girl needs. E-mail personalshopMOA@americangirl.com.

Ann Taylor

S218, ☎ 952-854-9220, anntaylor.com

Store size Small. **Target market** 20s+, upscale, female. **Inventory description** Upscale professional dresses, separates, and casual wear. **Inventory** 9. **Average cost of goods** 7. **Value** 6. **Sales and discounts** 5.

COMMENTS The friendly staff is always happy to offer their expertise.

Anthropologie (opening late 2016)

C128, anthropologie.com

Store size Large. **Target market** 20s+, mid-range to upscale, female. **Inventory description** Luxury apparel, accessories, home decor, and beauty products. **Inventory** 8. **Average cost of goods** 7. **Value** 2. **Sales and discounts** 4.

COMMENTS This location is set to open in late 2016 in a 10,000-square-foot store in the new Phase II expansion. While this location was not open at press time, we are familiar with Anthropologie and highly recommend it. We are basing this entry off other store locations, but we have a feeling it will be everything we expect.

Apple

S132, ☎ 952-229-5630, apple.com/retail/mallofamerica

Store size Large. **Target market** Teens+, upscale, male/female. **Inventory description** Home of Mac, iPhone, iPad, Apple Watch, and the ever-busy Genius Bar. **Inventory** 10. **Average cost of goods** 9. **Value** 7. **Sales and discounts** 1.

COMMENTS This slick i-everything store welcomes its fan boys and girls to play with the latest and greatest. Customer service is good; however, making an appointment is a must for tech services, and don't be surprised if you have to wait a long time, even with an appointment. A short table has iPads with games and shows for kids.

The Art of Shaving

W125, ☎ 952-854-1441, theartofshaving.com

Store size Medium. **Target market** 20s+, mid-range to upscale, male. **Inventory description** Men's skin care to help achieve the perfect shave. **inventory** 10. **Average cost of goods** 7. **Value** 5. **Sales and discounts** 8.

COMMENTS Find products based off of the "4 Elements of the Perfect Shave Prepare. . . Lather Up! . . Shave. . . and Moisturize."

Athleta

S145, ☎ 952-854-9387, athleta.gap.com

Store size Medium. **Target market** 20s+, mid-range, female. **Inventory description** Performance apparel for ladies. **Inventory** 9. **Average cost of goods** 6. **Value** 6. **Sales and discounts** 5.

COMMENTS The staff offers attentive customer service.

AT&T

S104, ☎ 952-851-9029, att.com

Store size Large. Target market All, mid-range, male/female. Inventory description Smartphones and the latest related technology. Inventory 10. Average cost of goods 5. Value 5. Sales and discounts 1.

COMMENTS This new store is fun! Find more than phones at this AT&T location. Guests can get hands-on with the latest accessories to the latest smart-phones. In other words, this isn't just a store—it's an experience.

Aveda

W288, ☎ 952-854-0595, aveda.com

Store size Small. Target market All, mid-range, male/female. Inventory description Healthy hair products and salon. Inventory 8. Average cost of goods 4. Value 3. Sales and discounts 5.

COMMENTS This is a local brand with an excellent reputation.

A/X Armani Exchange

S141, ☎ 952-854-9400, armaniexchange.com

Store size Small. Target market 30s+, upscale, male/female. Inventory description Accessible designer clothes for men and women. Inventory 9. Average cost of goods 8. Value 6. Sales and discounts 5.

COMMENTS This shop has a nice denim selection in the $100+ range.

 # B

BabyGap & GapKids

S210, ☎ 952-854-1011, gap.com

Store size Large. Target market Kids, mid-range, male/female. Inventory description Trendy, preppy clothes for kids based off the adult store Gap. Inventory 10. Average cost of goods 5. Value 5. Sales and discounts 6.

COMMENTS The staff is always friendly and willing to assist.

Banana Republic

W100, ☎ 952-854-1818, bananarepublic.gap.com

Store size Large. Target market 30s+, upscale, male/female. Inventory description What started out as a safari retailer in the 1970s has evolved into an upscale men's and women's retailer. Inventory 10. Average cost of goods 8. Value 6. Sales and discounts 5.

COMMENTS The clothing is high-end and of a nicer quality than what you'll find at other stores under the Gap umbrella, but it's more affordable than other luxury brands.

bareMinerals

Location #1 E110, ☎ 952-854-9205; Location #2 N294, ☎ 952-854-8554; bareescentuals.com

Store size Small. **Target market** 20s+, budget to mid-range, female. **Inventory description** Natural makeup and skin care. **Inventory** 9. **Average cost of goods** 3. **Value** 7. **Sales and discounts** 5.

COMMENTS Prices are comparable to other makeup lines.

Barnes & Noble

E118, ☎ 952-854-1455, barnesandnoble.com

Store size Large. **Target market** All, budget to mid-range, male/female. **Inventory description** The only bookstore in MOA; also carries magazines, toys, and games. **Inventory** 10. **Average cost of goods** 2. **Value** 1. **Sales and discounts** 10.

COMMENTS The spacious coffee shop is a wonderful, quiet escape from the mall madness. Check the website for the store's calendar of events.

Bath & Body Works

Location #1 S234, ☎ 952-854-5252; Location #2 N172, ☎ 952-858-8377; bathandbodyworks.com

Store size Location #1, medium; Location #2, small. **Target market** Teens+, budget to mid-range, female. **Inventory description** Lotions, fragrant sprays, body care, and candles. **Inventory** 8. **Average cost of goods** 1. **Value** 2. **Sales and discounts** 9.

COMMENTS Semi-annual (winter/summer) sales offer the best discounts of the year, but it seems like there's always a promotion of some sort going on at Bath & Body Works.

BCBGeneration

N221, ☎ 952-854-5393, bcbgeneration.com

Store size Medium. **Target market** 20s, mid-range to upscale, female. **Inventory description** Fresh, trendy clothes for the millennial generation. **Inventory** 8. **Average cost of goods** 7. **Value** 6. **Sales and discounts** 5.

COMMENTS These cute, trendy clothes are overpriced compared to other fast-fashion options.

BCBGMAXAZRIA

S140, ☎ 952-687-4525, bcbg.com

Store size Medium. **Target market** 20s+, upscale, female. **Inventory description** Styles for the sophisticated grown-up. **Inventory** 8. **Average cost of goods** 8. **Value** 4. **Sales and discounts** 5.

COMMENTS Some items lean toward the pricey side, but this high-quality line is unlike anything you'll find elsewhere.

bebe

N104, ☎ 952-814-3548, bebe.com

Store size Small. Target market Teens+, mid-range, female. Inventory description Trendy fashions and accessories. Inventory 9. Average cost of goods 5. Value 6. Sales and discounts 6.

COMMENTS Moms, leave this store for your daughters. Fun store name fact: *bebe* is a portmanteau from *Hamlet*'s "To be or not to be."

Ben Bridge Jeweler

W136, ☎ 952-814-9356, benbridge.com

Store size Medium. Target market 30s+, mid-range to upscale, male/female. Inventory description Classic jewelry shop. Inventory 9. Average cost of goods 6. Value 5. Sales and discounts 4.

COMMENTS This shop is ideal for event jewelry and carries Pandora charms.

Best Buy

W340, ☎ 952-853-1359, bestbuy.com

Store size Large. Target market 20s+, mid-range to upscale, male/female. Inventory description Electronics. Inventory 9. Average cost of goods 7. Value 5. Sales and discounts 9.

COMMENTS While this store may not be as big as a stand-alone Best Buy, there is plenty of selection, as well as an open-box offering for discounted prices.

Body Corner

Location #1 E6109, ☎ 952-854-5757; Location #2 N6113

Store size Kiosk. Target market Teens+, mid-range, male/female. Inventory description Jewelry for pierced body parts. Inventory 10. Average cost of goods 2. Value 3. Sales and discounts 2.

COMMENTS This kiosk has an impressive selection of jewelry and frequently has decent sales.

The Body Shop

W148, ☎ 952-858-9752, thebodyshop-usa.com

Store size Medium. Target market Teens+, budget to mid-range, male/female. Inventory description Face and body care. Inventory 10. Average cost of goods 2. Value 2. Sales and discounts 9.

COMMENTS Free makeovers and samples are available.

Boot Barn

N386, ☎ 952-854-1063, bootbarn.com

Store size Medium. **Target market** All, upscale, male/female. **Inventory description** Western wear and boots. **Inventory** 8. **Average cost of goods** 8. **Value** 3. **Sales and discounts** 4.

COMMENTS There aren't a lot of boot stores in MOA, or Minnesota in general, but Boot Barn's offerings are comparable to other boot stores across the United States.

Bose

W156, ☎ 952-854-6978, bose.com

Store size Medium. **Target market** 20s+, upscale, male/female. **Inventory description** Music systems, speakers, and headphones. **Inventory** 8. **Average cost of goods** 7–10. **Value** 7. **Sales and discounts** 5.

COMMENTS Bose products hardly come cheap, but you won't be disappointed.

BOSS Hugo Boss

S176, ☎ 952-854-4403, hugoboss.com

Store size Medium. **Target market** All, upscale, male/female. **Inventory description** Luxury fashion line for men, women, and kids, plus accessories and fragrances. **Inventory** 10. **Average cost of goods** 10. **Value** 8. **Sales and discounts** 3.

COMMENTS Prices are high, but in this case you get what you pay for with zero regrets. Men, these aren't your grandfather's suits. Expect a warm welcome upon entering and to walk out looking runway-worthy.

Brevena

W6120, ☎ 651-407-8131, brevena.com

Store size Tiny. **Target market** 30s+, upscale, female. **Inventory description** Luxury skin care products. **Inventory** 9. **Average cost of goods** 8. **Value** 6. **Sales and discounts** 5.

COMMENTS Brevena is a locally based skin care company using Macro B Complex (oat beta glucan) with a fantastic reputation for good results. If you have skin care issues, this is one brand worth checking out.

Brickmania

E352, ☎ 952-854-9850, brickmania.com

Store size Medium. **Target market** All, budget to mid-range, male/female. **Inventory description** Specialized building kits made from genuine LEGO brand parts with a military flair. **Inventory** 9. **Average cost of goods** 1–3. **Value** 3. **Sales and discounts** 5.

COMMENTS LEGO lovers will appreciate the opportunity to expand their collections.

Brighton Collectibles

S224, ☎ 952-854-8043, brighton.com

Store size Medium. Target market 20s+, upscale, female. Inventory description Women's leather and hand-crafted accessories, including belts, handbags, wallets, jewelry, and charms for bracelets. Inventory 9. Average cost of goods 9. Value 6. Sales and discounts 3.

COMMENTS Like any designer brand, prices are high at Brighton, but the quality and craftsmanship are well worth it.

Brookstone

W162, ☎ 952-858-8848, brookstone.com

Store size Large. Target market 20s+, upscale, male/female. Inventory description Cool gadgets and unique gifts. Inventory 10. Average cost of goods 7–8. Value 5. Sales and discounts 3.

COMMENTS Brookstone is pretty predictable, but it's always fun to see the latest gadgets. There are always plenty of floor models to explore and play with.

Brow Art

E362, ☎ 952-854-1270, browart23.com

Store size Small. Target market 20s+, mid-range, female. Inventory description Body, facial, and eyebrow threading and waxing, plus henna tattoos, makeup, and body care. Inventory 8. Average cost of goods 6. Value 7. Sales and discounts 4.

COMMENTS Ladies looking for temporary body enhancers will appreciate Brow Art.

Buckle

E203, ☎ 952-854-4388, buckle.com

Store size Medium. Target market Teens–20s, mid-range to upscale, male/female. Inventory description Trendy clothing for young teens and young men/women. Inventory 8. Average cost of goods 8. Value 7. Sales and discounts 5.

COMMENTS Fun young fashions line the racks. The Buckle Exclusive line is worth checking out but a little on the pricey side.

Build-A-Bear Workshop

E172, ☎ 952-854-1164, buildabear.com

Store size Large. Target market Kids, mid-range, male/female. Inventory description A hands-on bear-building experience (from stuffing to dressing) and accessories for every occasion in a newly remodeled shop with multiple stations. Inventory 10. Average cost of goods 3. Value 5. Sales and discounts 1.

COMMENTS The newly remodeled space has multiple stations, which makes for quicker service. Look for the MOA-themed bear clothing.

Burberry

S178, ☎ 952-854-7000, us.burberry.com

Store size Medium. **Target market** 30s+, upscale, male/female. **Inventory description** British brand best known for its iconic trench coat and plaid. **Inventory** 9. **Average cost of goods** 10. **Value** 5. **Sales and discounts** 1.

COMMENTS The nice staff will help you find pricey but high-quality accessories and apparel.

 C

Call It Spring

N166, ☎ 952-854-5753, callitspring.com

Store size Small. **Target market** 20s, mid-range, male/female. **Inventory description** Trendy, reasonably priced footwear for adults. **Inventory** 9. **Average cost of goods** 4. **Value** 2. **Sales and discounts** 3.

COMMENTS Find fun fashions at affordable prices, especially during end-of-season sales.

Calvin Klein Performance

S130, ☎ 952-854-1318, explore.calvinklein.com

Store size Small. **Target market** 20s+, mid-range, male/female. **Inventory description** Men's and women's athletic wear and underwear inspired by the classic brand. **Inventory** 8. **Average cost of goods** 4. **Value** 5. **Sales and discounts** 4.

COMMENTS The store is easy to browse, with lots of practical choices.

Carhartt

N144, ☎ 612-318-6422, carhartt.com

Store size Medium. **Target market** All, mid-range, male/female. **Inventory description** Retail for the rugged worker on and off the job. **Inventory** 7. **Average cost of goods** 7. **Value** 8. **Sales and discounts** 5.

COMMENTS This is one of the more practical stores in the mall for facing the Minnesota outdoors.

Carter's Baby

S254, ☎ 952-854-4522, carters.com

Store size Small. **Target market** Kids, budget to mid-range, male/female. **Inventory description** Children's wear, including babies and toddlers. **Inventory** 10. **Average cost of goods** 2–3. **Value** 1. **Sales and discounts** 1.

COMMENTS Carter's has a reputation for cute, good-quality, affordable baby clothes.

Cellairis

N1, ☎ 651-317-9495, cellairis.com

Store size Kiosk. **Target market** All, mid-range, male/female. **Inventory description** Smartphone and cell accessories. **Inventory** 7. **Average cost of goods** 5. **Value** 5. **Sales and discounts** 5.

COMMENTS Teens seem to really like this cart.

Champs Just Hats

E276, ☎ 952-854-6739, champssports.com

Store size Medium. **Target market** All, mid-range, male/female. **Inventory description** Hats-only version of Champs Sports, featuring sport and collegiate hats. **Inventory** 10. **Average cost of goods** 3. **Value** 3. **Sales and discounts** 4.

COMMENTS There is a good chance your team is featured here. Check out the clearance rack for cheap hats ($5 clearance hats pop up from time to time).

Champs Sports

Location #1 W358, ☎ 952-858-9215; Location #2 E205, ☎ 952-854-4980; champssports.com

Store size Large. **Target market** Teens+, mid-range, male/female. **Inventory description** Athletic footwear, attire, and accessories. **Inventory** 9. **Average cost of goods** 5. **Value** 5. **Sales and discounts** 4.

COMMENTS It's a sports fan's paradise.

Chapel Hats

N170, ☎ 952-854-6707, chapelhats.com

Store size Medium. **Target market** All, mid-range, male/female. **Inventory description** Men's and women's hats. **Inventory** 10. **Average cost of goods** 5. **Value** 2. **Sales and discounts** 4.

COMMENTS The store carries an affordable and diverse collection.

Charlotte Russe

E141, ☎ 952-854-6862, charlotterusse.com

Store size Large. **Target market** 20s, budget, female. **Inventory description** Affordable trends for young ladies. **Inventory** 9. **Average cost of goods** 2. **Value** 3. **Sales and discounts** 2.

COMMENTS Here's a great place for shopping for a night on the town.

Chico's

S160, ☎ 952-851-0882, chicos.com

Store size Large. **Target market** 30s+, upscale, female. **Inventory description** Ladies fashions. **Inventory** 10. **Average cost of goods** 6. **Value** 4. **Sales and discounts** 7.

COMMENTS It's a nice-size store in an ideal location.

The Children's Place

S272, ☎ 952-854-5641, childrensplace.com

Store size Medium. **Target market** Kids, budget to mid-range, male/female. **Inventory description** Low-priced clothing for little ones. **Inventory** 10. **Average cost of goods** 1–2. **Value** 1. **Sales and discounts** 10.

COMMENTS The store carries infant sizes 0 up to boys/girls size 16.

Christopher & Banks and CJ Banks

S270, ☎ 952-858-8512, christopherandbanks.com

Store size Medium. **Target market** 30s+, mid-range, female. **Inventory description** Women's professional and casual wear. **Inventory** 10. **Average cost of goods** 5. **Value** 4. **Sales and discounts** 3.

COMMENTS CJ Banks provides plus sizes 14 and up.

City Shirts

W383, ☎ 952-854-6221, cityshirts.com

Store size Small. **Target market** Teens+, budget, male/female. **Inventory description** Fun printed T-shirts. **Inventory** 10. **Average cost of goods** 3. **Value** 5. **Sales and discounts** 3.

COMMENTS Find movie-, TV show–, and superhero-themed shirts, and more.

Claire's Boutique

Location #1 E179, ☎ 952-854-5504; Location #2 N394, ☎ 952-851-0050; Location #3 E292, ☎ 952-858-9903; claires.com

Store size Small. **Target market** Tweens–20s, budget, female. **Inventory description** Inexpensive female accessories, ear piercing. **Inventory** 10. **Average cost of goods** 3. **Value Scale** 1. **Sales and discounts** 10.

COMMENTS Find hair accessories, jewelry, and trinkets for kids and teens.

Clark's

E146, ☎ 952-854-4462, clarksusa.com

Store size Large. **Target market** All, mid-range to upscale, male/female. **Inventory description** Classic footwear for men, women, and children. **Inventory** 10. **Average cost of goods** 6. **Value** 7. **Sales and discounts** 5.

COMMENTS These shoes are best described as classic and high quality.

Club Monaco

N102, ☎ 952-854-2200, clubmonaco.com

Store size Small. **Target market** 30s+, upscale, male/female. **Inventory description** Nice men's and women's clothing line for urban professionals. **Inventory** 10. **Average cost of goods** 9. **Value** 6. **Sales and discounts** 3.

COMMENTS The clothes are elegant and beautiful.

Coach

W274, ☎ 952-858-8600, coach.com

Store size Large. **Target market** 20s+, upscale, female. **Inventory description** Fine leather handbags, belts, shoes. **Inventory** 10. **Average cost of goods** 8. **Value** 7. **Sales and discounts** 4.

COMMENTS This store carries the latest Coach styles.

Columbia Sportswear

W117, ☎ 952-854-5260, columbia.com

Store size Large. **Target market** 20s+, mid-range to upscale, male/female. **Inventory description** Outdoor wear for active people. **Inventory** 10. **Average cost of goods** 7. **Value** 4. **Sales and discounts** 5.

COMMENTS A friendly sales staff is ready to help at this skiwear brand that has expanded into sportswear and footwear for men, women, and kids.

CordaRoy's

E348, ☎ 952-854-0335, cordaroys.com

Store size Small. **Target market** All, mid-range to upscale, male/female. **Inventory description** Foam-filled chairs and sofas that convert to beds. **Inventory** 8. **Average cost of goods** 7. **Value** 6. **Sales and discounts** 5.

COMMENTS A unique concept; the products can be carried out or shipped to your home in boxes.

CottonOn

N278, ☎ 952-854-5060, cottonon.com

Store size Large. **Target market** All, budget to mid-range, male/female. **Inventory description** Affordable fashions. **Inventory** 10. **Average cost of goods** 3. **Value** 1. **Sales and discounts** 7.

COMMENTS Find incredible bargains, including jeans for $40.

Cowgirl Tuff Company

N302, ☎ 952-546-1601, cowgirltuffco.com

Store size Small. **Target market** 20s+, mid-range to upscale, female. **Inventory description** A wide range of sizes for the western girl in you. **Inventory** 8. **Average cost of goods** 7. **Value** 5. **Sales and discounts** 5.

COMMENTS Stop here before your next rodeo, and find a nice range of ladies sizes.

Crabtree & Evelyn

W270, ☎ 952-854-3986, crabtree-evelyn.com

Store size Tiny. **Target market** 20s+, budget to mid-range, male/female. **Inventory description** Body care for women and men. **Inventory** 10. **Average cost of goods** 3. **Value** 4. **Sales and discounts** 3.

COMMENTS There's a scent for everyone.

Creative Kidstuff

E148, ☎ 612-524-6630, creativekidstuff.com

Store size Medium. **Target market** Kids, mid-range, male/female. **Inventory description** Fun, educational, and traditional toys. **Inventory** 10. **Average cost of goods** 5. **Value** 4. **Sales and discounts** 9.

COMMENTS This is the best toy store in the mall, with lots of hands-on toys to play with while mom shops.

Crocs

N108, ☎ 952-854-5278, crocs.com

Store size Small. **Target market** All, budget to mid-range, male/female. **Inventory description** Casual boat shoes. **Inventory** 10. **Average cost of goods** 3. **Value** 3. **Sales and discounts** 8.

COMMENTS Look here for extensive offerings at reasonable prices.

Cut Above Home

S238, ☎ 952-854-1157, cutabovehome.com

Store size Large. **Target market** 30s+, mid-range, male/female. **Inventory description** Home decor, home staging, and wedding registries. **Inventory** 10. **Average cost of goods** 6. **Value** 4. **Sales and discounts** 6.

COMMENTS Browsing the seemingly endless merchandise will easily turn into buying.

 D

Dance District

E370, ☎ 952-854-5266, dancedistrictmoa.com

Store size Small. **Target market** All, mid-range, female. **Inventory description** Dance and gymnastics attire and accessories. **Inventory** 9. **Average cost of goods** 6. **Value** 5. **Sales and discounts** 5.

COMMENTS This is the place to find your daughter's dance class needs.

Deck the Walls

W368, ☎ 952-858-8335, twincitiesdeckthewalls.com

Store size Medium. **Target market** 30s+, mid-range to upscale, male/female. **Inventory description** Frame experts and wall decor. **Inventory** 9. **Average cost of goods** 6. **Value** 4. **Sales and discounts** 5.

COMMENTS In addition to framing, you'll find Minnesota and sports-themed works.

Destination Maternity

S258, ☎ 952-854-1144, destinationmaternity.com

Store size Medium. **Target market** 20s+, mid-range, female. **Inventory description** Maternity wear for mothers-to-be. **Inventory** 10. **Average cost of goods** 5. **Value** 6. **Sales and discounts** 7.

COMMENTS This full maternity store has comfy couches to rest on and is very welcoming to nursing moms.

Disney Store

S118, ☎ 952-854-9119, disneystore.com

Store size Large. **Target market** Kids, mid-range, male/female. **Inventory description** The latest and greatest Disney-themed merchandise. **Inventory** 10. **Average cost of goods** 6. **Value** 5. **Sales and discounts** 3.

COMMENTS This is the store for planning your Disney vacation (princess dresses and clothing) or buying the hottest Disney toys.

Dr. Martens

N101, ☎ 952-854-9006, drmartens.com

Store size Medium. **Target market** 20s, mid-range to upscale, male/female. **Inventory description** Shoes created for every generation's unique youth subculture. **Inventory** 8. **Average cost of goods** 7. **Value** 6. **Sales and discounts** 5.

COMMENTS Expect cool, helpful staff.

DSW

W124, ☎ 952-876-0991, dsw.com

Store size Large. **Target market** 20s+, mid-range, male/female. **Inventory description** Designer, casual, and athletic shoes for less, plus handbags. **Inventory** 9. **Average cost of goods** 4. **Value** 4. **Sales and discounts** 8.

COMMENTS Count on DSW to have huge offerings of casual and dressy shoes.

 # E

Eagle Anime

N365, ☎ 612-293-8697, eagleanime.com

Store size Small. **Target market** Teens–20s, mid-range, male/female. **Inventory description** Pop culture merchandise. **Inventory** 5. **Average cost of goods** 4. **Value** 4. **Sales and discounts** 5.

COMMENTS This niche, hip store has a nice selection of T-shirts.

ECCO

N218, ☎ 952-854-5177, ecco.com

Store size Small. **Target market** 20s+, upscale, male/female. **Inventory description** Danish shoe company created with the purpose of forming the shoe to the foot. **Inventory** 8. **Average cost of goods** 7. **Value** 4. **Sales and discounts** 5.

COMMENTS ECCO shoes easily cost in the $100 range, but the investment is worth it.

Eddie Bauer

S214, ☎ 952-851-0727, eddiebauer.com

Store size Medium. **Target market** 20s+, upscale, male/female. **Inventory description** Outerwear, gear, and outdoor attire for men and women. **Inventory** 10. **Average cost of goods** 8. **Value** 6. **Sales and discounts** 5.

COMMENTS This nice-size store offers high-quality merchandise.

Emoji Pillows

W6108

Store size Kiosk. **Target market** Kids, mid-range, male/female. **Inventory description** Pillows with emoji faces. **Inventory** 6. **Average cost of goods** 5. **Value Scale** 5. **Sales and discounts** 8.

COMMENTS Teens like this cute trend mirroring our digital age.

Everything But Water

W290, ☎ 952-858-9563, everythingbutwater.com

Store size Medium. **Target market** 20s+, upscale, female. **Inventory description** Resort and swimwear. **Inventory** 10. **Average cost of goods** 7. **Value** 6. **Sales and discounts** 5.

COMMENTS Ladies, Everything But Water carries D+ cups and has much more than swimwear, including sundresses, hats, and jewelry.

EXPRESS

W204, ☎ 952-851-0741, express.com

Store size Large. **Target market** 20s, mid-range, male/female. **Inventory description** Forward fashion brand for young men and women. **Inventory** 10. **Average cost of goods** 6. **Value** 6. **Sales and discounts** 4.

COMMENTS This is one of the brand's more spacious stores with an abundance of merchandise.

Fabletics

S142, ☎ 651-583-5511, fabletics.com

Store size Small. **Target market** 20s+, budget, female. **Inventory description** Athletic apparel for ladies. **Inventory** 6. **Average cost of goods** 3. **Value** 2. **Sales and discounts** 8.

COMMENTS If you're searching for stylish yet affordable athletic wear, this is the place. Actress Kate Hudson is cofounder of the brand.

Famous Footwear

Location #1 W310, ☎ 952-854-5188; Location #2 N151; famousfootwear.com

Store size Medium. **Target market** All, mid-range, male/female. **Inventory description** Diverse shoe wear from athletic to dress for adults and kids. **Inventory** 8. **Average cost of goods** 7. **Value** 8. **Sales and discounts** 9.

COMMENTS Famous Footwear tends to have overpriced shoes, but sales and buy-one-get-one deals help lesson the blow.

FBFG Farm Boy/Farm Girl

N380, ☎ 952-854-1311, farmboybrand.com

Store size Small. **Target market** 20s, mid-range, male/female. **Inventory description** Celebrating all things farm for men, women, kids, dogs, and cats via apparel and accessories. **Inventory** 9. **Average cost of goods** 4. **Value** 4. **Sales and discounts** 7.

COMMENTS The farm theme is fun, and the T-shirts are worth the stop. Country star James Wesley has a collection here, and John Deere has a presence.

The Finish Line

E241, ☎ 952-814-0116, finishline.com

Store size Large. **Target market** All, mid-range to upscale, male/female. **Inventory description** Athletic brand-name footwear, apparel, and accessories for men, women, and children. **Inventory** 10. **Average cost of goods** 7. **Value** 7. **Sales and discounts** 8.

COMMENTS Find top-brand shoes (Nike, Puma, Under Armour, and so on) for the sporty lifestyle.

Fixology

N390, ☎ 952-854-4205, fixologyrepair.com

Store size Small. **Target market** 20s+, mid-range, male/female. **Inventory description** Fast watch, jewelry, tablet, Apple watch, and phone repair. **Inventory** N/A. **Average cost of goods** 5. **Value** 2. **Sales and discounts** N/A.

COMMENTS The staff can repair jewelry, watches, cell phones, and even Zippo lighters.

Fjällräven

S128, ☎ 651-255-3050, fjallraven.us

Store size Small. **Target market** Kids, upscale, male/female. **Inventory description** Durable Swedish outdoor equipment and apparel. **Inventory** 8. **Average cost of goods** 10. **Value** 6. **Sales and discounts** 3.

COMMENTS This isn't a fashion-only retailer. Prices are steep, but the quality is well worth it due to the modern technology and function.

Flip Flop Shops

N103, ☎ 952-767-7528, flipflopshops.com

Store size Small. Target market 20s+, mid-range, male/female. Inventory description Flip-flops of all shapes and sizes. Inventory 9. Average cost of goods 5. Value 4. Sales and discounts 4.

COMMENTS The store carries top names like REEF, OluKai, Quiksilver, and ROXY, to name a few.

Fly Zone

E272B, ☎ 952-858-8928, kidsfootlocker.com/flyzone

Store size Tiny. Target market Kids, upscale, male/female. Inventory description Nike and Jordan basketball shoes. Inventory 8. Average cost of goods 8. Value 9. Sales and discounts 6.

COMMENTS Do kids really need $160 shoes? With that said, the occasional sale or end-of-season prices are a little easier on the wallet.

Footaction

E102, ☎ 952-858-8937, footaction.com

Store size Large. Target market 20s+, mid-range to upscale, male/female. Inventory description Street-style athletic shoes and apparel for men, women, and kids. Inventory 9. Average cost of goods 8. Value 6. Sales and discounts 6.

COMMENTS This division of Foot Locker has flashy, colorful footwear.

Foot Locker

N162, ☎ 952-854-5728, footlocker.com

Store size Medium. Target market 20s+, mid-range to upscale, male/female. Inventory description Athletic shoes and wear for men, women, and kids. Inventory 8. Average cost of goods 8. Value 6. Sales and discounts 6.

COMMENTS The shop carries a wide variety of basketball, running, and training shoes, including the Jordan collection.

Forever 21

E144, ☎ 952-854-1890, forever21.com

Store size Large. Target market Teens–20s, budget to mid-range, male/female. Inventory description Affordable women's, men's, and kids' attire. Inventory 10. Average cost of goods 2–4. Value 2. Sales and discounts 10.

COMMENTS Shoppers looking for the latest fashions at a reasonable price will want to carve out some time here. The store is huge, and inventory is fresh and constantly updated.

Fossil

E168, ☎ 952-854-1935, fossil.com

Store size Medium. Target market 20s+, upscale, male/female. Inventory description American designer and manufacturer featuring mostly watches and accessories. Inventory 9. Average cost of goods 8. Value 6. Sales and discounts 4.

COMMENTS Fossil has been around since 1954 and has always provided high-quality merchandise best described as modern vintage. This store is in a great location off the Rotunda. The staff is friendly and always ready to help.

Francesca's Collections

S116, ☎ 952-854-9985, francescas.com

Store size Small. **Target market** 20s, mid-range, female. **Inventory description** Eclectic women's clothing boutique at affordable prices. **Inventory** 9. **Average cost of goods** 6. **Value** 4. **Sales and discounts** 5.

COMMENTS Shoppers will find the latest trends here, but here's the catch: If it fits and you like it, buy it, as stock is limited. New fashions float in daily, so check back often.

Free People

S149, ☎ 952-854-9905, freepeople.com

Store size Medium. **Target market** 20s+, upscale, female. **Inventory description** Bohemian-inspired women's clothing. **Inventory** 8. **Average cost of goods** 8. **Value** 7. **Sales and discounts** 5.

COMMENTS The unique styles here are unrivaled by other MOA stores.

 G

Games by James

E358, ☎ 952-854-4747, gamesbyjames.com

Store size Small. **Target market** Kids, mid-range, male/female. **Inventory description** board games, jigsaw puzzles, mind teasers, chess, darts, dominoes, family games, military games, card games, casino games, and much more. **Inventory** 10. **Average cost of goods** 5. **Value** 4. **Sales and discounts** 3.

COMMENTS Find a great selection and friendly, knowledgeable staff.

Game Stop

Location #1 N378, ☎ 952-854-6191; Location #2 E284, ☎ 952-814-0082; gamestop.com

Store size Location #1, medium; Location #2, small. **Target market** Kids+, mid-range, male/female. **Inventory description** Assortment of new and used video games. **Inventory** 8. **Average cost of goods** 4. **Value** 4. **Sales and discounts** 5.

COMMENTS The game selection varies, so visit regularly for the newest arrivals.

G&B Custom Embroidery

W6114, ☎ 720-401-3606, moa-embroidery.com

Store size Kiosk. **Target market** 20s+, mid-range, male/female. **Inventory description** Customization for hats, shirts, jackets, and more. **Inventory** 8. **Average cost of goods** 5. **Value** 5. **Sales and discounts** 5.

COMMENTS Have your order filled while you shop.

Gap

S110, ☎ 952-854-1011, gap.com

Store size Large. **Target market** All, mid-range, male/female. **Inventory description** Classic, casual wear for the entire family. **Inventory** 10. **Average cost of goods** 5. **Value** 4. **Sales and discounts** 4.

COMMENTS You really can dress the entire family in the Gap for family photos.

Garage

N140, ☎ 952-854-4592, garageclothing.com/us

Store size Large. **Target market** Teens/20s, mid-range, female. **Inventory description** Fun clothing for the trendy teen girl. **Inventory** 9. **Average cost of goods** 3. **Value** 2. **Sales and discounts** 3.

COMMENTS Young ladies can find the hottest fashions at affordable prices. Don't miss the candy counter.

General Nutrition Center (GNC)

N370, ☎ 952-851-0880, gnc.com

Store size Small. **Target market** 20s+, mid-range, male/female. **Inventory description** Nutritional supplements. **Inventory** 7. **Average cost of goods** 3. **Value** 5. **Sales and discounts** 5.

COMMENTS Find sports nutrition, protein, and diet supplements.

GLITZ!

N306, ☎ 952-854-5257, glitzgowns.com

Store size Medium. **Target market** Teens–20s, upscale, female. **Inventory description** Family-owned dress store for young ladies planning for pageants, prom, homecoming, or quinceañeras. **Inventory** 8. **Average cost of goods** 8. **Value** 3. **Sales and discounts** 7.

COMMENTS Find a lovely gown selection for special occasions.

Godiva Chocolatier

W126, ☎ 952-858-9306, godiva.com

Store size Tiny. **Target market** All, upscale, male/female. **Inventory description** Gourmet chocolates, truffles, and gifts in a newly remodeled space. **Inventory** 8. **Average cost of goods** 2. **Value** 4. **Sales and discounts** 6.

COMMENTS Sign up for the Godiva Rewards Card for free chocolate.

Go! Games/Go! Toys

N134, ☎ 952-854-4694, calendarholdings.com

Store size Large. **Target market** Kids, mid-range, male/female. **Inventory description** Games, toys, coloring books, puzzles, and more. **Inventory** 10. **Average cost of goods** 5. **Value** 8. **Sales and discounts** 5.

COMMENTS This is a great place to find birthday gifts.

Gold Guys

E357, ☎ 952-465-3489, goldguys.com

Store size Small. **Target market** 20s+, mid-range, male/female. **Inventory description** Sell your coins and Bullion, dental gold, diamonds, jewelry, sterling silver, platinum, and gold karats (10k, 14k, 16k, 18k, 21k, 22k, and 24k). **Average cost of goods** No cost; they pay you. Purchases vary across the board. **Value** 8. **Sales and discounts** N/A.

COMMENTS This is the Gold Guys flagship store. Accept the offer and walk away with a check.

Goldy's Locker Room

W366, ☎ 952-858-9585, mygophersports.com

Store size Small. **Target market** All, mid-range, male/female. **Inventory description** All things Minnesota, including sportswear, collectibles, and sports-fan products from Minnesota teams (Gophers, Vikings, Twins, Timberwolves, and Wild). **Inventory** 9. **Average cost of goods** 5. **Value** 5. **Sales and discounts** 4.

COMMENTS Here's a must-stop for the Minnesota sports fan.

Greater Good

S236, ☎ 612-524-6830, greatergood.com

Store size Medium. **Target market** Teens+, mid-range, male/female. **Inventory description** Proceeds benefit people, pets, and the planet. **Inventory** 8. **Average cost of goods** 6. **Value** 7. **Sales and discounts** 4.

COMMENTS Feel good about helping others when you make a purchase here.

GUESS

S260, ☎ 952-858-8241, guess.com

Store size Medium. **Target market** 20s, mid-range, male/female. **Inventory description** Jeans and other fashionable attire. **Inventory** 8. **Average cost of goods** 6. **Value** 7. **Sales and discounts** 4.

COMMENTS Racks are filled with the latest trends.

H

H&M

W117, ☎ 855-466-7467, hm.com

Store size Large. **Target market** All, budget to mid-range, male/female. **Inventory description** Fast-fashion clothing for men, women, teenagers, and children. **Inventory** 10. **Average cost of goods** 2. **Value** 2. **Sales and discounts** 10.

COMMENTS You'll find killer bargains on the clearance racks.

Hallmark

N308, ☎ 952-858-9455, hallmark.com

Store size Medium. **Target market** All, mid-range, male/female. **Inventory description** Card and gift shop. **Inventory** 10. **Average cost of goods** 4. **Value** 4. **Sales and discounts** 6.

COMMENTS Shop here for cards, gifts, and knickknacks.

Hammer Made

S150, ☎ 952-854-9097, hammermade.com

Store size Small. **Target market** 30s+, upscale, male. **Inventory description** Specialty high-end men's shirts and accessories. **Inventory** 8. **Average cost of goods** 8. **Value** 5. **Sales and discounts** 5.

COMMENTS This is not your traditional stuffy men's shop; the items on the racks are cool, colorful, and of high quality.

Hanna Andersson

N190, ☎ 952-854-9598, hannaandersson.com

Store size Medium. **Target market** Kids, mid-range to upscale, male/female. **Inventory description** Swedish kids' clothing store. **Inventory** 10. **Average cost of goods** 7. **Value** 4. **Sales and discounts** 4.

COMMENTS This brand has a focus on organic clothing.

Harley-Davidson Motor Company

W344, ☎ 952-854-1225, americanroad.biz

Store size Medium–large. **Target market** 20s+, mid-range to upscale, male/female. **Inventory description** Harley-Davidson motorcycle accessories, apparel, boots, gloves, and jackets. **Inventory** 9. **Average cost of goods** 4. **Value** 4. **Sales and discounts** 4.

COMMENTS Find Harley-Davidson gear galore.

Hat World

E178, ☎ 952-853-0056

Store size Small. **Target market** Teens+, mid-range, male/female. **Inventory description** Sports, fashion, and collegiate hats. **Inventory** 9. **Average cost of goods** 3. **Value** 4. **Sales and discounts** 4.

COMMENTS With so many great choices, picking only one hat can be a challenge—actually, picking only two hats would be hard!

Helzberg Diamonds

W154, ☎ 952-851-0057, helzberg.com

Store size Large. **Target market** 30s+, mid-range, male/female. **Inventory description** Jewelry and diamonds, including engagement and wedding rings. **Inventory** 9. **Average cost of goods** 5. **Value** 5. **Sales and discounts** 4.

COMMENTS The staff is helpful, and the store carries a nice selection.

Henri Bendel

S156, ☎ 952-854-9206, henribendel.com

Store size Medium. **Target market** 30s+, upscale, female. **Inventory description** Designer handbags, fashion jewelry, and accessories. **Inventory** 9. **Average cost of goods** 9. **Value** 7. **Sales and discounts** 5.

COMMENTS Prices aren't inexpensive, but the high-quality products are gorgeous.

Hockey Minnesota by Goldy's Locker Room

E160, ☎ 952-854-9484, mygophersports.com

Store size Small. **Target market** All, mid-range, male/female. **Inventory description** Minnesota-themed sportswear and collectibles. **Inventory** 10. **Average cost of goods** 6. **Value** 5. **Sales and discounts** 5.

COMMENTS Find goods from the State of Hockey and all of the other beloved sports teams.

Holiday Stationstore

W123, ☎ 952-854-6660, holidaystationstores.com

Store size Medium. **Target market** All, budget to mid-range, male/female. **Inventory description** Convenience store. **Inventory** 10. **Average cost of goods** 2. **Value** 2. **Sales and discounts** 7.

COMMENTS Think gas station convenience store; it's appreciated for personal needs like painkillers or diapers.

Hollister

W210, ☎ 952-854-1139, hollisterco.com

Store size Large. **Target market** Teens–20s, mid-range, male/female. **Inventory description** Selections for guys and girls, inspired by the coolness of So-Cal, including hoodies. **Inventory** 10. **Average cost of goods** 4. **Value** 3. **Sales and discounts** 9.

COMMENTS Find casual attire you'd be happy to let your kids wear.

Hot Topic

N168, ☎ 952-858-9150, hottopic.com

Store size Large. **Target market** Teen–20s, mid-range, male/female. **Inventory description** Music-inspired clothing, rock T-shirts, gifts, posters, books, and music. **Inventory** 8. **Average cost of goods** 7. **Value** 4. **Sales and discounts** 4.

COMMENTS You can always find the latest music-themed tees here.

House of Hoops by Foot Locker

N356, ☎ 952-854-5644, footlocker.com

Store size Large. **Target market** Teen–20s, mid-range to upscale, male/female. **Inventory description** Nike and Jordan kicks (athletic shoes). **Inventory** 8. **Average cost of goods** 7. **Value** 5. **Sales and discounts** 5.

COMMENTS Young people really seem to like this place.

House of Samsonite

W158, ☎ 952-854-9139, samsonite.com

Store size Small. **Target market** 30s+, upscale, male/female. **Inventory description** Upscale luggage. **Inventory** 7. **Average cost of goods** 7. **Value** 4. **Sales and discounts** 6.

COMMENTS The store is nice and easy to navigate.

iAccessories

Location #1 W6105, ☎ 952-854-6606; Location #2 S6107, ☎ 952-854-6626; Location #3 S6311

Store size Kiosk. **Target market** Teens, mid-range, male/female. **Inventory description** Accessories for iPads, iPods, and iPhones. **Inventory** 7. **Average cost of goods** 5. **Value** 5. **Sales and discounts** 5.

COMMENTS Popular with the younger crowd, this kiosk offers a fun variety of electronic-device accessories.

iCandy Sugar Shoppe

E154, ☎ 952-767-0224, icandyliciousstore.com

Store size Small. **Target market** All, mid-range, male/female. **Inventory description** Traditional candy store. **Inventory** 10. **Average cost of goods** 4. **Value** 5. **Sales and discounts** 8.

COMMENTS The shop has a nice selection.

Icing

E247, ☎ 952-858-8851, icing.com

Store size Small. **Target market** 20s+, budget, female. **Inventory description** Ladies fashion and clothing accessories. **Inventory** 8. **Average cost of goods** 4. **Value** 4. **Sales and discounts** 9.

COMMENTS This shop is marketed toward ladies who have outgrown sister store Claire's tween-geared supply.

I Love Minnesota

W372, ☎ 952-854-9100, lovefromcompanies.com

Store size Medium. **Target market** All, mid-range, male/female. **Inventory description** Minnesota-themed merchandise. **Inventory** 8. **Average cost of goods** 5. **Value** 5. **Sales and discounts** 4.

COMMENTS Get your Minnesota souvenirs and sweatshirts here.

Impulse

E314, ☎ 952-854-1195

Store size Small. Target market 20s+, mid-range, male/female. Inventory description Jewelry. Inventory 9. Average cost of goods 6. Value 6. Sales and discounts 8.

COMMENTS Look here for affordable jewelry and accessories.

Impulse II

E7302

Store size Kiosk. Target market 20s+, mid-range, male/female. Inventory description Lots of chain jewelry. Inventory 7. Average cost of goods 6. Value 4. Sales and discounts 8.

COMMENTS Kiosk is located directly in front of the main store.

IN

S158, ☎ 952-567-1324, intelligentnutrients.com

Store size Small. Target market 20s+, mid-range, male/female. Inventory description Organic health and beauty products, featuring skin, body, and lip care items. Inventory 8. Average cost of goods 5. Value 4. Sales and discounts 3.

COMMENTS If it's good enough to go on your body, it should be good enough to go into your mouth.

Indulge + Bloom

N314, ☎ 612-343-0000, Ext. 3, indulgeandbloom.com

Store size Medium. Target market 30s+, mid-range, female. Inventory description Floral and gift store. Inventory 9. Average cost of goods 8. Value 5. Sales and discounts 7.

COMMENTS Find fresh flowers for sale on display outside the store.

ISmart Massager

Location # 1 E6316; Location #2 E6101

Store size Kiosk. Target market 30s+, mid-range, male/female. Inventory description Personal electronic simulation technology. Inventory 6. Average cost of goods 4. Value 5. Sales and discounts 5.

COMMENTS Products here are similar to what you find at chiropractic offices.

IT'SUGAR

N270, ☎ 952-854-9245, itsugar.com

Store size Large. Target market All, mid-range, male/female. Inventory description Trendy candy store. Inventory 10. Average cost of goods 2. Value 4. Sales and discounts 3.

COMMENTS This is a vibrant candy shop.

ivivva

S143, ☎ 952-854-1191, ivivva.com

Store size Medium. **Target market** Tweens–teens, upscale, female. **Inventory description** Girls athletic gear by lululemon. **Inventory** 7. **Average cost of goods** 7. **Value** 7. **Sales and discounts** 5.

COMMENTS Find a fun selection here, and check the store's schedule for upcoming classes.

 J

Janie and Jack

S168, ☎ 952-854-2009, janieandjack.com

Store size Small. **Target market** Kids, upscale, male/female. **Inventory description** Children's clothes. **Inventory** 8. **Average cost of goods** 9. **Value** 4. **Sales and discounts** 5.

COMMENTS Find heart-meltingly cute boutique clothes for newborns to age 12.

Jared The Galleria of Jewelry

W278, ☎ 952-814-9230, jared.com

Store size Large. **Target market** 20s+, upscale, male/female. **Inventory description** Fine jewelry. **Inventory** 9. **Average cost of goods** 5. **Value** 4. **Sales and discounts** 4.

COMMENTS The store carries a nice selection.

J.CREW

S200, ☎ 952-814-7419, jcrew.com

Store size Large. **Target market** 20s+, upscale, male/female. **Inventory description** Men's and women's apparel, shoes, and accessories. **Inventory** 9. **Average cost of goods** 7. **Value** 5. **Sales and discounts** 4.

COMMENTS This clothing brand is a bit pricey but classic.

J.Jill

S228, ☎ 952-876-0031, jjill.com

Store size Small. **Target market** 30s+, upscale, female. **Inventory description** Misses and women's casual attire. **Inventory** 10. **Average cost of goods** 7. **Value** 4. **Sales and discounts** 7.

COMMENTS These ageless styles come with a hefty price tag.

JM Cremp's The Boys Adventure Store

N240, ☎ 952-854-9105, jmcremps.com

Store size Large. **Target market** Kids, mid-range, male. **Inventory description** Classic kids' adventure store, focusing on hunting, fishing, survival, camping, and toys. **Inventory** 10. **Average cost of goods** 5. **Value** 4. **Sales and discounts** 9.

COMMENTS Active, outdoorsy kids will be in paradise with the massive amounts of camping, science, fishing, and military-themed toys and activities. Boy Scouts won't want to miss this location.

Johnston & Murphy

W144, ☎ 952-854-1930, johnstonmurphy.com

Store size Small. **Target market** 30s+, upscale, male/female. **Inventory description** Premium, classic shoes for adults. **Inventory** 8. **Average cost of goods** 8. **Value** 5. **Sales and discounts** 5.

COMMENTS Shoppers can't go wrong, especially with the Oxfords.

Journeys

N154, ☎ 952-858-9923, journeys.com

Store size Medium. **Target market** All, mid-range, male/female. **Inventory description** Cool, trendy shoes for the entire family. **Inventory** 9. **Average cost of goods** 6. **Value** 5. **Sales and discounts** 4.

COMMENTS Hipsters especially dig the offerings here.

Just Dogs! Gourmet

Macy's Court, ☎ 952-854-6951, justdogsar.com

Store size Tiny. **Target market** All, mid-range, male/female. **Inventory description** Doggy gear galore. **Inventory** 7. **Average cost of goods** 5. **Value** 6. **Sales and discounts** 6.

COMMENTS This is a spoil-your-dog shop.

Justice

S255, ☎ 952-851-9557, shopjustice.com

Store size Large. **Target market** Tweens, mid-range, female. **Inventory description** Trendy, blingy, sparkly tween fashions. **Inventory** 8. **Average cost of goods** 6. **Value** 10. **Sales and discounts** 4.

COMMENTS This is a fun line for the tween girl.

 # K

kate spade

S106, ☎ 952-854-1003, katespade.com

Store size Medium. **Target market** 20s+, upscale, female. **Inventory description** The latest handbag fashions and accessories. **Inventory** 10. **Average cost of goods** 9. **Value** 7. **Sales and discounts** 3.

COMMENTS Kate Spade is one of MOA's newer tenants; the store is beautiful.

KAY Jewelers

N174, ☎ 952-876-0700, kay.com

Store size Small. **Target market** 20s+, mid-range, female. **Inventory description** Jewelry. **Inventory** 7. **Average cost of goods** 6. **Value** 4. **Sales and discounts** 8.

COMMENTS This location is consistent with other KAY Jewelers locations.

KD Designs

W6111, kddesignsjewelry.com

Store size Kiosk. **Target market** 20s, mid-range, male/female. **Inventory description** Jewelry made with natural stones. **Inventory** 7. **Average cost of goods** 5. **Value** 4. **Sales and discounts** 3.

COMMENTS Find creative workmanship here.

Kids Foot Locker

E272A, ☎ 952-858-8928, kidsfootlocker.com

Store size Medium–large. **Target market** Kids, mid-range, male/female. **Inventory description** Athletic shoes. **Inventory** 8. **Average cost of goods** 7. **Value** 5. **Sales and discounts** 8.

COMMENTS Find footwear for your athletic kids.

Kiehl's

N121, ☎ 952-854-9541, kiehls.com

Store size Small. **Target market** 20s+, mid-range, male/female. **Inventory description** Natural skin and hair care formulas. **Inventory** 10. **Average cost of goods** 4. **Value** 4. **Sales and discounts** 4.

COMMENTS The shop offers top-notch customer service and a nice body care selection.

Kit Ace

S108, kitandace.com

Store size Small. **Target market** 30s+, upscale, male/female. **Inventory description** Luxury attire for men and women. **Inventory** 9. **Average cost of goods** 9. **Value** 5. **Sales and discounts** 5.

COMMENTS Find the original Technical Cashmere for which this brand is known.

 L

Lacoste

S172, ☎ 952-854-9929, lacoste.com/us

Store size Small. **Target market** 20s+, upscale, male. **Inventory description** Men's sportswear. **Inventory** 9. **Average cost of goods** 7. **Value** 6. **Sales and discounts** 6.

COMMENTS Go for the Lacoste polo shirts; stay for everything else.

Lane Bryant

S229, ☎ 952-356-3325, lanebryant.com

Store size Medium. Target market 20s+, mid-range, female. Inventory description Women's plus-size clothing, sizes 14–28. Inventory 10. Average cost of goods 6. Value 5. Sales and discounts 8.

COMMENTS Find fashionable clothes for plus-size ladies.

The LEGO Store

S164, ☎ 952-858-8949, lego.com

Store size Large. Target market All, mid-range, male/female. Inventory description LEGO bricks and sets, plus a 180-choice pick-a-brick wall. Inventory 10. Average cost of goods 5. Value 6. Sales and discounts 5.

COMMENTS Formerly known as LEGOLAND, the name was a bit misleading if you'd been to the theme parks by the same name. This location has oversize LEGO formations looming above the store with smaller-scale LEGO creations inside. Typical MOA merchandise is for sale at average LEGO prices. Several LEGO tables outside the store provide free play for children. MOA says 170,000+ LEGOs have been lost over the years.

len

N300, ☎ 952-358-6969, shoplen.com

Store size Large. Target market 30s+, mid-range, male/female. Inventory description Affordable men's and women's clothing. Inventory 10. Average cost of goods 6. Value 4. Sales and discounts 6.

COMMENTS Shop this locally owned store for stylish apparel.

LensCrafters

N304, ☎ 952-858-8410, lenscrafters.com

Store size Small. Target market All, mid-range, male/female. Inventory description Eyewear and exams. Inventory 9. Average cost of goods 6. Value 5. Sales and discounts 7.

COMMENTS Schedule an appointment online.

Levi's

S262, ☎ 952-814-9980, levi.com

Store size Large. Target market Teens+, mid-range, male/female. Inventory description Classic denim retailer. Inventory 10. Average cost of goods 6. Value 4. Sales and discounts 7.

COMMENTS This trusted brand keeps up with the latest styles.

L.L.Bean

S100, ☎ 952-854-1017, llbean.com

Store size Large. **Target market** All, mid-range to upscale, male/female. **Inventory description** Outdoors apparel, gear, boots, and shoes, including the Original Duck Boot. **Inventory** 10. **Average cost of goods** 7. **Value** 6. **Sales and discounts** 8.

COMMENTS The oversize Duck Boot outside the store makes for a fun photo opportunity.

Lids

Location #1 E134, ☎ 952-858-9670; Location #2 E346, ☎ 952-814-0150; Location #3 W369, ☎ 952-854-2794; lids.com

Store size Location #1, medium; Location #2, tiny; Location #3, small. **Target market** 20s+, mid-range, male/female. **Inventory description** Sports, fashion, and college team hats. **Inventory** Location #1, 9; Location #2, 6; Location #3, 6. **Average cost of goods** 3. **Value** 3. **Sales and discounts** 6.

COMMENTS You'll find hats galore.

The Limited

S206, ☎ 952-854-1970, thelimited.com

Store size Medium. **Target market** 20s+, mid-range, female. **Inventory description** Sophisticated women's fashions. **Inventory** 10. **Average cost of goods** 6–7. **Value** 5. **Sales and discounts** 8.

COMMENTS This store offers classy casual and professional wear.

Lindt Master Swiss Chocolatier

S284, ☎ 952-854-1917, lindtusa.com

Store size Small. **Target market** All, mid-range, male/female. **Inventory description** Swiss chocolates. **Inventory** 10. **Average cost of goods** 3. **Value** 3. **Sales and discounts** 10.

COMMENTS Buy one or a whole box.

Live Love Dream

N262, ☎ 952-854-9446, aeropostale.com

Store size Small. **Target market** 20s+, mid-range, female. **Inventory description** Female athletic and active wear by Aéropostale. **Inventory** 8. **Average cost of goods** 5. **Value** 5. **Sales and discounts** 6.

COMMENTS This store is adjacent to Aéropostale.

Local Charm

E104, ☎ 952-854-6562

Store size Small. **Target market** 20s+, mid-range, female. **Inventory description** Specializes in sterling and gemstone jewelry. **Inventory** 10. **Average cost of goods** 6–9. **Value** 5. **Sales and discounts** 5.

COMMENTS Find a wide range of prices and jewelry styles.

LOFT

N184, ☎ 952-854-2323, loft.com

Store size Medium. Target market 20s+, mid-range, female. Inventory description Fashionable women's clothing for all occasions. Inventory 10. Average cost of goods 7. Value 6. Sales and discounts 6.

COMMENTS LOFT pieces are easy to mix and match. Owned and operated by the Ann Taylor collection of companies.

Long Tall Sally

W282, ☎ 952-858-9360, us.longtallsally.com

Store size Small. Target market 20s+, mid-range, female. Inventory description Fashions for ladies of height. Inventory 9. Average cost of goods 7. Value 6. Sales and discounts 6.

COMMENTS This specialty shop carries clothing for women who are 5'8" and above in sizes 4–18.

Lotus Beads and Jewelry

N368, ☎ 952-854-9951, lotusbeadsandjewelry.com

Store size Medium. Target market All, mid-range, female. Inventory description Jewelry making. Inventory 10. Average cost of goods 4. Value 4. Sales and discounts 5.

COMMENTS This make-your-own-jewelry shop has beads and gems from around the world, as well as locally crafted offerings. Table reservations can be made for 6 or 12 people.

Love from Minnesota

W380, ☎ 952-854-7319, lovefromcompanies.com

Store size Medium. Target market All, mid-range, male/female. Inventory description Minnesota-themed goods. Inventory 9. Average cost of goods 4. Value 3. Sales and discounts 8.

COMMENTS Shop for Minnesota-themed souvenirs, gifts, and apparel.

Lovesac

W327, ☎ 952-854-5105, lovesac.com

Store size Small. Target market 20s+, mid-range, male/female. Inventory description Unique furniture, including foam-filled Sacs. Inventory 7. Average cost of goods 10. Value 6. Sales and discounts 8.

COMMENTS It's a unique concept, and you can ship items home.

Lucky Brand

S170, ☎ 952-854-9289, luckybrand.com

Store size Medium. Target market 20s+, mid-range, male/female. Inventory description Denim and T-shirts. Inventory 9. Average cost of goods 6. Value 6. Sales and discounts 5.

COMMENTS It's easy to become a Lucky fan, if the jean styles fit you.

lululemon athletica

S152, ☎ 952-854-6785, shop.lululemon.com

Store size Medium. **Target market** 20s+, upscale, female. **Inventory description** Trendy athletic wear. **Inventory** 10. **Average cost of goods** 7. **Value** 8. **Sales and discounts** 5.

COMMENTS Fitness trainers and active ladies swear that once you try lululemon, you're stuck.

LUSH

E112, ☎ 952-854-9672, lush.com

Store size Small. **Target market** 20s+, mid-range, female. **Inventory description** Handmade cosmetics. **Inventory** 8. **Average cost of goods** 3. **Value** 3. **Sales and discounts** 7.

COMMENTS Bath bombs will get you hooked on LUSH.

 M

MAC Cosmetics

W294, ☎ 952-814-9800, maccosmetics.com

Store size Small. **Target market** 20s+, mid-range, female. **Inventory description** Trendy cosmetics. **Inventory** 9. **Average cost of goods** 3. **Value** 3. **Sales and discounts** 6.

COMMENTS MAC carries the latest and greatest in colors and products. If it's hot, MAC will show you.

Macy's

SW Court 4000, ☎ 952-888-3333, macys.com

Store size Large (anchor). **Target market** All, mid-range to upscale, male/female. **Inventory description** Clothes, shoes, cosmetics, housewares. **Inventory** 10. **Average cost of goods** 7. **Value** 6. **Sales and discounts** 10.

COMMENTS This is a classic department store with a huge inventory.

Madewell

S143, ☎ 952-854-1863, madewell.com

Store size Small. **Target market** 20s+, upscale, female. **Inventory description** Cute ladies' denim and other fashions. **Inventory** 10. **Average cost of goods** 7. **Value** 6. **Sales and discounts** 6.

COMMENTS The store accepts used jeans for Blue Jeans Go Green recycling, used to insulate Habitat for Humanity homes. Donations are exchanged for a Madewell discount coupon.

Mall of America Gift Store

Location #1 S225, ☎ 952-883-8423; Location #2 W388, ☎ 952-883-8918; Location #3 E372; mallofamericagifts.com

Store size Locations #1 and #2, small; Location #3, tiny. **Target market** All, mid-range, male/female. **Inventory description** Mall of America branded merchandise and gifts. **Inventory** Locations #1 and #3, 3; Location #2, 7. **Average cost of goods** 3. **Value** 3. **Sales and discounts** 5.

COMMENTS This is the place for Mall of America souvenirs.

Marbles The Brain Store

N216, ☎ 952-854-5804, marblesthebrainstore.com

Store size Medium. **Target market** All, mid-range, male/female. **Inventory description** Brain-sharpening games. **Inventory** 10. **Average cost of goods** 4. **Value** 3. **Sales and discounts** 8.

COMMENTS Shop for adult coloring books, puzzles, brainteasers, educational games, and more.

Marshalls

E320, ☎ 952-851-0750, marshallsonline.com

Store size Large. **Target market** All, budget to mid-range, male/female. **Inventory description** Fashions and shoes for men, women, and children. **Inventory** 8. **Average cost of goods** 3. **Value** 2. **Sales and discounts** 10.

COMMENTS This off-price department store sells brand names and designer goods for the whole family.

maurices

E212, ☎ 952-851-0027, maurices.com

Store size Large. **Target market** 20s+, mid-range, female. **Inventory description** Young ladies' fashions. **Inventory** 10. **Average cost of goods** 5. **Value** 4. **Sales and discounts** 8.

COMMENTS While the store is marketed to young ladies in their 20s, ladies 30+ can easily shop here too (sizes 1–24).

ME3D

E356, ☎ 952-658-8868, me3dstore.com

Store size Small. **Target market** All, upscale, male/female. **Inventory description** Cutting-edge technology, combining photogrammetry and 3-D printing. **Inventory** 8. **Average cost of goods** 8. **Value** 5. **Sales and discounts** 8.

COMMENTS Figurines start at $100 for personal, sports, or even group replicas. It's the new selfie!

Merrell

N282, ☎ 952-854-5778, merrell.com

Store size Medium. **Target market** All, mid-range to upscale, male/female. **Inventory description** Outdoorsy shoes. **Inventory** 10. **Average cost of goods** 7. **Value** 5. **Sales and discounts** 5.

COMMENTS Merrell is teaming with Tough Mudder in 2016.

Michael Hill

S292, ☎ 952-854-9292, michaelhill.com

Store size Small. **Target market** 20s+, mid-range to upscale, female. **Inventory description** Jewelry. **Inventory** 9. **Average cost of goods** 7–10. **Value** 4. **Sales and discounts** 4.

COMMENTS The store has an in-house team of master craftsmen.

Michael Kors

S184, ☎ 952-814-1900, michaelkors.com

Store size Small. **Target market** 20s+, upscale, female. **Inventory description** Designer handbags, watches, shoes, and clothing. **Inventory** 10. **Average cost of goods** 9. **Value** 6. **Sales and discounts** 5.

COMMENTS Think jet-setter styles.

Microsoft

S162, ☎ 952-487-7372, microsoftstore.com

Store size Large. **Target market** Teens+, mid-range to upscale, male/female. **Inventory description** Computers and the latest technology. **Inventory** 10. **Average cost of goods** 8–10. **Value** 5. **Sales and discounts** 8.

COMMENTS This is a nice space with lots of hands-on opportunities.

Minnesot-ah!

E157, ☎ 952-858-8531, lovefromcompanies.com

Store size Medium. **Target market** 30s+, mid-range, male/female. **Inventory description** Minnesota-themed souvenirs, gifts, and apparel. **Inventory** 10. **Average cost of goods** 4. **Value** 4. **Sales and discounts** 9.

COMMENTS Here's some easy North Star State souvenir shopping.

Minnesota Vikings Locker Room

E126, ☎ 952-854-5473, vikingsfanshop.com

Store size Small. **Target market** Kids+, mid-range, male/female. **Inventory description** Official Vikings' football team store. **Inventory** 8. **Average cost of goods** 7. **Value** 7. **Sales and discounts** 5.

COMMENTS This shop carries Vikings items galore. There's a good chance you'll find what you're looking for.

Mona Williams

W132, monawilliams.com

Store size Medium. **Target market** 20s+, mid-range, female. **Inventory description** Upscale consignment clothing. **Inventory** 8. **Average cost of goods** 6. **Value** 3. **Sales and discounts** 7.

COMMENTS Shop here for vintage designer apparel and exclusive brands.

 N

New Era

N274, ☎ 952-854-5714, neweracap.com

Store size Medium. **Target market** Teens+, mid-range, male/female. **Inventory description** Sports hats. **Inventory** 10. **Average cost of goods** 2. **Value** 3. **Sales and discounts** 5.

COMMENTS This brand is best known as the official on-field cap for Major League Baseball and the National Football League.

New York & Company

S276, ☎ 952-858-8815, nyandcompany.com

Store size Large . **Target market** 20s+, mid-range, female. **Inventory description** Trendy clothes for the ladies. **Inventory** 10. **Average cost of goods** 4–5. **Value** 3. **Sales and discounts** 9.

COMMENTS These cute, affordable finds are easily half the price of similar styles found in designer stores.

Nike

W244, ☎ 952-854-5042, nike.com

Store size Large. **Target market** Teens+, mid-range to upscale, male/female. **Inventory description** Athletic wear. **Inventory** 10. **Average cost of goods** 7. **Value** 7. **Sales and discounts** 6.

COMMENTS This is one of four stores with Nike's new hip shopping experience; it includes team customization services.

Nordstrom

1000 NW Court, ☎ 952-883-2121, shop.nordstrom.com

Store size Large (anchor). **Target market** All, upscale, male/female. **Inventory description** Upscale fashion retailer. **Inventory** 10. **Average cost of goods** 8. **Value** 8. **Sales and discounts** 6.

COMMENTS There are three floors of high-quality lines and top-tier service.

Nordstrom Rack

W324, ☎ 952-854-3131, nordstromrack.com

Store size Large. Target market All, budget to upscale, male/female. Inventory description Discounted fashions from Nordstrom. Inventory 10. Average cost of goods 6. Value 4. Sales and discounts 10.

COMMENTS There is always something good to be swooped up at the Rack.

The North Face

S166, ☎ 952-854-1493, thenorthface.com

Store size Large. Target market All, mid-range to upscale, male/female. Inventory description Athletic apparel, equipment, and footwear for the outdoors. Inventory 10. Average cost of goods 8. Value 6. Sales and discounts 7.

COMMENTS Find innovative, high-quality outdoors wear.

Northwoods Candy Emporium

N312, ☎ 952-373-4959, northwoodscandy.com

Store size Medium. Target market All, mid-range, male/female. Inventory description Gourmet candy. Inventory 8. Average cost of goods 2. Value 2. Sales and discounts 8.

COMMENTS An entire section is dedicated to nostalgic candies, and the fudge is delectable.

NYX Professional Makeup

E106, nyxcosmetics.com

Store size Small. Target market Teens+, budget, female. Inventory description Fun, trendy makeup. Inventory 8. Average cost of goods 2. Value 2. Sales and discounts 8.

COMMENTS This is a great place to pick up a new lipstick.

Oakley

Location #1 N107, ☎ 952-854-2007; Location #2 N260, ☎ 952-854-6620; oakley.com

Store size Medium. Target market 20s+, mid-range, male/female. Inventory description High-performance sunglasses. Inventory 8. Average cost of goods 7. Value 4. Sales and discounts 7.

COMMENTS Find a large selection of colors and styles.

L'Occitane En Provence

W268, ☎ 952-854-5581, usa.loccitane.com

Store size Small. Target market 30s+, upscale, male/female. Inventory description Beauty and skin care products inspired by the Mediterranean region of Provence. Inventory 9. Average cost of goods 5. Value 6. Sales and discounts 5.

COMMENTS Find fancy French products for the bath.

Old Navy

E138, ☎ 952-853-0100, oldnavy.gap.com

Store size Large (Flagship store). **Target market** All, budget, male/female. **Inventory description** Affordable update fashions for men, women, and kids. **Inventory** 10. **Average cost of goods** 4. **Value** 3. **Sales and discounts** 10.

COMMENTS The back-room clearance section is teeming with discounts and bargains.

Old Vine Wine + Spirits

W326, ☎ 952-858-8800

Store size Large. **Target market** 21+, mid-range to upscale, male/female. **Inventory description** Wine and spirits. **Inventory** 10. **Average cost of goods** 3–7. **Value** 4. **Sales and discounts** 5.

COMMENTS The only wine and spirits store in the mall, it has a nice selection of good wines but also inexpensive choices, including the funny-named, affordable gift wine.

Origins

W292, ☎ 952-858-9665, origins.com

Store size Medium. **Target market** 20s+, mid-range, male/female. **Inventory description** Skin care, makeup, bath and body products. **Inventory** 9. **Average cost of goods** 3. **Value** 3. **Sales and discounts** 7.

COMMENTS Origins isn't just for ladies; there is a men's line too.

  P

PacSun

E246, ☎ 952-854-4090, pacsun.com

Store size Large. **Target market** Teens–20s, mid-range, male/female. **Inventory description** The latest California-inspired styles. **Inventory** 9. **Average cost of goods** 6. **Value** 6. **Sales and discounts** 8.

COMMENTS Find hot brands like Billabong, Hurley, Roxy, Nike, Vans, and more.

Pandora

N127, ☎ 952-252-1495, becharming.com

Store size Small. **Target market** 20s+, upscale, female. **Inventory description** Jewelry. **Inventory** 10. **Average cost of goods** 6. **Value** 6. **Sales and discounts** 8.

COMMENTS Best known for its Pandora charms and bracelets, the store also has a selection of rings, necklaces, earrings, and watches.

Paper Source

N116, papersource.com

Store size Small. **Target market** All, mid-range to upscale, male/female. **Inventory description** Personalized invitations and stationery, gift wrap. **Inventory** 10. **Average cost of goods** 6. **Value** 6. **Sales and discounts** 6.

COMMENTS This is a great shop for birthday gifts.

Paradise Pen

S222, ☎ 952-854-9494, paradisepen.com

Store size Small. **Target market** 20s+, mid-range to upscale, male/female. **Inventory description** Fine writing utensils. **Inventory** 10. **Average cost of goods** 8. **Value** 6. **Sales and discounts** 6.

COMMENTS Find an exquisite selection of pens.

Payless Shoe Source

N150, ☎ 952-858-8132, payless.com

Store size Small. **Target market** All, budget, male/female. **Inventory description** Affordable footwear. **Inventory** 9. **Average cost of goods** 2. **Value** 2. **Sales and discounts** 8.

COMMENTS This is one of the less expensive shoe stores in the mall.

Pearle Vision

W385, ☎ 952-854-4500, pearlvision.com

Store size Small. **Target market** All, mid-range, male/female. **Inventory description** Service provider of eye exams, frames, lenses, and contacts. **Inventory** 8. **Average cost of goods** 4. **Value** 4. **Sales and discounts** 7.

COMMENTS Get your eyes checked, and then order new specs.

Peeps & Company

Nickelodeon Universe, ☎ 952-854-5130, marshmallowpeeps.com

Store size Large. **Target market** Kids, budget, male/female. **Inventory description** Candy shop teeming with Peeps, Hot Tamales, and Peeps-themed attire and gifts. **Inventory** 10. **Average cost of goods** 2. **Value** 2. **Sales and discounts** 10.

COMMENTS Peeps are marshmallow candy in the shape of baby chickens, bunnies, and more. Peeps brand shirts, stuffed animals, and lots of candy.

Pepper Palace

E360, ☎ 952-456-2714, pepperpalace.com

Store size Large. **Target market** All, mid-range, male/female. **Inventory description** Seemingly endless rows of barbecue sauce, salsa, pickled items, jellies and jams, and a variety of gift ideas. **Inventory** 10. **Average cost of goods** 2. **Value** 2. **Sales and discounts** 8.

COMMENTS Taste before you buy.

Perfumania

N219, ☎ 952-851-0790, perfumania.com

Store size Small. Target market 20s+, budget, male/female. Inventory description Discount perfume, cologne, and other fragrances. Inventory 10. Average cost of goods 3. Value 3. Sales and discounts 9.

COMMENTS Find cheaper offerings than at department stores.

Persepolis

W360, ☎ 612-382-8393

Store size Tiny. Target market 20s+, mid-range, male/female. Inventory description Eclectic jewelry, T-shirts, and accessories. Inventory 6. Average cost of goods 5. Value 5. Sales and discounts 5.

COMMENTS Shoppers who are into skulls will like this store.

Piercing Pagoda

S1803, ☎ 952-853-0843, pagoda.com

Store size Tiny. Target market All, mid-range, male/female. Inventory description Ear-piercing services, earrings, and jewelry. Inventory 10. Average cost of goods 5. Value 4. Sales and discounts 8.

COMMENTS Pick out one-step, single-use, sterilized, prepackaged piercing earrings.

PINK

N120, ☎ 952-854-1615, victoriassecret.com/pink

Store size Large. Target market Teens–20s, mid-range, female. Inventory description Victoria's Secret for the teen/college-age girl; sportswear. Inventory 10. Average cost of goods 6. Value 5. Sales and discounts 7.

COMMENTS This is more appropriate for young ladies than its sister store Victoria's Secret. In addition to lingerie, PINK offers comfy activewear, including hoodies, tank tops, and sweatpants.

Pinook Massager

N6141, ☎ 952-854-5599, pinookcanada.com

Store size Kiosk. Target market 30s+, mid-range, male/female. Inventory description Personal massagers. Inventory 5. Average cost of goods 5. Value 5. Sales and discounts 4.

COMMENTS Shop for relief from back pain.

proactiv

E6110, ☎ 877-275-2561, theproactivstore.com

Store size Kiosk. Target market Teens+, mid-range, male/female. Inventory description Acne treatment, moisture, sheer cover mineral makeup. Inventory 10. Average cost of goods 6. Value 4. Sales and discounts 6.

COMMENTS This brand has been going strong for a long time. It's worth a try if you suffer from acne and haven't tried it yet.

Pro Image Sports

N258, ☎ 952-960-0783, proimageamerica.com

Store size Medium. **Target market** All, mid-range, male/female. **Inventory description** Sports fan merchandise. **Inventory** 10. **Average cost of goods** 7. **Value** 4. **Sales and discounts** 7.

COMMENTS Buy a T-shirt here to show everyone which professional team is your favorite.

Professor Bellows Specialty Photography

N374, ☎ 952-853-9804, professorbellows.com

Store size Medium. **Target market** All, mid-range, male/female. **Inventory description** Old-time, Santa, and event photos. **Inventory** 10. **Average cost of goods** 6. **Value** 5. **Sales and discounts** 6.

COMMENTS Reservations are recommended for Santa photos.

 R

Ragstock

Location #1 N275, ☎ 952-854-9377; Location #2 E214, ☎ 952-854-9017; ragstock.com

Store size Location #1, medium; Location #2, large. **Target market** 20s, budget, male/female. **Inventory description** New and vintage clothing. **Inventory** 10. **Average cost of goods** 4. **Value** 3. **Sales and discounts** 10.

COMMENTS Ragstock sometimes has temporary pop-up stores with holiday-themed attire, such as Halloween costumes and ugly Christmas sweaters.

Rainbow

E330, ☎ 952-858-9363, rainbowshops.com

Store size Large. **Target market** Kids+, mid-range, male/female. **Inventory description** Trendy fashions for good value, for kids and women. **Inventory** 10. **Average cost of goods** 1. **Value** 1. **Sales and discounts** 2.

COMMENTS Shop a wide variety of sizes for a great deal.

Relax•a•daisical/Life is Good

W342, ☎ 952-854-5485, relaxadaisical.com

Store size Small. **Target market** All, mid-range, male/female. **Inventory description** Life is Good attire, hats, and apparel. **Inventory** 9. **Average cost of goods** 3. **Value** 3. **Sales and discounts** 2.

COMMENTS The T-shirt designs will bring a smile to your face.

Rockport Shop

S280, ☎ 952-883-0331, rockport.com

Store size Small. Target market 20s+, mid-range, male/female. Inventory description Dress and casual shoes. Inventory 9. Average cost of goods 7. Value 5. Sales and discounts 4.

COMMENTS The shoes are lightweight due to advanced athletic technologies.

Rocky Mountain Chocolate Factory

E128, ☎ 952-858-8826, rmcf.com

Store size Tiny. Target market All, budget, male/female. Inventory description Specialty chocolates and confections. Inventory 8. Average cost of goods 1. Value 3. Sales and discounts 6.

COMMENTS Come get your sugar fix here.

Rogers & Hollands

W146, ☎ 952-814-9400, rogersandhollands.com

Store size Medium. Target market 20s, mid-range, male/female. Inventory description Family-owned jewelry store. Inventory 9. Average cost of goods 6. Value 4. Sales and discounts 5.

COMMENTS Find gorgeous, updated styles.

Running Room

W161, ☎ 952-854-1996, runningroom.com

Store size Small. Target market 20s+, mid-range, male/female. Inventory description Running and walking shoes. Inventory 8. Average cost of goods 8. Value 4. Sales and discounts 5.

COMMENTS Find your running gear here.

Rybicki Cheese, Ltd.

W382, ☎ 952-854-3330, rybickicheese4u.com

Store size Small. Target market All, budget, male/female. Inventory description Fresh cheeses and Wisconsin Green Bay Packer merchandise. Inventory 10. Average cost of goods 2. Value 3. Sales and discounts 5.

COMMENTS A sample cart is always set up outside the store.

 # S

Sabon

W166, ☎ 952-657-5861, sabonnyc.com

Store size Tiny. Target market 20s, mid-range, male/female. Inventory description Israeli countryside–inspired herbs and oils. Inventory 8. Average cost of goods 3. Value 3. Sales and discounts 6.

COMMENTS Shop for body scrubs and gifts.

Sears

2000 NE Court, ☎ 952-853-0500, sears.com

Store size Large (anchor). **Target market** All, budget to mid-range, male/female. **Inventory description** Department store covering home, automotive, apparel, shoes, and optical. **Inventory** 10. **Average cost of goods** 4. **Value** 4. **Sales and discounts** 10.

COMMENTS It's sometimes challenging to find salespeople here.

See's Candies

N284, ☎ 952-854-5772, sees.com

Store size Small. **Target market** All, mid-range, male/female. **Inventory description** Classic old-time candy. **Inventory** 8. **Average cost of goods** 3. **Value** 3. **Sales and discounts** 4.

COMMENTS See's never disappoints in the candy world.

Sephora

W200, ☎ 952-854-1517, sephora.com

Store size Large. **Target market** 20s+, mid-range, male/female. **Inventory description** Head-to-toe body and skin care products. **Inventory** 10. **Average cost of goods** 7. **Value** 5. **Sales and discounts** 5.

COMMENTS Come for a mini makeover.

shï by Journeys

E268, ☎ 952-854-6991, journeys.com

Store size Medium. **Target market** 20s+, mid-range, female. **Inventory description** Journeys' women's-only concept store. **Inventory** 9. **Average cost of goods** 7. **Value** 5. **Sales and discounts** 5.

COMMENTS The female focus is nice.

Sigma

W286, ☎ 952-405-6684, sigmabeauty.com

Store size Small. **Target market** 20s+, mid-range, female. **Inventory description** High-quality beauty products at an affordable price. **Inventory** 9. **Average cost of goods** 1. **Value** 1. **Sales and discounts** 5.

COMMENTS Find inexpensive prices at this shop.

Silver Jeans Co.

S220, ☎ 952-607-5328, silverjeans.com

Store size Medium. **Target market** All, mid-range, male/female. **Inventory description** Jeans with a mixture of modern and vintage flair. **Inventory** 10. **Average cost of goods** 5. **Value** 4. **Sales and discounts** 8.

COMMENTS Find something for all sizes, including women's plus.

SIX

E125, ☎ 952-854-5448, click-six.com

Store size Small. **Target market** 20s+, mid-range, male/female. **Inventory description** Trendy accessories for women and men. **Inventory** 9. **Average cost of goods** 5. **Value** 5. **Sales and discounts** 5.

COMMENTS Find purses, sunglasses, jewelry, and more.

Skechers

N214, ☎ 952-854-3000, skechers.com

Store size Small. **Target market** All, mid-range, male/female. **Inventory description** Trendy athletic and casual footwear for the entire family. **Inventory** 8. **Average cost of goods** 7. **Value** 6. **Sales and discounts** 5.

COMMENTS These shoes are always on-trend.

Sleep Number

S256, ☎ 952-858-9531, sleepnumber.com

Store size Small. **Target market** 30s+, mid-range to upscale, male/female. **Inventory description** Adjustable and foam beds. **Inventory** 7. **Average cost of goods** 8. **Value** 6. **Sales and discounts** 5.

COMMENTS *Warning:* Don't shop here when you're tired—you may fall asleep!

Sole Mio

W296, ☎ 952-858-8910

Store size Small. **Target market** 20s+, upscale, male/female. **Inventory description** High-end sunglasses. **Inventory** 8. **Average cost of goods** 7. **Value** 7. **Sales and discounts** 5.

COMMENTS Find sport and designer sunglasses and luxury eyewear.

Solstice Sunglasses

W131, ☎ 952-854-4720, solsticesunglasses.com

Store size Small. **Target market** 20s+, upscale, male/female. **Inventory description** Fashionable sunglasses. **Inventory** 8. **Average cost of goods** 7. **Value** 5. **Sales and discounts** 5.

COMMENTS Trained stylists will help you find the pair that's right for you.

Soma

W135, ☎ 952-854-1230, soma.com

Store size Medium. **Target market** 20s+, upscale, female. **Inventory description** Sleepwear, bras, underwear. **Inventory** 10. **Average cost of goods** 7. **Value** 6. **Sales and discounts** 6.

COMMENTS The store offers an elegant line and personal service.

Sox Appeal

W391, ☎ 952-858-9141

Store size Tiny. **Target market** All, budget to mid-range, male/female. **Inventory description** Socks, hosiery, and slippers. **Inventory** 8. **Average cost of goods** 2. **Value** 3. **Sales and discounts** 7.

COMMENTS Go here for easy sock shopping.

Spencer's

N354, ☎ 952-851-0878, spencersonline.com

Store size Medium. **Target market** Teens and 20s, mid-range, male/female. **Inventory description** Goofy T-shirts and gifts. **Inventory** 10. **Average cost of goods** 3. **Value** 5. **Sales and discounts** 9.

COMMENTS Think twice before dragging children in here because many items are kitschy and inappropriate.

Sprint

Location #1 W387, ☎ 952-854-9070; Location #2 E220, ☎ 612-225-9136; sprint.com

Store size Location #1, medium; Location #2, tiny. **Target market** All, mid-range, male/female. **Inventory description** Wireless and wire line communications services. **Inventory** Location #1, 9; Location #2, 4. **Average cost of goods** 6. **Value** 5. **Sales and discounts** 7.

COMMENTS Location #2 is located near the escalators, kiosk-style.

Steve Madden

W142, ☎ 952-876-0370, stevemadden.com

Store size Small. **Target market** 20s+, upscale, male/female. **Inventory description** Fashionable shoes for men and women. **Inventory** 3–4. **Average cost of goods** 7. **Value** 8. **Sales and discounts** 5.

COMMENTS You can always find the latest footwear trends at Steve Madden.

Street Corner News

E122, ☎ 952-858-8539

Store size Tiny. **Target market** All, budget, male/female. **Inventory description** Mini convenience store. **Inventory** 4. **Average cost of goods** 2. **Value** 2. **Sales and discounts** 4.

COMMENTS Grab a quick bottled drink or snack here.

Stuart Weitzman

S180, ☎ 952-854-4080, stuartweitzman.com

Store size Small. **Target market** 20s+, upscale, female. **Inventory description** Designer shoes for women. **Inventory** 10. **Average cost of goods** 9. **Value** 7. **Sales and discounts** 6.

COMMENTS Shop the latest runway fashions with steep price tags.

Sunglass Depot

Location #1 W6109, Location #2 S6203, Location #3 E6101

Store size Kiosk. **Target market** 20s+, mid-range, male/female. **Inventory description** Sunglasses. **Inventory** 5. **Average cost of goods** 5. **Value** 5. **Sales and discounts** 7.

COMMENTS These shops are easy to access.

Sunglass Hut

Location #1 N256, ☎ 952-858-8910; Location #2 N118, ☎ 952-858-8547; Location #3 W362, ☎ 952-858-9963; Location #4 W296; sunglasshut.com

Store size Small. **Target market** Teens+, mid-range to upscale, male/female. **Inventory description** Sunglasses and sunglass accessories. **Inventory** 10. **Average cost of goods** 7. **Value** 6. **Sales and discounts** 7.

COMMENTS Keep up with trends or find classic styles.

Swarovski

N288, ☎ 952-853-2130, swarovski.com

Store size Small. **Target market** 30s+, upscale, male/female. **Inventory description** Precision-cut crystal glass jewelry, accessories, and gifts. **Inventory** 10. **Average cost of goods** 8. **Value** 6. **Sales and discounts** 7.

COMMENTS These are classic gifts.

Swatch

E162, ☎ 952-853-9000, swatch.com

Store size Small. **Target market** All, upscale, male/female. **Inventory description** Contemporary Swiss-made watches. **Inventory** 10. **Average cost of goods** 7. **Value** 6. **Sales and discounts** 4.

COMMENTS This is a newly remodeled store near the Rotunda.

Swim'n Sport

S286, ☎ 952-236-7028, swimnsport.com

Store size Small. **Target market** 20s+, mid-range, female. **Inventory description** Designer swimwear. **Inventory** 9. **Average cost of goods** 6. **Value** 4. **Sales and discounts** 4.

COMMENTS Find high-quality pieces at affordable prices.

 T

T-Mobile

Location #1 N382, ☎ 952-854-7469; Location #2 E156, ☎ 763-251-0671; t-mobile.com

Store size Medium. **Target market** All, mid-range, male/female. **Inventory description** Phone and cell service. **Inventory** 7. **Average cost of goods** 5. **Value** 5. **Sales and discounts** 7.

COMMENTS The staff is friendly and helpful.

Tervis

W370, ☎ 952-854-4054, tervis.com

Store size Small. **Target market** 20s+, mid-range, male/female. **Inventory description** Hot and cold cups with natural heating/cooling insulating technology. **Inventory** 8. **Average cost of goods** 1. **Value** 3. **Sales and discounts** 7.

COMMENTS Tumblers have a made-for-life guarantee.

Things Remembered

E290, ☎ 952-858-9066, thingsremembered.com

Store size Small. **Target market** All, mid-range to upscale, male/female. **Inventory description** Personally engraved gifts for all occasions. **Inventory** 7. **Average cost of goods** 7. **Value** 5. **Sales and discounts** 5.

COMMENTS Metal and glass engraving is done in the store. Another option is to order online and pick up on the same day. Most items are finished in 4 hours.

Tilly's

N246, ☎ 952-814-1035, tillys.com

Store size Medium. **Target market** Kids and teens, mid-range, male/female. **Inventory description** Casual clothing and accessories. **Inventory** 10. **Average cost of goods** 5. **Value** 4. **Sales and discounts** 6.

COMMENTS Find fun, trendy clothes aimed at younger people.

Tommy Bahama

W235, ☎ 952-351-9888, tommybahama.com

Store size Medium. **Target market** 30s+, upscale, male/female. **Inventory description** Luxury island lifestyle clothing and accessories. **Inventory** 10. **Average cost of goods** 8. **Value** 4. **Sales and discounts** 4.

COMMENTS The staff is knowledgeable and classy.

Tomodachi

N316, ☎ 952-582-1739, tomodachi.us

Store size Medium. **Target market** Teens, mid-range to upscale, male/female. **Inventory description** Pop culture and toys; the place for Hello Kitty items. **Inventory** 10. **Average cost of goods** 7. **Value** 7. **Sales and discounts** 6.

COMMENTS Look for the free unique classes (jewelry, origami) held on weekends at this fun store with a Japanese flair.

TORRID

N148, ☎ 952-854-5330, torrid.com

Store size Medium. **Target market** 20s+, mid-range, female. **Inventory description** Fashion for plus-size ladies. **Inventory** 10. **Average cost of goods** 4–6. **Value** 4. **Sales and discounts** 6.

COMMENTS This fashionable line is suited for voluptuous ladies, sizes 12–28.

True Religion

S174, ☎ 952-851-7975, truereligion.com

Store size Medium. **Target market** All, upscale, male/female. **Inventory description** Designer clothing for young women, men, and children. **Inventory** 9. **Average cost of goods** 8. **Value** 7. **Sales and discounts** 7.

COMMENTS Whatever jeans style is hot, you will find it here.

Tumi

W140, ☎ 952-854-4767, tumi.com

Store size Small. **Target market** 20s+, upscale, male/female. **Inventory description** Luxury travel, business, and lifestyle accessories. **Inventory** 7. **Average cost of goods** 9. **Value** 6. **Sales and discounts** 4.

COMMENTS This is upscale luggage done right.

Typo

N132, ☎ 952-854-5873, shop.cottonon.com/typo

Store size Small. **Target market** 20s+, mid-range, male/female. **Inventory description** Writing utensils, notebooks, and gifts. **Inventory** 10. **Average cost of goods** 4. **Value** 4. **Sales and discounts** 8.

COMMENTS Shop an exquisite selection of pens, paper, and gifts for reasonable prices.

 U

UGG Australia

S144, ☎ 952-854-5166, ugg.com

Store size Medium. **Target market** All, upscale, male/female. **Inventory description** Comfortable shoes for the entire family. **Inventory** 10. **Average cost of goods** 8. **Value** 6. **Sales and discounts** 4.

COMMENTS The brand is best known for sheepskin-lined boots and shoes.

Under Armour

W240, ☎ 612-235-4190, underarmour.com

Store size Large. **Target market** All, mid-range, male/female. **Inventory description** Sportswear. **Inventory** 10. **Average cost of goods** 6. **Value** 8. **Sales and discounts** 2.

COMMENTS This newer store is easy to navigate.

Urban Outfitters

W122, ☎ 952-854-8448, urbanoutfitters.com

Store size Large. **Target market** 20s, mid-range, male/female. **Inventory description** Hipster, bohemian, retro styles. **Inventory** 10. **Average cost of goods** 6. **Value** 5. **Sales and discounts** 9.

COMMENTS Here's a clothing line for the young or young at heart.

Vaase

E315, ☎ 952-854-9474

Store size Small. **Target market** 20s+, mid-range, male/female. **Inventory description** Italian- and Asian-inspired vases and home decor. **Inventory** 8. **Average cost of goods** 4. **Value** 4. **Sales and discounts** 7.

COMMENTS You can't miss the Buddha statues in the window.

Vans

N254, ☎ 952-854-2942, vans.com

Store size Medium. **Target market** All, mid-range, male/female. **Inventory description** Traditional skateboarding-inspired shoes. **Inventory** 10. **Average cost of goods** 6. **Value** 5. **Sales and discounts** 4.

COMMENTS The store carries shoes for skaters, snowboarders, surfers, and BMX bikers.

Vera Bradley

S288, ☎ 952-854-1822, verabradley.com

Store size Medium. **Target market** Teens+, upscale, female. **Inventory description** Cotton quilt handbags, accessories, and luggage. **Inventory** 10. **Average cost of goods** 9. **Value** 6. **Sales and discounts** 5.

COMMENTS The brand is equally loved by teen girls and older women.

Verizon

E264, ☎ 952-853-0022, verizon.com

Store size Large. **Target market** All, mid-range, male/female. **Inventory description** Tech experience. **Inventory** 10. **Average cost of goods** 7–9. **Value** 5. **Sales and discounts** 8.

COMMENTS See the latest consumer technologies with product demos.

Victoria's Secret

Location #1 N178, ☎ 952-854-9289; Location #2 S220, ☎ 952-854-5614; victoriassecret.com

Store size Large. Target market Adult, mid-range to upscale, female. Inventory description Lingerie, sleepwear, and beauty products. Inventory 10. Average cost of goods 6. Value 5. Sales and discounts 8.

COMMENTS The sales ladies are happy to help measure to size.

Victorinox Swiss Army

S138, ☎ 952-876-0200, victorinox.com

Store size Medium. Target market Kids+, mid-range, male/female. Inventory description Iconic Original Swiss Army knives, plus rustic attire, luggage, and time-pieces. Inventory 8. Average cost of goods 7. Value 7. Sales and discounts 5.

COMMENTS This is the only store outside of Switzerland where the Swiss Army Knife can be made and purchased.

VILLA

N244, ☎ 952-854-9114, ruvilla.com

Store size Medium. Target market Teens+, mid-range, male/female. Inventory description Fun, high-energy fashion shopping for men, women, and children. Inventory 8. Average cost of goods 10. Value 10. Sales and discounts 5.

COMMENTS Find a nice selection.

VomFASS

E280, ☎ 952-426-3222, vomfassusa.com

Store size Medium. Target market 20s+, upscale, male/female. Inventory description Oils, vinegars, and spirits. Inventory 10. Average cost of goods 1–2. Value 2. Sales and discounts 3.

COMMENTS VomFASS is divided into two stores. One features oils and vinegars; the other has spirits and wine. Prices are reasonable. You could spend the day tasting offerings from barrels filled with flavored oils, vinegars, and maple syrups. Let the employees do their job and help you with the samples. The knobs can be tricky, and the staff are trained professionals. As for sampling the liquor, have your ID ready. Tasters must be 21+.

The Walking Company

W160, ☎ 952-854-0380, thewalkingcompany.com

Store size Medium. Target market 20s+, mid-range, male/female. Inventory description Top shoe brands from around the world. Inventory 8. Average cost of goods 6. Value 5. Sales and discounts 6.

COMMENTS Benefit from 3-D technology sizing and customized fit analysis.

Wet Seal

N158, ☎ 952-851-0966, wetseal.com

Store size Medium. **Target market** Teens+, mid-range, female. **Inventory description** Cute, casual, and affordable wear for the teen and 20-something. **Inventory** 9. **Average cost of goods** 4. **Value** 4. **Sales and discounts** 3.

COMMENTS Wet Seal has been around for ages and always keeps up with the latest fashions at affordable prices.

White House Black Market

S148, ☎ 952-854-2006, whitehouseblackmarket.com

Store size Medium. **Target market** 20s+, upscale, female. **Inventory description** Chic line for ladies, mostly in black and white. **Inventory** 9. **Average cost of goods** 6. **Value** 5. **Sales and discounts** 6.

COMMENTS Find power dress outfits here, as well as casual wear for lunch with the ladies. There is always something good on these racks.

Williams-Sonoma

W262, ☎ 952-854-4553, williams-sonoma.com

Store size Medium. **Target market** 20s+, upscale, male/female. **Inventory description** Specialty home furnishings focusing on gourmet foods, professional-quality cookware, and small kitchen appliances. **Inventory** 10. **Average cost of goods** 7. **Value** 4. **Sales and discounts** 5.

COMMENTS Shoppers who are serious about their culinary endeavors will appreciate the quality of Williams-Sonoma. The staff is friendly and always happy to offer help and advice.

Yankee Candle

N286, ☎ 952-854-9222, yankeecandle.com

Store size Small. **Target market** 20s+, mid-range, female. **Inventory description** Candles and home fragrances. **Inventory** 7. **Average cost of goods** 1–3. **Value** 4. **Sales and discounts** 2.

COMMENTS The shop has an astounding selection of scents, including holiday options.

Z

Zagg, Invisible Shield, Frogz

W6122, ☎ 612-810-9244, zagg.com

Store size Kiosk. **Target market** 20s+, mid-range, male/female. **Inventory description** Phone shields. **Inventory** 3. **Average cost of goods** 1–3. **Value** 5. **Sales and discounts** 3.

COMMENTS Check here for phone covers for a reasonable price.

Zales

E240, ☎ 952-883-2063, zales.com

Store size Small. **Target market** 20s+, mid-range, male/female. **Inventory description** Modern and classic jewelry and diamonds. **Inventory** 8. **Average cost of goods** 9. **Value** 4. **Sales and discounts** 3.

COMMENTS Zales has a long history of offering good quality at a decent price; the store has great sales.

Zumiez

N236, ☎ 952-814-9260, zumiez.com

Store size Medium. **Target market** Teen–20s, mid-range, male/female. **Inventory description** Shoes, attire, and goods for snowboarders and skaters. **Inventory** 8. **Average cost of goods** 7. **Value** 5. **Sales and discounts** 5.

COMMENTS The coolest store for cold and hot "riders," this is a great place to relax.

PART SEVEN

NICKELODEON UNIVERSE

THEME PARK HISTORY

ACCORDING TO THE International Association of Amusement Parks and Attractions (IAAPA) survey, Global Theme and Amusement Park Outlook: 2014-2018, and Oxford Economics' report: The Economic Impacts of the U.S. Attractions Industry, there are approximately 400 amusement parks in the United States. Serving roughly 360 million people, these parks boast collective revenues of $18 billion. Impressed? We are.

Most amusement parks, at least in the mid to northern parts of the United States, are seasonal due to weather. That's why putting a covered theme park in the center of a shopping mall is rather brilliant. It's sort of like having the ice-cream man in the neighborhood. Not many kids can resist the promise of cold treats in front of the house on a boring summer day, much like a range of rides promising thrills and excitement lures families to the mall on an otherwise uneventful day. Mall of America (MOA) is a family destination that draws visitors for all reasons. Naturally, there must be a plan to make such an attraction a success, and often it takes some tweaking.

If there's one thing Minnesotans are proud of, besides lakes, hockey, the State Fair, and Mall of America, it's their former or current renowned residents—think F. Scott Fitzgerald, Prince, and Lindsey Vonn (who learned to ski on Buck Hill in Burnsville). Winona Ryder was named for Winona, Minnesota, and, most recently, Minnesota-transplant Andrew Zimmern of the Travel Channel has become a beloved resident who loves to talk State Fair food and even has his own food truck. He proved his residency by giving the Scandinavian lutefisk a try (he didn't like it).

Farther back in time is a local who, to this day, is especially cherished: Charles Schulz, creator of the *Peanuts* comic strip. Born in

1922 and raised in Minnesota, his presence is still upon us. Cruise around Saint Paul and you will see colorful, 5-foot-tall Snoopy, Charlie Brown, and Lucy statues welcoming you at restaurant entrances, in store windows, and on downtown sidewalks. These were part of the Peanuts on Parade event, which was held shortly after Schulz's death, in the year 2000, and ran for three summers. Most of the statues were auctioned off—sometimes you will see them displayed in private front yards—but many figures still remain in public view. Visit the south IKEA entrance (8000 Ikea Way, Bloomington, MN 55425), located north of MOA, and you will spy a Snoopy statue painted by IKEA employees called "Swede Dreams of Home."

What do these dandy details have to do with Mall of America? The original theme park in MOA was called Knott's Camp Snoopy (1992–2005) and was then updated to Camp Snoopy (2005–2006). The theme park displayed a massive blow-up Snoopy, while the other *Peanuts* character faces graced rides. Mall visitors had fun at *Peanuts* character meet and greets. Naturally, all good things must end, and in 2006 MOA lost the rights to the *Peanuts* branding, so off marched Snoopy and the gang. Today, *Peanuts* fans can head to Valleyfair (1 Valley Fair Drive, Shakopee, MN 55379; ☎ 952-445-7600), an outdoor theme park in the Minneapolis suburb of Shakopee that is open during the summer months through Halloween for Valley Scare.

Valley Fair sits under the umbrella of 14 theme parks—sister parks include the popular Knott's Berry Farm and Cedar Point. The Minnesota location opened in 1976 and sits on 175 acres, compared to MOA's 7 acres. It's obviously a much more extensive theme park, with 75 rides and attractions, including eight roller coasters. In 2011 a $9-million expansion included a renovation of the children's section into a Planet Snoopy, with *Peanuts*-themed rides and character photo ops for the younger crowd.

Back at the mall, the theme park became The Park at MOA (2006–2008). In July 2007 it was announced that the generic indoor park was getting a new identity. This time the makeover would be called Nickelodeon Universe (NU) and entail a new group of famous faces: SpongeBob, Patrick, Dora, Diego, the Backyardigans, and many other beloved Nickelodeon characters. Rides, decorations, foods, and gift shops were rebranded, while "real" famous faces, such as the casts from *Victorious, iCarly,* and *Big Time Rush,* make guest appearances at MOA.

Only a couple of years after the transition from Camp Snoopy to NU, the branding company Preston Kelly went on a mission to attract the attention of the tween and teen clientele, who had been passing the park off as a "little kid" theme park. The "We want your scream" campaign was born, and the theme park hasn't been quiet since.

Waltz into NU from any of the four entrances, and it's apparent that the Nickelodeon brand is present. The massive, rotating ball suspended from the ceiling printed with Nickelodeon Universe is one clue, but what you will most likely notice first are the popular Nickelodeon and Nick Junior characters' faces splashed everywhere you look. Backyardigans, Bubble Guppies, Dora, Diego, Swiper the Fox, SpongeBob and Patrick, Jimmy Neutron, Fairy Odd Parents, Blue and Magenta from Blue's Clues, the Teenage Mutant Ninja Turtles, and other show characters pop up on pictures, as statues, and even as, again, the famous meet and greet characters. SpongeBob is featured as the park's souvenir all-you-can-drink cup (on the day of purchase).

WHEN *to* GO

WHILE MOST GUESTS ARE INITIALLY IMPRESSED at their first gander of Nickelodeon Universe, the truth is the theme park is manageable. This means your strategy can be flexible in how you approach the rides, unlike a massive outdoor theme park with various themed areas.

Frankly, your success at riding all of the rides on your wish list in your allotted time will depend upon one thing—how busy the mall is. If you visit during weekends, holidays, or summer, being in NU upon opening is hands-down your best chance to get a number of rides under your belt before the lines get too long. We have waited an hour in line for Teenage Mutant Ninja Turtles, as well as the Log Chute. On the other hand, we went to the mall at the end of the school year, a couple of days before the public schools were out for the summer, and the kids literally rode the Log Chute consistently for two hours without anyone else in line. If you can visit any time of year, we suggest visiting NU the initial few weeks of school in September or the first week of June for the best chance of a vacant park. There is one caveat: The park may be on the Non-Peak Ride Schedule (for more on this, see the next page). While school is in session the rest of the year, schoolchildren on field trips and other groups keep the park more active than during those shoulder seasons.

NICKELODEON UNIVERSE HOURS

NU IS OPEN MONDAY–THURSDAY, 10 A.M.–9:30 P.M.; Friday and Saturday, 10 a.m.–10 p.m.; and Sunday, 10:30 a.m.–7:30 p.m. Special events and holidays may extend these hours. Weekdays, when local schools are in session, are the best days to go.

Dutchman's Deck Adventure Course and Barnacle Blast Zip Line have different hours than the rest of the rides: Monday–Thursday, noon–8 p.m.; Friday and Saturday, 10 a.m.–10 p.m.; and Sunday, 10:30 a.m.–7:30 p.m. These two attractions and Nickelodeon Universe as a whole are sometimes rented out for group events, so check the MOA website for any upcoming closings.

SCHEDULED MAINTENANCE AND PARK CLOSURES

NU ANNOUNCES UPCOMING ride maintenance on the lower right side of the nickelodeonuniverse.com website. Below that is the link to the schedule maintenance calendar and permanent ride closures. Occasionally, the park will be bought out for several hours or an evening. These temporary closures will be announced on the right side of the site.

NON-PEAK RIDE SCHEDULE

OFF-SEASON IS SEPTEMBER–MAY, MONDAY–THURSDAY (with the exception of holidays), and the park operates on the Non-Peak Ride Schedule. This means some rides run only at the top or the bottom of the hour for 20 minutes. However, there are plenty of rides that are open the entire day.

We showed up one evening to find that NU was on this schedule. We left because we didn't want to deal with the opening and closing of rides. What the informant didn't tell us was that not all rides close down. Our favorite rides ended up being open the entire evening. Here's an idea of what the Non-Peak Ride Schedule looks like.

RUNNING 10 A.M.–9 P.M. THESE RIDES ARE OPEN FOR 20 MINUTES

- Avatar Airbender • Blue's Skidoo • Crazy Cars • Diego's Rescue Rider
- El Circulo del Cielo • La Aventura de Azul • Pineapple Poppers
- Shredder's Mutant Masher

RUNNING 10:30 A.M.–8:30 P.M. THESE RIDES ARE OPEN FOR 20 MINUTES

- Back at the Barnyard • Backyardigans Swing-Along • Big Rigs
- Brain Surge • Bubble Guppies Guppy Bubbler
- Jimmy Neutron's Atomic Collider • Rugrats Reptarmobiles
- Splat-O-Sphere

ALWAYS OPEN

- Carousel • Dutchman's Deck Adventure Course (noon–8 p.m.)
- Fairly Odd Coaster • Ghost Blasters • Log Chute (noon–8 p.m.)
- Pepsi Orange Streak • SpongeBob SquarePants Rock Bottom Plunge
- Swiper's Sweeper • Teenage Mutant Ninja Turtles Shell Shock
- Wonder Pets Flyboat

THEME PARK CUSTOMERS

THERE ARE SEVERAL TYPES of Nickelodeon Universe customers, from the "Let's ride again!" to the (yawning) "Can we go yet?" people. Analyzing your group's riding habits and schedule will help you decide how to plan your ride purchase. Entry into the actual park is free. You can come and go as needed or use it as a shortcut to stores or restaurants. Here are some customer types you may encounter.

"WE LOVE NICKELODEON UNIVERSE AND GO THERE EVERY CHANCE WE GET!" Usually, these are Minnesotans, some of whom live outside the Twin Cities, who find MOA to be the best entertainment in the world. The best ticket option for this category is the new year-round pass ($139).

THE ALL-YOU-CAN-RIDE-ALL-DAY-LONG PEOPLE The majority of these are children and teens, but parents are often included in this group too. Often, the mom shops while the kids play. This group visits occasionally. If your main reason for visiting MOA is the theme park, or you're planning on spending more than an hour riding, then the Unlimited Ride Wristband is for your party.

THE ONE- OR TWO-RIDE PEOPLE The low-key parent, perhaps, who is watching an infant, or a grandparent who already knows that one ride means a week of recovery. This category applies to those who don't have much time or think the lines are too long. The points option is for you.

THE WATCHER This visitor has no interest in riding rides or can't due to medical reasons or pregnancy. If you need to sit, there are plenty of metal benches throughout the park, as well as stone pony walls at sitting level. Caribou Coffee has a couple of tables and chairs for customers, and Hard Rock Cafe's patio dining is in NU. If you don't mind a bird's-eye view, the South Street food court overlooks the park and has hundreds of tables and chairs with a view.

THE ADULT WITH A YOUNG CHILD Parents, grandparents, or any other guardian need not purchase a wristband or points. Some rides allow children under a certain height to ride with a guardian. Visiting on Toddler Tuesday for

> *unofficial* **TIP**
> Unofficial fun fact: There are 30,000 live plants in the park, and a natural pesticide is used—ladybugs.

discounted wristbands is the best scenario; otherwise, purchase points or a wristband, depending on how much time you have to ride.

WHERE *to* START

THE FIRST THING YOU SHOULD DO is pick up a Nickelodeon Universe Guide at any of the park's kiosks or Guest Services. Next, stash your belongings in a locker under the Ferris wheel. Lockers are electronic and can be used all day. There are four locker sizes: regular ($6), large ($8), extra large ($11), and jumbo ($13). Next, designate a meeting place for your group in case a phone gets lost or loses a charge, as there are no charging stations in NU. You can purchase tickets at either Guest Services in Nickelodeon Universe (not to be confused with Mall of America Guest Services located at mall entrances), located across from the carousel, or at any of the self-service, credit-card-only kiosks located at each entrance. Ticket discounts, coupons, cash, or any other redemptions must be handled at Guest Services. If you need an ATM, you have two options in NU: one is located across from the entrance to the Log Chute, and the other is across from the SpongeBob SquarePants Rock Bottom Plunge.

Families with preschool-age kids may want to start off at the Ferris wheel. Look for the new stair entrance in NU. This ride offers a great view of the park to get you acquainted with your surroundings. After climbing down the stairs, jet left to find several of the preschooler rides on the northern side. Bubble Guppies is to the far left, nestled behind the red Jimmy Neutron ride, past Swiper's Sweeper. The best advice is to look for the zip line tower for the Bubble Guppies entrance and follow the path. After that, simply follow the trail of preschool rides that extend toward the west entrance and loop around to the Pineapple Poppers Bounce House and across from Hard Rock Cafe.

Older kids and adults looking for thrills may want to consider hitting the Log Chute first because that is one ride line that stays pretty long on busy days. Be forewarned that you may get a little damp. Next, either make a right for Shredder's Mutant Masher or make a left and follow the path to the Fairly Odd Coaster. Whichever way you go, continue the loop on the outside of the park for the remaining thrill rides, including Jimmy Neutron's Atomic Collider, SpongeBob SquarePants Rock Bottom Plunge, and Teenage Mutant Ninja Turtles. Brain Surge, Avatar Airbender, and Splat-O-Sphere are located in the center of the park. Several avenues from all directions lead you to the center.

TICKETS:
Prices, Deals, and Choices

ADMISSION INTO NICKELODEON UNIVERSE IS FREE. Yes, as in zero, zilch, nada. There are no fences to climb over or secret back doors to sneak through. No one is guarding entrances or accepting tickets, and there aren't any turnstiles or metal detectors to pass through. If grandma wants to watch or mom is expecting a baby and can't ride, they need not pay. In fact, NU is often used as a shortcut to get from one side of the mall to the other.

As far as rides go, you must have a wristband or points pass to board all rides; however, you can get in line with riders, then exit before their wristband is scanned to board the ride. Depending upon the ride, to exit you may have to swim upstream or squeeze between or duck under rails, but in our experience you can certainly keep your friend or family member company during the wait.

Ride tickets come in a few forms. In 2015 a year-round unlimited pass was announced for $139. If you frequent Mall of America, this is a great deal. The Annual Pass includes one All-Day Wristband (good for unlimited rides) per day, four passes to Moose Mountain Adventure Golf, plus $5 golf admission once you've used your passes. Annual Pass holders receive 25% off at NU retail stores and food locations (with the exception of Caribou Coffee), 50% off the SpongeBob souvenir cup (which includes unlimited refills on day of purchase), and other discounts and invitations offered throughout the year.

Daily passes can be purchased with credit cards online (recommended because you get a discount) or at any of the multiuser automated ticket kiosks found inside each NU entrance. Tickets can be purchased with either cash or credit card at any Level 1 MOA Guest Services desk located at each entrance, Nickelodeon Guest Services (the stand-alone office near the carousel), or any NU retail location.

WRISTBANDS

THE ALL-DAY WRISTBAND ALLOWS you to experience any ride as many times as you wish. If your main goal of the day is to ride, this is your best option. At press time, All-Day Wristbands cost $34.99 at MOA or $29.99 online (save $5). Sometimes you can find coupons at Dairy Queen, Subway, and other local businesses. Better yet, ask if your hotel offers a Nickelodeon Universe package. Oftentimes, hotel deals can't be beat and can provide an assortment of other perks.

Beware: The term "unlimited" can be misleading, as there are some add-ons. Dutchman's Deck zip line plus ropes course (one-time pass) costs $15.99 alone. The Barnacle Blast Zip Line is an extra $13.99 for a one-time pass, and the ropes course is $11.99 for a one-time pass.

If you're not arriving until later in the evening, you can save a few bucks. The Twilight Savings Unlimited Ride Wristband is $21.99 and is offered after 5 p.m. But keep in mind that evenings can get busy.

POINT PASSES

IT'S EASY TO HAVE A LOVE-HATE RELATIONSHIP with the Point Pass. Don't get us wrong: it has its place and purpose, but it's tricky. Unless you know exactly how to dispense your points (see below), there is a good chance your point pass will have a couple of leftover points, which means you waste points or have to purchase more points.

If you choose to walk away, don't trash your ticket. Instead, drop your bracelet into the Boys & Girls Club donation boxes located in beams near the NU electronic kiosks. The kids appreciate your generosity! Another option is to play the "pay it forward" game and give your remaining points to an unsuspecting person or family and watch their eyes twinkle with excitement.

The points system works like this:

84-Point Pass	$67.99 = 14 (6-point) rides or 28 (3-point) rides
48-Point Pass	$44.99 = 8 (6-point) rides or 16 (3-point) rides
30-Point Pass	$28.99 = 6 (6-point) rides or 12 (3-point) rides
18-Point Pass	$19.99 = 3 (6-point) rides or 6 (3-point) rides
6-Point Pass	$6.90 = 1 (6-point) ride or 2 (3-point) rides
3-Point Pass	$3.45 = 1 (3-point) ride

POINT PASS PROS Multiple riders can use the pass (mom and dad are only going on two rides each or sister only had time for one ride because she had to attend an event). The points don't expire, so you can bring the band on the next trip. The pass is less expensive than the unlimited option if multiple people are riding only a few rides each.

POINT PASS CONS You may end up with leftover points (remember to donate or save them for next time) or you may be short points for that one last ride.

How do you know which option to choose? If one person is going to ride more than six rides, the unlimited-ride All-Day Wristband is the ideal option. That is, assuming the ride lines are not excessive.

PACKAGE DEALS

NU HAS PLENTY OF CASH-SAVING OPTIONS, but you need to know where to look. To start, if you plan to hit NU, an unlimited-ride All-Day Wristband is $34.99. Order online ($29.99) and save $5. Sea Life on its own is $24.25 per adult and $17.25 per child. Opt for the MOA Entertainment Pass (All-Day Wristband plus Sea Life pass) for $50.99 ($45.99 online) for a $10 savings per person. Sometimes special offers throughout the year will feature even steeper discounts. The only con about this pass is that both attractions must be used the same day. On the other hand, if you throw in Moose Mountain Miniature Golf ($9.99/one-time pass), $5 gets knocked off the price, but you can use the golf passes any day. The online price for an All-Day Wristband plus Moose Mountain Golf is $40.99. Another option is the Evening Unlimited Ride Wristband after 5 p.m. for $26.99.

unofficial **TIP**
MOA offers Toddler Tuesday, a discount-laden day for parents on food, shopping, and rides. Tots can ride 5 hours for $11.95. Parents need not pay for rides where a chaperone must be present.

Shop-and-Ride Offer

During certain times of the year, usually over the holidays and summer months, shoppers can partake in a generous promotion consisting of two one-day Nickelodeon Universe wristbands ($70 value) for every $250 spent at MOA between certain dates. Usually the offer lasts about a month. Employees verify and tally receipts before issuing rewards. Watch for signs throughout Nickelodeon Universe for where to turn in receipts. The wristbands are restricted to certain dates and have an expiration date, which means you can't turn around and use them that day. There are other restrictions, including a limit of 16 wristbands per person, shoppers must present a photo ID to receive their promotional wristbands, receipts cashed in must be from purchases made between certain dates, some mall locations are not included, and receipts must be original and from personal purchases.

NICKELODEON UNIVERSE RIDES

NICKELODEON UNIVERSE RIDES RANGE from the stomach-dropping Rock Bottom Plunge roller coaster to the mellow toddler-size rides for the young ones and everything in between.

THRILL RIDES
Avatar Airbender

What it is Half-pipe coaster. **Height requirement** 48″. **Scope and scale** Medium attraction. **Author's rating** One of the best thrill rides in the park; ★★★★★ **Ride duration** 45-60 seconds. **Average wait in line** 10 minutes. **Loading speed** Fast. **Points** 6.

DESCRIPTION AND COMMENTS Avatar Airbender features the character Aang from the popular animated show. The ride swoops from side to side, half-pipe style, and reaches 70 feet high, while riders on the two sides, Firebending or Waterbending, spin. Motion sickness is possible.

Brain Surge

What it is 16-person UniCoaster. **Height requirement** 48″. **Scope and scale** Minor attraction. **Author's rating** Prepare to get dizzy; ★★. **Ride duration** 1½-2 minutes. **Average wait in line** 15-20 minutes. **Loading speed** Fast. **Points** 5.

DESCRIPTION AND COMMENTS Riders control their experience with options of spinning forward, backward, upside down, or not at all. Motion sickness is possible.

A parent warns:

My school-age daughter went on this ride one too many times while visiting the park with friends and ended up with a spinning sensation for several days. She has refused any rides since. I think her legs were a little short to reach the floor, so she couldn't brace herself. She used to be a thrill-seeker, but that one shook her up. Parents may need to limit the number of times their children ride on this one.

Fairly Odd Coaster

What it is Spinning steel coaster. **Height requirement** 47″ (or 43″ with a chaperone). **Scope and scale** Major attraction. **Author's rating** Prepare to get dizzy;

Nickelodeon Universe

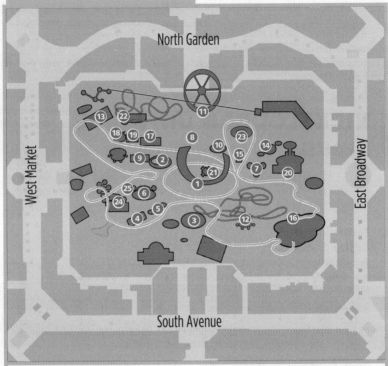

North Garden

West Market

East Broadway

South Avenue

1. Avatar Airbender
2. Back at the Barnyard
3. Backyardigans Swing-Along
4. Big Rigs
5. Blue's Skidoo
6. Brain Surge
7. Bubble Guppies Guppy Bubbler
8. Carousel
9. Crazy Cars
10. Diego's Rescue Rider
11. El Circulo del Cielo
12. Fairly Odd Coaster
13. Ghost Blasters
14. Jimmy Neutron's Atomic Collider
15. La Aventura de Azul
16. Log Chute
17. Pepsi Orange Streak
18. Pineapple Poppers
19. Rugrats Reptarmobiles
20. Shredder's Mutant Masher
21. Splat-O-Sphere
22. SpongeBob Square Pants Rock Bottom Plunge
23. Swiper's Sweeper
24. Teenage Mutant Ninja Turtles Shell Shock
25. Wonder Pet's Flyboat

★★★★★. **Ride duration** 1½ minutes. **Average wait in line** 10–15 minutes. **Loading speed** Fast. **Points** 6.

DESCRIPTION AND COMMENTS The green carts on purple tracks occupy the south-central part of Nickelodeon Universe. Carts spin while cruising the tracks, with occasional jerky turns, spirals, and various speeds and the suspense of a chain-lift hill. Riders should have good head control. Motion sickness is possible.

Jimmy Neutron's Atomic Collider

What it is Hexentanz. **Height requirement** 47". **Scope and scale** Medium attraction. **Author's rating** ★★★★★. **Ride duration** 3–3½ minutes. **Average wait in line** 15–20 minutes. **Loading speed** Fast. **Points** 6.

DESCRIPTION AND COMMENTS This ride has been at MOA since opening day but has been rebranded (it was formerly Treetop Tumbler). Jimmy Neutron, the fifth-grade boy genius, now has his own ride. It's located in the northeast corner of NU, near the arcades and American Girl store. Two cars on each arm rotate over each other at various speeds while the arms spin. This one will make your stomach drop. Motion sickness is possible.

Pepsi Orange Streak

What it is Steel roller coaster. **Height requirement** 47" (or 42" with a chaperone). **Scope and scale** Major attraction. **Author's rating** Fun but mellow thrill ride, with awesome views of the park; not too scary; ★★★★★. **Ride duration** 2½ minutes. **Average wait in line** 20–25 minutes. **Loading speed** Fast. **Points** 6.

DESCRIPTION AND COMMENTS Pepsi Orange Streak is the longest roller coaster in NU. A few dips give the experience a thrill, but it's not over-the-top scary. Riders get a unique view of the entire park while passing many other rides.

Shredder's Mutant Masher

What it is Chance Revolution 20. **Height requirement** 48". **Scope and scale** Major attraction. **Author's rating** ★★★★. **Ride duration** 2 minutes. **Average wait in line** 15 minutes. **Loading speed** Fast. **Points** 6.

DESCRIPTION AND COMMENTS Shredder's Mutant Masher is one of the latest rides themed to the Teenage Mutant Ninja Turtles. It's best described as a giant pendulum, spinning and swinging riders more than 60 feet in the air.

Splat-O-Sphere

What it is Thrill ride with 60-foot climb and drop. **Height requirement** 42". **Scope and scale** Medium attraction. **Author's rating** Fun, especially with the 10-second suspense of final big drop toward the end; ★★★★★. **Ride duration** 2 minutes. **Average wait in line** 15 minutes. **Loading speed** Fast. **Points** 6.

DESCRIPTION AND COMMENTS This spring ride can accommodate 16 passengers. It is rather impressive, as it has some fun drops.

SpongeBob SquarePants Rock Bottom Plunge

What it is Steel sit-down coaster with two inversions and a vertical chain-lift hill. **Height requirement** 48". **Scope and scale** Top thrill ride. **Author's rating** ★★★★★. **Ride duration** 2 minutes. **Average wait in line** 15 minutes. **Loading speed** Fast. **Points** 6.

DESCRIPTION AND COMMENTS SpongeBob and Patrick tempt the daredevils with this one, as it's probably the scariest ride in the park. With that said, roller coaster enthusiasts will enjoy this ride, but it's certainly less intense than, say, The Hulk at Universal's Islands of Adventure or the Eagle at Dollywood. Accommodates 8 passengers per ride.

unofficial **TIP**
Ride photos are available for purchase at the Log Chute (photo taken at final plunge), Pepsi Orange Streak (photo taken after first curve), and SpongeBob SquarePants Rock Bottom Plunge (photo taken during big plunge).

Teenage Mutant Ninja Turtles Shell Shock

What it is Mellow circular flying sensation; riders can opt to flip upside down. **Height requirement** 48″. **Scope and scale** Major attraction. **Author's rating** ★★★★ (★★★★★ if you can get your seat to flip). **Ride duration** 60–90 seconds. **Average wait in line** 45 minutes. **Loading speed** Fast. **Points** 6.

DESCRIPTION AND COMMENTS Every rider turns into a Teenage Mutant Ninja Turtle on this ride, which was manufactured in the Bavarian village of Munsterhausen, Germany.

FAMILY RIDES
Backyardigans Swing-Along

What it is Wave swinger. **Height requirement** 47″ (43″ with harness or 39″ with a chaperone). **Scope and scale** Major attraction. **Author's rating** ★★★★★. **Ride duration** 2½ minutes. **Average wait in line** 5-10 minutes. **Loading speed** Fast. **Points** 3.

DESCRIPTION AND COMMENTS Formerly Kite-Eating Tree, this classic wave swinger is now in full Backyardigan fashion. Note the cute statues of the adorable neighborhood gang facing Hard Rock Cafe. The swings fly in circles and reach heights of up to 27 feet. Shoes can be left in cubbies, along with personal belongings. Motion sickness is possible.

Bubble Guppies Guppy Bubbler

What it is Spinning tower ride. **Height requirement** 42″. **Scope and scale** Minor attraction. **Author's rating** Fun if you like spinning, but may bring on the dizzies; ★★★. **Ride duration** 2 minutes. **Average wait in line** 5-10 minutes. **Loading speed** Fast. **Points** 3.

DESCRIPTION AND COMMENTS The Bubble Guppies Guppy Bubbler replaced the long-time Balloon Race ride that had been running since the theme park's opening day in 1992. This latest ride is similar in the sense that rides rotate 360 degrees, but the difference is the gondolas spin like the traditional Tea Cups found at Disney parks but at the same time move up, offering a view from up high. That is, if your spinning body can focus on anything outside the ride. Riders have control over how fast their gondola spins, but even if you're not making your ride spin it will still rotate.

Carousel (formerly Americana Carousel)

What it is Carousel. **Height requirement** 42″ (unless accompanied by a chaperone). **Scope and scale** Medium attraction. **Author's rating** Exactly what you'd expect from a carousel; ★★★★. **Ride duration** 2 minutes. **Average wait in line** 5-10 minutes. **Loading speed** Slow. **Points** 3.

DESCRIPTION AND COMMENTS This classic carousel has all of the favorite animals (horses, zebras, antelope) to sit on, complete with required safety belts. Some animals move, some are stationary, and benches are available for sitting.

Crazy Cars

What it is Bumper cars. Height requirement 48″ (or 42″ with a chaperone). Scope and scale Minor attraction. Author's rating Fun, nice, and modern; ★★★★. Ride duration Average wait in line 5–10 minutes. Loading speed Fast. Points 6.

DESCRIPTION AND COMMENTS Nickelodeon's version of classic bumper cars.

El Circulo del Cielo
(formerly Dora and Boots Sun Wheel Ferris Wheel)

What it is Ferris wheel. Height requirement 42″ (unless accompanied by a chaperone). Scope and scale Minor attraction. Author's rating Nice for relaxing and views of NU if you can see through the finger smudges; ★★★. Ride duration 5-8 minutes with loading/unloading. Average wait in line 3–10 minutes. Loading speed Moderate/slow. Points 3.

DESCRIPTION AND COMMENTS This classic Ferris wheel, often referred to as the Dora Ferris Wheel because of its Dora and Boots faces, overlooks the theme park. Found on the north side of Nickelodeon Universe, it is a useful landmark when offering directions or planning meet-ups (you can say I will meet you under the Ferris wheel). Reaching over seven stories high, it makes for a great way to see the park from overhead. Each gondola is surrounded by Plexiglas; don't let the kids touch the Plexiglas. Reaching the entrance to this ride is tricky because it's the only ride that doesn't offer ground-level boarding. There is a new entrance for El Circulo del Cielo on Level 1 inside NU. To the left of the Ferris wheel is a staircase leading to the entrance. To the right of the stairs is stroller parking and an elevator for those unable to utilize the stairs. No single riders allowed.

Ghost Blasters

What it is Haunted mansion with laser guns. Height requirement 42″ (unless accompanied by a chaperone). Scope and scale Minor attraction. Author's rating ★★★. Ride duration 2 minutes. Average wait in line 10–20 minutes. Loading speed Medium. Points 6.

DESCRIPTION AND COMMENTS This is Nickelodeon Universe's only dark ride. Riders use laser guns to aim for the ghosts and score points.

Log Chute

What it is Log flume ride. Height requirement 47″ (or 36″ with a chaperone). Scope and scale Major attraction. Author's rating ★★★★★. Ride duration 5 minutes. Average wait in line 20–25 minutes. Loading speed Fast. Points 6.

DESCRIPTION AND COMMENTS Despite the name change, Paul Bunyan and Babe the Blue Ox still make appearances on this Log Chute (log flume). It's the only ride that wasn't rebranded during the theme park's transitions. As the only water ride, the attraction has two lifts and two drops. The second, steeper drop has a ride photo, and at the end the landing does mist or dampen riders. Remember: the heavier, the wetter. In other words, if two kids go alone, they will barely get wet. If the entire family goes, expect a nice splash. When the park is rocking, expect a long line for this one.

A fifth grader told us the favorite part of his day at MOA was the Log Chute ride:

The worst part was that the ride was a 1.5-hour wait and it only lasted 5 minutes.

Another fifth grader agrees that the wait is always long and declared that she's not a fan of the ride because of the big drop at the end that makes her stomach turn.

Father and husband Dave Sniadak of Minnesota says:

One of the best log-flume rides in America, in my opinion. We could ride that thing all day, every day!

KIDDIE RIDES
Back at the Barnyard

What it is Kiddie roller coaster. **Height requirement** 42″ (unless accompanied by a chaperone). **Scope and scale** Minor attraction. **Author's rating** Fun transition ride if the little ones are not ready for the Orange Streak; ★★★★★. **Ride duration** 1½ minutes. **Average wait in line** 3–7 minutes. **Loading speed** Fast. **Points** 3.

DESCRIPTION AND COMMENTS This kiddie coaster is the perfect transition ride for growing children wanting something a little more exciting than Blues Skidoo but who aren't ready for the bigger rides. The ride goes in an oval and offers enough excitement to make little kids feel big. Parents may want to ride with their child first because unexpected jerks occur. Motion sickness is possible.

Big Rigs

What it is Convoy. **Height requirement** 36″ (unless accompanied by a chaperone). **Scope and scale** Preschool ride. **Author's rating** Cute for kids; ★★★★★. **Ride duration** 2½ minutes. **Average wait in line** 5–10 minutes. **Loading speed** Fast. **Points** 3.

DESCRIPTION AND COMMENTS Tots have fun riding and honking the horn of their own kid-size Big Rig.

Blue's Skidoo

What it is Rotating ride where riders control up-down motion. **Height requirement** 36″ (unless accompanied by a chaperone). **Scope and scale** Preschool ride. **Author's rating** Great for kids; ★★★★. **Ride duration** 1½ minutes. **Average wait in line** 5–10 minutes. **Loading speed** Fast. **Points** 3.

DESCRIPTION AND COMMENTS Blue and Magenta from *Blues Clues* are the theme of this children's ride. Tots can use the on-board controls to fly up and down as the ride moves in a circular motion. Motion sickness is possible. Parents of size may not be comfortable or fit in the seat.

Diego's Rescue Rider

What it is Crazy bus. **Height requirement** 42″ (unless accompanied by a chaperone). **Scope and scale** Preschool ride. **Author's rating** ★★★★. **Ride duration** 2 minutes. **Average wait in line** 5–10 minutes. **Loading speed** Fast. **Points** 3.

DESCRIPTION AND COMMENTS Riders climb aboard the Rescue Rider for an up-and-down journey in a circular motion. Motion sickness is possible.

La Aventura de Azul

What it is Mini train. **Height requirement** 36" (unless accompanied by a chaperone). **Scope and scale** Preschool ride. **Author's rating** ★★★★. **Ride duration** 2 minutes. **Average wait in line** 5–10 minutes. **Loading speed** Fast. **Points** 3.

DESCRIPTION AND COMMENTS Dora the Explorer's preschool fans excitedly line up for a ride on the blue train.

Pineapple Poppers

What it is Bounce house. **Height requirement** 36"–58". **Scope and scale** Minor attraction. **Author's rating** ★★★★. **Ride duration** 2 minutes. **Average wait in line** 5–15 minutes. **Loading speed** Slow-medium. **Points** 3.

DESCRIPTION AND COMMENTS This busy bounce house is meant for the little ones and has a maximum height of 58 inches. Rounding up the tots for the next group can be tedious for the employees and make a wait seem longer than necessary. Socks are required but can be purchased at the Peeps store around the corner.

Rugrats Reptarmobiles

What it is Kids-size bumper cars. **Height requirement** 39"– 52". **Scope and Scale** Preschool ride. **Author's rating** Kids like it, but it gets annoying listening to parents shout commands to help their kids get their cars to go; ★★★. **Ride duration** 1½ minutes. **Average wait in line** 5–10 minutes. **Loading speed** Fast. **Points** 3.

DESCRIPTION AND COMMENTS Kids love these bumper cars made just for them.

Swiper's Sweeper

What it is Oval circular. **Height requirement** 42". **Scope and scale** Preschool ride. **Author's rating** ★★★. **Ride duration** 1½ minutes. **Average wait in line** 5–10 minutes. **Loading speed** Fast. **Points** 3.

DESCRIPTION AND COMMENTS The most surprising kiddie ride—riders get whipped. If you don't plan to ride, at least stop by and watch parents' surprised faces and howls.

Wonder Pet's Flyboat

What it is Frog hopper. **Height requirement** 36". **Scope and scale** Preschool ride. **Author's rating** ★★★. **Ride duration** 1 minute. **Average wait in line** 5–10 minutes. **Loading speed** Fast. **Points** 3.

DESCRIPTION AND COMMENTS This mini-version of the Splat-O-Sphere lifts the little ones 20 feet in the air and goes up and down.

OTHER ATTRACTIONS
FlyOver America

What it is Flight simulator ride. **Height requirement** 40". **Scope and scale** Major attraction. **Author's rating** ★★★★★. **Ride duration** 25 minutes. **Average wait in line** 10–30 minutes. **Loading speed** Fast. **Cost** $16.96 adults, $12.95 children age 12 and under.

DESCRIPTION AND COMMENTS The newest attraction in NU, FlyOver America is similar to Disney's Soarin' attraction. The experience is outstanding

—passengers fly through mist as regional scents and sounds bring the experience to life. Guests wishing to ride a second time the same day can opt for a discount.

Dutchman's Deck Adventure Course

What it is Ropes course, spiral slides, and zip line. **Height requirement** 48" (40" for Anchor Drop Spiral Slides only; 42" for Ghostly Gangplank Ropes Course with paid chaperone). **Scope and scale** Major attraction. **Author's rating** ★★★★★. **Ride duration** Depends on what you do. **Cost** $15.99 for one-time pass to ropes course, slides, and zip line; $3.99 for one-time pass on Anchor Drop Spiral Slides only; $13.99 for one-time pass on Barnacle Blast Zip Line; $11.99 for one-time pass on Ghostly Gangplank Ropes Course.

DESCRIPTION AND COMMENTS Located on the west side of Nickelodeon Universe, Dutchman's Deck offers three adventures in one. The **Ghostly Gangplank Ropes Course** is the tallest ropes course in the world. If they can make it to the top, climbers have the opportunity to survey NU from 56 feet up. What goes up must come down, and that's where the **Anchor Drop Spiral Slides** come in. And the new two-way Barnacle Blast Zip Line is the longest indoor zip line in the United States, at 405 feet long, and takes visitors flying 55 feet above Nickelodeon Universe. Closed-toe and closed-heel shoes must be worn at all times on the course. Crocs are available for use but must be worn with socks, which are available for purchase for $1. No skirts, dresses, or shorts shorter than 6 inches.

Moose Mountain Adventure Golf

What it is Indoor miniature golf. **Height requirement** None. **Scope and scale** Major attraction. **Author's rating** ★★★. **Duration of experience** Varies, depending on the size of your party. **Cost** $9.99 per person or $31.99 for a family of four.

DESCRIPTION AND COMMENTS Moose Mountain Adventure Golf (N376; ☎ 952-883-8777) is named for a peak in the Sawtooth Mountains of northeastern Minnesota. Like the mall's theme park, the area where the golf course sits now has seen transition. Formerly it was another mini-golf course, Golf Mountain, with different branding; then it became General Mills's Cereal Adventure, a farm-to-factory cereal-themed family attraction that closed in 2003; next came the Dinosaur Walk Museum. In 2008 Moose Mountain opened and seems to be sticking around. The course winds through "mountains" with an abandoned mine theme. You can't miss the Moose Mountain gold mine train and stacks of dynamite along the course, which make for fun obstacles. The course is relatively flat, with a few options to putt the ball over a hill or into a watermill that rides down a pipe. It is very accessible for wheelchairs, electric carts, and strollers; we played the course with a stroller and didn't encounter any problems. There is one caveat: golfers need to be mindful of how hard they hit the ball. Some of the greens do not have full barriers due to the accessibility access for wheelchairs. Moose Mountain is best enjoyed on a slow day when there aren't a lot of people. If there is a wait, the back hole offers nice view of Nickelodeon Universe, especially SpongeBob SquarePants Rock Bottom Plunge. While the course is not overly challenging, we did have balls get caught in a couple of the pipe holes (where your ball goes in and comes out on another level or part of the course). In most cases, we were able to push the stuck balls through with another ball. Finally, if you get a hole-in-one at the end, you win another round of golf.

HEIGHT REQUIREMENTS

36 INCHES TALL TO RIDE ALONE

• Big Rigs • Blue's Skidoo • La Aventura de Azul

36 INCHES TALL TO RIDE

• Wonder Pets Flyboat • Log Chute • Pineapple Poppers

39 INCHES TALL TO RIDE

• Rugrats Reptarmobiles • Backyardigans Swing-Along

42 INCHES TALL TO RIDE ALONE

• Back at the Barnyard • Bubble Guppies Guppy Bubbler • Carousel
• Diego's Rescue Rider • El Circulo del Cielo • Ghost Blasters
• Splat-O-Sphere • Swiper's Sweeper

42 INCHES TALL TO RIDE

• Crazy Cars • Dutchman's Deck Ghostly Gangplank and Anchor Drop
• Pepsi Orange Streak

47 INCHES TALL TO RIDE ALONE

• Fairly Odd Coaster • Jimmy Neutron's Atomic Collider
• Pepsi Orange Streak

48 INCHES TALL TO RIDE ALONE

• Avatar Airbender • Brain Surge • SpongeBob SquarePants Rock
Bottom Plunge • Teenage Mutant Ninja Turtles Shell Shock

CHARACTER APPEARANCES

NICKELODEON UNIVERSE HAS TWO COLORED "SPOTS" offer-
ing meet and greets with Nickelodeon characters. The **Blue Spot** is located
across from Teenage Mutant Ninja Turtles Shell Shock and adjacent to
Crazy Cars and Pineapple Poppers. The **Green Spot** is found directly
across from the Log Chute exit. Signs at both spots provide the daily
character appearance schedule. Guest Services should also be able to tell
you the schedule, or you can check the website at nickelodeonuniverse
.com/events/character-appearances.

The Blue Spot most recently tends to host the Teenage Mutant
Ninja Turtles since their beloved ride Shell Shock is across the walkway. SpongeBob and his friends also frequent this spot, which is no
surprise, considering it's adjacent to his pineapple house (Pineapple
Poppers bounce house). The Green Spot sees a lot of Dora and Friends,
Backyardigans, Blue from *Blues Clues,* and Wonder Pets. The characters are "on the spot" for 30-minute increments. Employees keep the
line moving quickly, so the wait is never miserable.

Because the roof of Nickelodeon Universe is glass, visiting characters midday on a sunny summer day will likely produce squinty-eyed

photos. The sun doesn't beat down on the spot for long, but when it does, you will know. Here's a great thing about Nickelodeon Universe: the staff welcomes, if not encourages, parents to take their own pictures. However, professional photographers will snap some pictures for your viewing pleasure (and in the hope that you will purchase a collection of that sacred moment). Photos can be viewed and purchased upon exiting the spots. We have to give NU credit. We have never been pressured to purchase photos. The photographer will hand you the slip and that's it. No "come this way" antics to view photos. In our experience, the photo quality of the NU photographers is much better than what our iPhone produces (at the moment). Therefore, if you meet a favorite character, or don't have your phone, the branded photos may be worth it, but be prepared to pay for it because the photos aren't cheap.

Serendipitous appearances sometimes happen near the bronze SpongeBob Statue by the East Entrance, usually right in front of the Nickelodeon Universe sign. *Warning:* If SpongeBob disappears from this spot, there is a good chance the undersea gods (or Nickelodeon maintenance) took him for a deep sea cleaning. Also, sometimes movie releases will bring in guest characters.

Note: If you child is intent on meeting a certain character, line up before the start time, even if another character is already on the spot (simply let other families pass you if you move to the front of the line). If you wait and end up in the back of the line, you may miss the character you wanted to see and end up meeting a completely different character. Trust us—avoid meltdowns by arriving early.

PHOTO PASSES

IN 2016 NICKELODEON UNIVERSE introduced a new day photo pass ($19.95) and annual photo pass for local residents ($19.95). All images taken on rides, with characters, or by roving photographers are downloaded to the online account. Photos are accessible from your home computer, smartphone (via downloadable app), and can be shared on Twitter and Facebook. The images can also be turned into souvenirs via the online shop: https://presale.amazingpictures.com/NickUniverse.aspx.

FOOD *at*
NICKELODEON UNIVERSE

JUST BECAUSE YOU'RE SPENDING the day or hours in Nickelodeon Universe doesn't mean you're limited to eating theme-park food. Two food courts are only a short elevator ride away. **Hard Rock Cafe** (5115 Center Court) and **American Girl Bistro** (5160 Center Court; Level 1,

East) are directly off NU and provide sit-down service. **Magic Pan Crepe Stand** (W114) is located outside the NU West Entrance.

Other quick grabs include **Caribou Coffee** (South Entrance), with hot and cold drinks and pastries; **Sweet Treats** (East and North Entrances), with Dippin' Dots; snack stands (popcorn, cotton candy, and more) throughout the park; and **Grub** (West Entrance), where guests can enjoy an ICEE Mix-It-Up Station with 12 flavor options (expect sticky shoes on busy days), traditional theme park funnel cake treats, local Rybicki Cheese Curds, as well as pizza, pretzels, and more.

ARCADE

NAMCO ARCADE & MIDWAY IN NICKELODEON UNIVERSE (located in the northeast corner) has all of the traditional video and ticket games. Games take tokens only: 3 tokens for $1, 18 tokens for $5; 40 tokens for $10, and 90 tokens $20. Machines only dispense tokens, and the tokens are nonrefundable.

PART EIGHT

OTHER ATTRACTIONS

AT FIRST SIGHT, Mall of America is an oversize shopping mall with a theme park in the middle. Before long, visitors realize there is an underground aquarium now called Sea Life. Yet, scattered around the mall are a number of other attractions nestled into the megamall's nooks and crannies.

A.C.E.S. Flight Simulation Center ★★★★★

E340, ☎ 952-920-3519, flyaces.com

Type of attraction Flight simulators. **Admission** $19.95–$44.95, depending on flight. **Hours** Monday–Saturday, 10 a.m.–9:30 p.m.; Sunday, 11 a.m.–7 p.m. **Special comments** Brings out the kid in you.

DESCRIPTION AND COMMENTS Here's a fun fact: the A.C.E.S. simulators are the same models designed and built for the world's largest defense contractor. Raytheon perhaps? We're not sure, but according to quotes on the A.C.E.S. website, trained pilots, including fighter pilots, give thumbs-up to an authentic experience. Choices include an F/A-18 Hornet, P-51 Mustang, and F4U Corsair. While we've never flown in the cockpit of a fighter jet, it sure seemed real to us. Motion, sound, and visual effects, including a wraparound view, all lend themselves to the real thing. Not to mention it's a little nerve-wracking to know you're doing all of the flying. This isn't one of those enjoy-the-ride experiences; you're in control and you can crash.

Amazing Mirror Maze ★★★★½

N353, ☎ 952-854-5345, mirrormazes.com

Type of attraction Mirror maze. **Admission** $8.95 per person. **Hours** Monday–Saturday, 10 a.m.–9:30 p.m.; Sunday, 11 a.m.–7 p.m.

DESCRIPTION AND COMMENTS This is the best mirror maze we have ever experienced. It's one of the largest, at 2,500 square feet. The reason this maze ranks high is guests must don plastic gloves (think food service rather than medical), which means there are no smudges or fingerprints along the route.

Guests can reenter immediately upon exiting, but you can't leave and then come back without paying for another admission. Some people say they made it through quickly; we did not. *Our tip:* Visit Groupon for a coupon. Amazing Mirror Maze is always offered at a steep discount.

Crayola Experience ★★★★★

S300, ☎ 952-851-5800, crayolaexperience.com

Type of attraction Interactive experience for kids. **Admission** $24.99 per person ages 2 and up, $34.99 for an annual pass. **Hours** Daily, 10 a.m.–7 p.m. **Special comments** Family fun. Truly something for everyone, from toddlers to teenagers.

DESCRIPTION AND COMMENTS 25 interactive, hands-on creative experiences keep the entire family entertained for 4–5 hours. Activities range from classic coloring to high-tech 4-D experiences. Each guest can personalize and wrap their own Crayola crayon (don't try to hand wrap; wrapping machines are found along the back wall), run through a digital Rainbow Rain, star in his or her own coloring page (a favorite), and so much more. Kids can burn off energy in one of two play areas (one for toddlers, another for older children). If you wish to visit more than once in a year, we highly recommend the annual pass for only $10 more.

Rick Bronson's House of Comedy ★★★★★

E408, ☎ 952-858-8558, houseofcomedy.net

Type of attraction Comedy club. **Admission** Prices vary by show. **Hours** Tuesday–Saturday, 11 a.m.–9 p.m.; Sunday, 2 p.m.–9 p.m. **Special comments** Best adult fun in the mall.

DESCRIPTION AND COMMENTS Located on the fourth floor of Mall of America, Rick Bronson's House of Comedy draws well-known comics and serves up more than laughs. Along with a fully stocked bar, guests can order appetizers, salads, burgers, sandwiches, flatbreads, full entrees, and desserts. (Groups of eight or more are subject to 18% gratuity.)

Bonus: Guests who sign up for the Birthday Club receive a free ticket on their birthday (excludes Special Presentations and Saturday evenings), while the rest of your party gets a discount. No walk-ups allowed; reservations must be made 30 days in advance.

Sea Life Minnesota Aquarium ★★★★

E120, ☎ 883-0202, visitsealife.com/minnesota

Type of attraction Aquarium. **Admission** $17.25 children ages 3–12, $24.25 adults; free for children under age 3; discounts available online. **Hours** Monday–Thursday, 10 a.m.–7 p.m.; Friday, 10 a.m.–8 p.m.; Saturday, 9:30 a.m.–8 p.m.; Sunday, 10 a.m.–6:30 p.m. **Special comments** Ideal for young children, and even better now that they lowered the prices.

DESCRIPTION AND COMMENTS Much like Mall of America's theme park, the mall's aquarium has gone through a number of transitions. A few years after opening, in 1996, the first Mall of America aquarium opened as Underwater World.

Four years later the name changed to Underwater Adventures Aquarium. Finally, in 2011, the now Merlin Entertainments–owned aquarium transitioned to the well-known Sea Life chain. We've experienced Sea Life at Mall of America, as well as other locations. How does it stack up to other aquariums? You can't compare it to Monterey Bay Aquarium in California or Shedd Aquarium in Chicago. Quite frankly, it's difficult to compete with an aquarium that is actually situated a few yards from a large body of water. With that said, it's a neat little aquarium. We joined a group of 3rd graders on a field trip, and they had a blast. The highlight for most of them was the underwater glass tunnel and the jellyfish. Little ones tend to enjoy the touch pools. This is a great opportunity for learning. In addition to field trips, there are discounted homeschool days and scouting opportunities.

Prices have recently come down, and that's a good thing, as we thought the former admission was a little overpriced. These new rates seem a little more reasonable. Coupons are easy to find. For one, Sharky, the aquarium mascot, walks around the mall passing out coupons and posing for photos, but stacks of coupons are also available at local Dairy Queens and other retail counters. We recommend purchasing your tickets online. GoldStar.com offers discounted tickets, and you can save as much as $6 per person by going directly through Sea Life online at visitsealife.com/minnesota. If you frequent the mall regularly, the annual pass is worth a peek ($49 per person or $199 per household). Not only do you get unlimited entry year-round but also a bevy of other discounts on guest admission, photo packages, behind-the-scenes tours, birthday party packages, gift store purchases, dive/snorkel programs, and the overnight "Sleep Under the Sea" program. Plus, you are the first to know about new exhibits, and the express membership entrance is certainly handy on busy days.

Sky Deck Sports Grille & Lanes ★★★

E401, ☎ 952-500-8700, skydecklanes.com

Type of attraction Bowling alley with arcade games, billiards, and restaurant and bar. **Admission** Bowling is $4–$5.50 per person per game, depending on day and time; shoe rentals are $3; game cards range from $5 for 20 credits to $37 for 260 credits. **Hours** Sunday–Thursday, 11 a.m.–midnight; Friday–Saturday, 11 a.m.–1 a.m. **Special comments** Happy hour Sunday–Thursday, 3–6 p.m. and 9 p.m.–close, features $1 off beverages and $2 off appetizers.

DESCRIPTION AND COMMENTS A "Welcome to Sky Deck Games" Las Vegas–style sign greets customers among a sea of arcade and ticket games, as well as bowling, pool tables, and a restaurant and bar. This place seems to have it all. We've given Sky Deck a few chances and found service to be slow at times but top-notch friendly. The games are hit or miss; the Skee-Ball games are not consistent with balls or tickets, but the best game in the house is Cycraft Simulator. During the day is a good time to visit, as evenings often bring the after-work crowd or company parties. The restaurant menu features appetizers such as wings, nachos, and sliders; salads; burgers, wraps, and sandwiches; pizzas and pastas; and more.

PHOTOS AT MALL OF AMERICA

In a day and age where #selfies are trending, Mall of America still has plenty of photo ops throughout the mall. As of this writing, selfie sticks are allowed and, in fact, encouraged. But first, keep an eye out for #selfie opportunities that can earn you discounts and free surprises when you post your pictures and #selfies with the proper hashtag and social media handles. Free advertising for them is a discount for you. When you don't feel like holding the selfie stick, there is a photo booth located adjacent to the Splat-O-Sphere in **Nickelodeon Universe** (NU), with options for themed borders and magazine covers.

Only a couple of rides at NU take pictures of passengers: the Log Chute, Pepsi Orange Streak, and SpongeBob SquarePants Rock Bottom Plunge. In 2013 MOA teamed with Colorvision International Inc, known as Amazing Pictures, to provide professional Nickelodeon Universe images. We've succumbed to these ride photos, and they are a fun souvenir if you have somewhere to display them. In addition to the traditional souvenir prints, guests can have their photos printed on various items such as mugs, T-shirts, and blankets. The Blue Spot on the west side of NU and the Green Spot on the southeast side of NU are where scheduled character meet and greets happen. See Part Seven, page 179, for more on character appearances and photos. If you see other characters roaming the park, you can certainly meet and pose with them, but no professional photographers will be available. Also see page 180 in Part Seven for details on the new daily photo pass.

Other photo ops available at MOA include Sharky from Sea Life and Bubba Gump Shrimp Co.'s shrimp mascot, who often frequents the front of the restaurant on weekends. Naturally, Santa and the Easter Bunny visit during appropriate holiday seasons, and various characters stop by to meet tots on Toddler Tuesday (for more information, see Part Five, page 102). The Rotunda often has celebrity events, which sometimes include chances for photos.

Professor Bellows (N374, ☎ 952-853-9804) is a year-round photo shop, where guests can dress up and take old-time photos (think cowboys and gangsters) and is a sponsor of the Professor Bellows Santa Experience. Shoppers looking for something especially creative will want to stop by **ME3D** (E356, ☎ 952-658-8868) and see how cutting-edge technology, combined with photogrammetry and 3-D printing, can turn you into a 3-D figure.

Theatres at Mall of America ★★★★★

S401, ☎ 952-883-8901, theatresmoa.com

Type of attraction Movie theater with 14 auditoriums. **Admission** Daily before 5 p.m., $6; Monday–Thursday after 5 p.m., $9.50; Friday–Sunday and holidays after 5 p.m., $10. **Hours** Daily, 11 a.m.–midnight. **Special comments** Happy hour is daily 4–6 p.m. and 9–11 p.m., with $3 domestic tap and bottled beer, $4 house wine, and $10 domestic pitchers.

DESCRIPTION AND COMMENTS This is not your typical movie theater. Saturday mornings feature free flicks for families, as well as free sensory flicks—movies especially for children with autism and other developmental disabilities. What's truly impressive is the technology here, which includes a 200-seat, 3-D theater with D-Box motion seats. The 21+ Theatre has comfy high-back rocker seats with lots of leg room, while the STARBAR offers beer and wine (have your ID ready).

PRINCE MEMORABILIA AT MALL OF AMERICA

Mall of America's Hard Rock Cafe is a stop on the **Experience Prince's Minneapolis** tour for the collection of Prince memorabilia, which includes the orange Minneapolis suit he wore during his *Sign o' the Times* tour in 1987. Other locations on the tour include his childhood home, the house from *Purple Rain,* and Paisley Park Studio (Prince's recording studio, home, and place of his death on April 21, 2016). For more information, visit minneapolis.org/princes-minneapolis.

PART NINE

GROUP ACTIVITIES

MALL *of* AMERICA IS *a* GROUP ATTRACTION

MORE THAN 12,000 GROUPS VISIT MALL OF AMERICA (MOA) per year. MOA makes for a good group outing or trip for many reasons. As we've said, MOA is easy to get to. For groups flying in, we can't reiterate enough that MOA is about as close to the airport as you can get. In addition to car rentals and hotel shuttles, the airport provides direct access to the mall on the light rail (read more in Part Three: Arriving and Getting Oriented).

For groups arriving by car or bus, the mall offers access from main highway arteries (specifically Interstate 494), parking is free, and buses and large vans have easy drop-off/pick-up and free parking locations at the east entrance. We've been on two school field trips to MOA, including one where we arrived on a bus, and the experience was easy. Plus, the parents loved having a Starbucks to descend upon before the event began and lunch options afterward for those of us who drove.

For those who don't live in the area, lodging is not a problem. There is a wide selection of hotels for all budgets (almost 40 within 10 minutes). If you are visiting MOA with a group from outside the Twin Cities and skipped to this section, we recommend you read Part Two: Where to Stay for tips on the best hotel options for groups.

School groups aren't the only groups MOA hosts. In addition to educational groups, the mall sees groups from various places and for different reasons, such as sports, church, scouts, homeschoolers, seniors, corporate, and fun celebrations such as birthdays and weddings.

GROUP EXPERIENCES
at MALL *of* AMERICA

THERE ARE MANY DIFFERENT GROUP EXPERIENCES at Mall of America. Some events are planned by MOA, while others are hosted by individual stores, attractions, and restaurants.

MEET AND GREET

GROUPS WITH 20 OR MORE PEOPLE can sign up to meet with an MOA representative who will provide a history of the mall, answer questions, and distribute the latest Mall of America Coupon Book ($9.50 value), a map and directory, and a souvenir shopping bag ($4 value). This program requires a two-week advance reservation and is offered Monday–Friday, 10 a.m.–4 p.m. Cost is $6.50 per person. For more information, call ☎ 952-883-8643.

unofficial TIP
Youth group rates can be found for Nickelodeon Universe, Moose Mountain Adventure Golf, Dutchman's Deck Adventure Course, and the Amazing Mirror Maze.

GROUP PRESENTATIONS

STUDENTS CAN LEARN ABOUT the background of MOA, business and marketing aspects, and job opportunities within MOA, or MOA can tailor presentations for individual group curriculums or interests. While fashion and retail are hot topics, other subjects the mall can cover include small business, security and law enforcement, and engineering. Presentations last 60 minutes, cost $6.50 per person, and include a Mall of America Coupon Book.

PHYSICS PROGRAM

THIS SELF-GUIDED PROGRAM SHOWS the awesomeness of science with hands-on opportunities in **Nickelodeon Universe.** Students get to study the laws via the theme park rides. The program is free with the purchase of a 3-hour ride wristband and lasts 3 hours; minimum group size is 15 people.

SEA LIFE MINNESOTA AQUARIUM

GROUPS CAN GO BEHIND THE SCENES at Sea Life Minnesota Aquarium to see how aquarists maintain habitats and learn about the medical treatments used on rescued and rehabilitated marine life. Cost is $6.99 per person, $5 per person group rate, and $4 per student for field trips. Programs last approximately 45 minutes. Groups must have a minimum of 10 and maximum of 90 participants. For more information, call ☎ 952-853-0612 or e-mail sales@sealifeus.com.

RICK BRONSON'S HOUSE OF COMEDY

RICK BRONSON'S HOUSE OF COMEDY (HOC) caters to businesses by hosting company or holiday parties of 15–300 people, with various options, including a preshow cocktail reception. HOC also hosts private parties, special events, awards ceremonies, charity functions, and team meetings. How to save: Special rates are available for groups larger than 25, with bargains on weeknights. A one-time-only group reservation fee saves on processing fees of individual tickets. In our experience, comedy is only as good as the joke teller, and luckily HOC has pretty high standards, so expect a fun night out for your group here. For more information, call ☎ 952-858-8558 or visit houseofcomedy.net/about/parties.

School and community groups can perform at MOA through the music series that runs January–mid-November. Visit mallofamerica.com/visit/group-experiences for more information.

HARD ROCK CAFE

LOCATED OFF NICKELODEON UNIVERSE, Hard Rock Cafe offers group experiences for 30–1,000 people in multiple event venues, depending on the group's needs. Hard Rock's immediate space incudes 15,000 square feet over two floors with seating for 408 guests, a live event stage, The Rock Shop, and music memorabilia from Hard Rock's iconic collection, including local icon Prince. For more information, call ☎ 952-853-7000.

SCAVENGER HUNTS

IT'S PRETTY COMMON TO SEE people huddled around the Metropolitan Stadium Home Plate marker in **Nickelodeon Universe** taking photos of their feet touching the home plate. Most often, the game at play is a scavenger hunt. Sometimes it's a school group, and other times it's a corporate team-building activity or a small birthday party.

Groups can make up their own scavenger hunt (keep reading for tips on planning your own), or for those who prefer to let someone else do the planning, Mall of America hosts a group scavenger hunt. MOA restaurant **Dick's Last Resort** also has an electronic-based scavenger hunt.

MALLQUEST SCAVENGER HUNT

MALLQUEST IS THE HOUR-LONG MOA SCAVENGER HUNT, with a list that includes stores, attractions, and products. Groups can pair the experience with a group presentation or additional activities. Reservations must be made at least two weeks in advance. Cost is

$10.95 per person or $6.95 per person for groups larger than 50. Group presentation and MallQuest combo is $14.95 per person. Each team receives a Mall of America Coupon Book. For more information and booking, call ☎ 952-883-8643.

DICK'S LAST RESORT SCAVENGER HUNT

DICK'S HUNT INCLUDES testing participants' Mall of America factual knowledge via a 32-question challenge on iPads to track answers and snap photos. When the game is concluded, photos can be viewed on the restaurant's big screens. The hunt lasts about an hour and requires a minimum of 20 participants. Cost is $18.95 per person or $12.95 per person with the purchase of a meal. For more information and booking, call ☎ 612-749-7955.

UNOFFICIAL SCAVENGER HUNT LIST

GROUPS WITH NO INTEREST IN ANYTHING official or who don't want to report to anyone at a certain time or place can create their own scavenger hunt list. Camera-inspired scavenger hunts are the best at MOA and can include any of these mall landmarks:

- Dora and Diego statues
- Backyardigan statues
- Red stadium chair on the wall
- Metropolitan Stadium Home Plate
- 9/11 Memorial
- Oversize L.L.Bean boot
- LEGO robot
- LEGO dragon
- WWII Battleship *Missouri*
- Hall of Fame
- Hotness Meter at Peeps (Place your hand on a sensor to rank your "hotness.")

Or, try taking photos of the following:

- A Vikings fan and a Packers fan in the same photo
- Any Nickelodeon character
- Sharky (the Sea Life character)
- A woman in super-high heels
- A LEGO creation
- Someone carrying more than 10 shopping bags
- A balloon
- Something priced at $19.99
- A dessert
- An arcade game

- Someone on a ride with hands in the air
- Someone reading a book
- Someone trying on Forrest Gump's shoes
- An ice cream cone
- A stuffed animal
- Someone sleeping
- Fried cheese curds
- Cotton candy
- The Mall of America Star

Note: The Wedding Chapel does not participate in scavenger hunts. If you do your own hunt, don't list "try on a wedding dress or veil" as an item, as you will only be rejected.

BIRTHDAY PARTIES

MALL OF AMERICA WORKS as a birthday party location for the same reasons we mention throughout the book: there are plenty of choices for all ages, free parking, everything is indoors, and there is a lot for parents to do while their child is enjoying the festivities. Choices range from create-your-own-party ideas to large reserved parties in private settings.

AMERICAN GIRL

BISTRO BIRTHDAY CELEBRATION PACKAGES ($28 per girl and $18 per adult, plus tax and gratuity) are for girls age 3 and up and cover a range of choices, including edibles such as meals and the signature American Girl pink-and-white cake and ice cream. Other options include goody bags and doll tiaras for each girl, commemorative keepsake for the birthday girl, and a set of invitations with matching thank-you notes. Deluxe Birthday Celebrations are designed for girls ages 8 and up ($45 per girl and $35 per adult, plus tax and gratuity) and are an all-inclusive experience with the same items as listed above plus space in a private room and a fun table activity and craft. Add-ons are available for an additional fee. For more information, call ☎ 877-247-5223.

BUILD-A-BEAR

BUILD-A-BEAR BIRTHDAY PARTY PACKAGES range from $12 to $44 per person. Parties include printable invitations and thank-you cards, birthday bonus points, a free party favor and virtual party favor, and a gift for the guest of honor. A party leader keeps the kids entertained and on task during the Build-A-Bear themed party. For more information, call ☎ 952-854-1164.

LOTUS BEADS AND JEWELRY

LOTUS BEADS AND JEWELRY is a make-your-own jewelry shop marketed as "an interactive bead store in a fun, zen-like environment." This shop is great for girls night out, Girl Scout troops, mother-daughter time, bridal showers, or any other gathering, including birthday parties. Tables for six can be reserved at $50 for 2 hours (add on 15-minute increments for $8). Table reservations include an instructor to lead the group. For more information, call ☎ 952-854-9951.

NICKELODEON UNIVERSE

HOSTING A PARTY AT THE INDOOR NICKELODEON UNIVERSE theme park means the birthday child rides for free. A minimum purchase of seven is required, and the wristband choices are 3-hour (18.95 per person) and 5-hour ($20.95 per person). Along with the wristband, each child receives a souvenir birthday cup to fill with ICEE or a Pepsi fountain soda. With the birthday ride wristband, Moose Mountain Adventure Golf and Dutchman's Deck Adventure Course are only an extra $5 admission for each birthday party participant. For more information, call ☎ 952-883-8800.

RICK BRONSON'S HOUSE OF COMEDY

HOUSE OF COMEDY, ON THE FOURTH FLOOR of MOA, hosts birthday parties, including kid parties. Guests who sign up for the Birthday Club receive a free ticket on their birthday (excludes Special Presentations and Saturday evenings), while the rest of your party gets a discount. No walk-ups allowed; reservations must be made 30 days in advance. For more information, call ☎ 952-858-8558.

SEA LIFE MINNESOTA AQUARIUM

STANDARD BIRTHDAY PARTY PACKAGES start at $225 plus tax (for up to 15 people) for ages 0–3 and include a decorated party room (1 hour), themed coloring and activity sheets, and interactive touch stations. For older kids, ages 4–12, there's the Deluxe Party Package for $325 plus tax (for up to 12 people), which includes the use of a decorated party room (1.5 hours), a behind-the-scenes tour, a shark tooth necklace craft, and live animal touching stations. The Extreme Party Package is $595 plus tax (for up to 12 people) and is for ages 9 and up. Guests have access to the party room (30 minutes) and get to swim with the fishes on the rainbow reef (8 people), take a behind-the-scenes tour, and receive a souvenir T-shirt. For more information, call ☎ 952-883-0202.

SKY DECK SPORTS GRILLE & LANES

LOCATED ON THE FOURTH FLOOR, Sky Deck Sports Grille & Lanes has several birthday packages, each of which includes assorted pizzas or chicken tenders with fries and all-you-can-drink soft drinks.

Bowling-and-game packages are $15.95 per person and include 2 hours of unlimited cosmic bowling, $5 game card for each guest, and $10 game card for the birthday guest of honor. Game-only packages are $15.95 per person and include a $10 game card for each guest and a $15 game card for the birthday boy or girl. The Unlimited Ultimate Package is $19.95 per person and includes 2 hours of unlimited cosmic bowling, $10 game card for each party guest, and a $15 game card for the birthday child. For more information, call ☎ 952-500-8700.

THEATRES AT MALL OF AMERICA

THEATRES AT MALL OF AMERICA BIRTHDAY PARTIES allow for large or small groups and can include concession packages and theatre tours if groups have more than 10 people. The Basic Birthday Package ($13 per person, minimum 10 guests) includes kids concession pack, movie admission, and a birthday gift for the guest of honor. The Premium Birthday Package ($220 for up to 10 people; additional guests are $18 per person) includes two large pizzas (pepperoni or cheese), souvenir cups, ice-cream bars, small popcorns, movie admission, and a birthday gift for the guest of honor. For more information, call ☎ 952-883-8900 or e-mail theatres@mallofamerica.com.

GROUP ACTIVITIES
for SCOUTS

IN THE SPRING OF 2012, 50,000 Girl Scouts, Brownies, Daisies, troop leaders, volunteers, alumni, and employees were expected to descend upon Mall of America for the Great Girl Gathering to celebrate the Girl Scout centennial. The actual count ended up exceeding that amount almost three times—the head count was roughly 140,000. Over that weekend, a temporary Girl Scout Store popped up, selling memorabilia, souvenirs, and cookies, along with a flash mob of badge-filled sash- and vest-wearing girls.

As for the boys, every summer the best of the best in the Cub Scouts' famous Pinewood Derby contest meet up at MOA for the challenge of the year.

Scouting events aren't limited to annual events at MOA. Many stores and attractions welcome scouts to learn, enjoy, and even earn awards. Below are some scout-friendly locations at MOA. (Please remember, events change often, so confirm with outlets to ensure offerings are still available.)

BUILD-A-BEAR

BUILD-A-BEAR WORKSHOP offers a Build-A-Party program. However, the partnership with the Girl Scouts ended in 2016, so the uniform options are no longer available, but troops can still partake in Build-A-Bear parties and events. Girl Scout leaders can purchase a Build a Buddy (not Build-A-Bear brand) fun patch or similar fun patches through official Girl Scouts. Party packages start at only $10 per person. For more information, call ☎ 888-560-2327.

MICROSOFT

MICROSOFT OFFERS REGULARLY SCHEDULED SCOUT EVENTS. All scouts must prepay and register via their scout headquarters. We've participated in this event with a Brownie troop, and the girls enjoyed it. Not only did they earn a badge, but Microsoft also gave them a fun patch. Double win! Girl Scout programs include Computer Expert Badge Day for Brownies, grades 2–3; Digital Photographer Badge Day for Juniors, grades 4–5; and Digital Movie Maker Badge Day for Girl Scouts, grades 6–8. All programs cost $11 per scout; adult chaperones are required but attend for free. For more information, call ☎ 952-487-7372.

RAINFOREST CAFE

MOST RAINFOREST CAFE LOCATIONS provide educational tours for 15 people or more on the plants and fish in the rain forest. Scout leaders can work in the earning of badges, loops, and awards. At press time we were told the new Rainforest Cafe at MOA will eventually offer educational tours to groups. You may request information via the online form under Parties and Group Events at rainforestcafe.com or call ☎ 952-854-7500.

SEA LIFE MINNESOTA AQUARIUM

SEA LIFE AQUARIUM PROVIDES an assortment of Scouting opportunities for both Boy and Girl Scout programs to earn or work toward specific loops, badges, pins, and awards.

Boy Scout Belt Loop Programs ($20 per scout) are 2 hours long and include Science and Wildlife Conservation. Academic Pin Programs ($20 per scout) are 2 hours long and also include Science and Wildlife Conservation. Discounts are available if you combine the Belt Loop and Academic Pin programs. Cub Scout Merit Badge Programs ($25 per scout) are 4 hours long and include Environmental Science and Oceanography.

Girl Scout Journey Programs for the "It's Your Planet—Love it" Journey are available for all levels: Daisies "Between Earth and Sky" ($20 per scout) can fulfill sessions 7–9 in earning the Clover Award. Brownies "Wonders of Water" ($20 per scout) fulfills sessions 1–3 in earning the Love Water Award. Juniors "Get Moving" ($22 per scout) fulfills sessions 3–5 in earning the Investigate Award. Cadettes "Breathe" ($22 per scout) helps build on the Aware Award. Seniors "Sow What" ($25 per scout) allows scouts to work toward the

Harvest Award. And Ambassadors "Justice" ($25 per scout) helps girls work toward the Sage Award.

Private group bookings must have a minimum of seven scouts; the booking includes one free chaperone. Scout Overnights are $65 per person and include a choice of three sleeping areas, T-shirt for all participants, souvenir photo, pizza party, light breakfast, activities, behind-the-scenes tour, and aquarium tour. Chaperone discounts do not apply for overnights. Add-on Snorkel Adventures ($40 per scout) are available to scouts ages 9 and up. For more information, call ☎ 952-853-0631 or e-mail sales@sealifeus.com. Sea Life requests a two-week notice for reservations.

OTHER SCOUT OUTINGS

WE MENTIONED THE BUILD A BUDDY fun patch option above, but you can create your own Mall of America scout outing and award your girls other fun patches. Here are a few ideas.

- Bead crafts or jewelry-making patches (Lotus Beads and Jewelry)
- Mall Mania
- Day at the Mall
- Amusement Park (Nickelodeon Universe)
- Shopping
- Aquatic Life (Sea Life)
- Block Building (LEGO)
- Mall Scavenger Hunt
- Bowling Party (Sky Deck Sports Grille & Lanes)
- Arcade (Sky Deck Sports Grille & Lanes)

Other stores in the mall worth visiting with Boy or Girl Scout groups or similar organizations are **Victorinox Swiss Army** (S138, ☎ 952-876-0200), the only location to build the classic knife outside of Switzerland, and **JM Cremp's The Boys Adventure Store** (N240, ☎ 952-854-9105), a store geared toward outdoors adventure and survival.

HOMESCHOOL WEEK

MALL OF AMERICA CELEBRATES homeschoolers by offering Homeschool Week twice a year. Recently, **Sea Life** offered $7 per person admission for children and adults (regular prices are $24.25 per adult and $17.25 per child). **Nickelodeon Universe** offered a rare 3-hour unlimited-ride wristband for $14.33 and a 5-hour unlimited-ride wristband for $16.45 with a special homeschooling coupon found on nickelodeonuniverse.com. Homeschoolers who bought a wristband received $5 admission to Moose Mountain or Dutchman's Deck. The temporary exhibits also provide specials to homeschoolers. If you are a homeschooler, we recommend you use hsadventures.org to keep up with the latest Mall of America and other Twin Cities homeschooling events.

WEDDINGS

COUPLES WHO LOVE MALLS and each other have ventured to Mall of America to get hitched—and sometimes in unexpected ways, such as getting married on the Pepsi Orange Streak roller coaster in Nickelodeon Universe or while SCUBA diving in the Sea Life Aquarium. More commonly, though, couples opt to exchange vows in the **Chapel of Love Wedding Chapel & Bridal Boutique** located on Level 3. Over the last 15 years, more than 7,000 couples have tied the knot or renewed wedding vows in the mall. For many years, the chapel was tucked away in the southeast corner where Bloomingdale's used to be located, but in 2015 it relocated to a new location on the same floor but with a lot more foot traffic, near the main entrance on the third floor by the Rotunda (E318, ☎ 952-854-4656). The former Bridal Boutique carried a wide selection of wedding gowns, but the new location has done away with the dresses; however, it is one of the largest bridal accessory sources in the Twin Cities.

Who would get married in a mall? At first thought, it might seem strange for couples to get hitched in a mall. The answers and people vary. Many couples are on their second or third marriage, while others are looking for an affordable or quick option. Other couples simply won the celebration through local contests. Today, after looking at resort quotes, a free wedding sounds pretty good. But even if you have to pay, MOA weddings are rather affordable.

The new chapel holds 35 wedding guests, half of what the former chapel held. The bride and groom can choose the Chapel of Love package that suits their needs. The midsize Petite Wedding prices range from $399 to $499 (depending upon the day), with a maximum of 35 guests, and include an officiate. Use of the chapel is up to 45 minutes and includes staff-selected processional, recessional, and unity candle music. The Dream Wedding runs $249–$349. The price includes the officiate and up to 15 guests. The Chapel of Love also offers License Signings without all of the hoopla. Couples need to provide a valid marriage license (see below) and two witnesses for the marriage to be official. The cost is $100–$150.

Couples married at the Chapel of Love can renew their vows for $99 for up to 12 guests. Any other couples looking for a renewal ceremony can opt for the Traditional Vow Renewal, which runs $499–$599 for 60 minutes and up to 35 guests. The Petite Vow Renewal is 30 minutes and up to 15 guests for $199.

Additional options include a Bridal Package: Chapel of Love unity candle, garter, toasting glasses, and bottle of champagne for $49. Pre–wedding day rehearsal is $100–$115. Custom music is $29. Videography/DVD packages cost $150 plus tax and shipping.

Marriage licenses for in-state couples can be obtained from any Minnesota county courthouse ($120). Out-of-state couples can contact the Chapel of Love for information regarding government center locations; the closest are in Edina and Minneapolis.

Wedding parties looking for a larger MOA wedding venue can turn to **Radisson Blu** (2100 Killebrew Drive, ☎ 952-881-5258 or 952-851-4011), located on the southern edge of the mall, attached by skyway. The hotel can accommodate up to 700 guests, and wedding dinners start at $37 per guest.

Elsewhere in the mall there is plenty of wedding-planning assistance. **Nordstrom** has a wedding stylist on hand to assist brides with their big day. Visit shop.nordstrom.com/c/wedding-stylist for more information.

WEDDING REGISTRIES

WHILE ONLINE REGISTRIES are rather popular these days, there are a handful of in-store registries at MOA: **Cut Above Home** (S238, ☎ 952-854-1157); **Macy's** (4000 SW Court, ☎ 952-888-3333); **Nordstrom** (1000 NW Court, ☎ 952-883-2121); **Sears** (2000 NE Court, ☎ 952-853-0500); and **Williams-Sonoma** (W262, ☎ 952-854-4553).

FUND-RAISERS *and* EVENTS

EVENTS ARE HELD IN SEVERAL LOCATIONS throughout the mall, the most common being the large Rotunda near the east exit. Other locations include Sears Court (Northeast Court), Macy's Court (Southwest Court), Nordstrom Court (Northwest), and Southeast Court (former Bloomingdale's Court). While a handful of events are held annually, there is not an annual events calendar; however, mallofamerica.com does have an event calendar marked with upcoming events looking ahead as far as two or three months.

Alex's Lemonade Stand is one notable event that pops up every spring to raise funds for and awareness of childhood cancer, specifically neuroblastoma. **Canstruction** is a food fund-raiser that calls on volunteer teams to build creative and often recognizable sculptures from food cans. The cans are then donated to Second Harvest Heartland.

TIPS FOR PLANNING A WALK

OVER THE LAST EIGHT YEARS, our friend Michelle Schlehuber has been organizing a team to participate in the JDRF Walk to Cure Diabetes, which is held every February at Mall of America. Her preteen daughter, Caroline, was diagnosed with diabetes when she was 3. Since their small beginnings, Team Caroline has grown to more than 80 walkers each year! She offers some tips for hosting a successful event:

- Send clear e-mail communication before the event, with information on where to park and what time to arrive, along with cell phone numbers in case of emergencies.
- Have a couple of large signs or balloons to make the team easy to spot. Kids love carrying the signs!
- Design a colorful team T-shirt for each year.
- Have a designated meeting place, but try to avoid the overcrowded Rotunda. JDRF does assign meeting places, but not all organizations make assignments. Stick with the same meeting place each year.
- Take a team photo to remember the day.
- Bring snacks and drinks for your group. People get hungry and thirsty.
- One additional treat for our walkers is a Team Caroline CD of special music selected by Caroline to send home with our friends after the walk. People love getting a new mix each year!
- Take a few breaks during the walk to allow the team to get all caught up and back together. Because our team is so large, we avoid walking on the crowded first floor. We avoid switching floors during the walk to accommodate folks with strollers or wagons.
- We pause before the end of the walk to thank our friends and family for attending. The past few years, we have used a battery-operated megaphone to help everyone hear.
- After the walk, send a thank-you photo card with updated stats on how much money you raise!

CORPORATE MEETINGS *and* EVENTS

LEVEL 4 HOUSES THE MALL OF AMERICA EXECUTIVE CENTER (E410), which includes the Boundary Waters Suite and two adjoining conference rooms (Grand Marais and North Shore). The 2,834-square-foot space is used for conferences, meetings, and parties.

Radisson Blu has more than 26,300 square feet of flexible meeting and event space spanning two ballrooms and 14 meeting rooms. Visit radissonblu.com/en/meetings-request for more information.

The new 4,000-square-foot **Parkview Meeting and Event Center** opened spring 2016. Located in the southwest corner of Nickelodeon Universe near the new FlyOver America attraction, it has an outdoor balcony overlooking the theme park.

The **Research Center at Mall of America** (W322, ☎ 952-883-8809) is ideal for face-to-face or one-way mirror experiences in Focus Group Rooms for focus or research groups.

PART TEN

HEALTH, FITNESS, *and* BEAUTY

BEYOND WHAT IS OFTEN REFERRED TO as the suburban exercise of mall walking, malls aren't typically considered an epicenter for fitness. However, Mall of America has multiple personalities, and health and fitness is one persona that pops up. The proof is in the Mayo Clinic Mile signage in the mall's corridors, as well as in fitness classes, retail shops, food courts, year-round health fairs, sports-inspired events, awareness walks and fund-raisers, fitness celebrities, and cooking demonstrations. There is even a General Nutrition Center (GNC) (N370, ☎ 952-851-0880) on Level 3.

WALKERS

MALL OF AMERICA STORES officially open daily at 10 a.m., but the main mall entrances are open as early as 7 a.m. for the mall-walking crowd. If you're staying at a local hotel and would rather avoid the hotel treadmill, consider taking the shuttle over to the mall to get some exercise. The mall provides a safe, comfortable environment for anyone to exercise year-round.

MOA MALL STARS

WHILE SOME PEOPLE SIMPLY SHOW UP to walk, there is an official group called MOA Mall Stars. For only $15 per person or $25 per couple per year, MOA Mall Stars walkers get the added benefit of a walker's card (scanned upon arrival and departure at the West Entrance), which tracks time spent at the mall, incentive prizes, and invitations to monthly seminars with guest speakers and breakfasts hosted by various stores. For more information, contact Dan Everson: PO Box 23406, Richfield, MN 55423; ☎ 612-866-0850.

MAYO CLINIC MILE

THE ESTEEMED MAYO CLINIC is based in Rochester, Minnesota (80 miles southeast of Mall of America), so teaming with MOA to promote activity only makes sense. Take a simple cruise around Mall of America, and, as previously mentioned, you will notice markers above eye level for the Mayo Clinic Mile (1 mile, 5K, and 10K walks around the mall). Pick up a Mayo Mile brochure for walking routes at any MOA Guest Services or check it out online at mallofamerica.com/content/doc/Mayo_Mile_Brochure.pdf.

HOW FAR WILL YOU WALK DURING A DAY AT MALL OF AMERICA?

Pedometers today make it easy to track activity. We have clipped on a Fitbit as we explored MOA, so we have a very good idea of what kind of activity level the experience entails—a lot. Looking back at records, one day, from 10 a.m. (opening) to midafternoon, at MOA we averaged 11,000 steps. Being that 10,000 steps—about 5 miles—a day is the recommended goal, that's pretty active. What does this mean for you? Wear comfortable shoes. It's unwise to wear new, uncomfortable, or, ladies, super-high heels. Unless you're going for a dinner date, leave the spikes at home. If you think we're kidding, take note of your fellow shoppers and you will see an assortment of heel heights; if it's late in the day, you may spy some shoes in hands or limping ladies. If you make a bad choice and wear the wrong shoes, at least you're at a mall and can buy a new pair. See Part Six for a list of stores.

RUNNERS

MINNESOTA IS ABOUT AS RUNNER, walker, and cyclist friendly as you can get, and it has the bike and jogging paths to prove it. There are hundreds of designated miles around the Twin Cities. And, yes, you will see fitness fanatics outdoors in the winter partaking in all activities, even on bikes, but we don't recommend cycling in the winter. While running is not allowed in Mall of America, MOA's Radisson Blu provides guests with running routes called Blu Routes. Ranging in different distances, routes include an indoor walking route through the mall, a 4-mile route outside the mall, another 4-mile course that provides views of the Minnesota Valley National Wildlife Refuge, and an 11-mile route that provides the challenge of hills along the Minnesota River in the Minnesota Valley National Wildlife Refuge, with the added benefit of playing I-spy Minnesota wildlife. *One important note:* Summer months can be very hot and muggy, so plan your hydration accordingly. For more information, visit radissonblu .com/hotel-mall-of-america/bluroutes.

unofficial **TIP**
Speaking of runners, head to Bubba Gump Shrimp Co. on Level 3 to sit on the bench to pose and "wear" the shoes of one of the most famous movie runners ever. "Run, Forrest, Run!"

Otherwise, we suggest plugging in Mall of America to mapmyrun.com to see routes other runners have previously charted.

STROLLER STRIDES

SOME MORNINGS AT MALL OF AMERICA, walkers may notice a group of parents with strollers in workout clothes lunging around the mall or doing floor exercises. This is the Stroller Strides workout group. We were lucky enough to get the scoop from the head instructor and owner of FIT-4MOM Twin Cities, Emily Christie.

Q: What is Stroller Strides?

A: Stroller Strides is a full-body fitness class that is customized for *any* level of fitness, specifically for moms or caregivers, that you do *with* your kids in a stroller. Each teacher is a nationally certified fitness instructor with a specialization in pre- and postnatal fitness.

We do a full hour-long, interval-based fitness class that includes cardio, strength, and core/balance, *while* we have fun with the kiddos by singing songs, playing games, reading books, and so on. Inside the malls, we move around from station to station to do a full-body workout. It's definitely not a mall-walking group. We work hard to help moms make the greatest strides in their fitness!

Among the many benefits are that moms get to socialize with other moms, kids get to socialize with other kids, moms emulate healthy behaviors for their kids showing that fitness can be fun, and we work hard to make the classes enriching for the little ones. What's more, in at least one study, moms who participated in a stroller-walking program with other moms had a lower incidence of postpartum depression than moms who did not.

Q: Who can attend?

A: Anyone who is a caregiver to a child may attend. This includes daddies, nannies, grannies, mamas, etc. We do require a stroller that is more sturdy than an umbrella stroller, but as long as you have that, you're welcome. Any fitness level can attend. As long as you are cleared to exercise by your health-care provider, you can participate. We offer different intensity levels for every exercise, so a new mom with a new baby can work out next to a mom with a toddler who is running marathons and using our class for cross-training. Our classes have children from about 6–8 weeks to 4 years old. Our first three classes are free to people who live nearby, but for visitors to the state who might be dropping in for a vacation, we do charge $15 per class.

Q: Why Mall of America?

A: We love Mall of America. MOA has so many amazing benefits, and not only as a shopping center. It has so much natural light during the cold dark winters, which is when we're inside (we're outside during the summertime). Yes, the shopping is great, but there are lots of open spaces where the kids can run around after class and we can set up a big bag of toys for sharing, umpteen coffee shops for mamas to get their favorite caffeinated beverage, and the amazing aquarium (a single-year pass is totally affordable, and my son and I go at least once every week or two).

Q: Do you have any insider tips for readers?

A: Tuesdays are Toddler Tuesday at MOA. So, there is a long list of places that offer free meals for kids on Tuesdays. While there are two food courts, many sit-down restaurants and fast sit-down places are great for kids, including the bistro at the American Girl store. Every kid wants what they want, so check the website—the list is enormous. (For more on Toddler Tuesdays, see Part Five: Mall of America with Kids.)

As for workout gear, the list is massive for that too. I'm a huge fan of Athleta and the Running Room. At the Running Room, they can fit you for an ideal running shoe that suits your foot shape or gait, and Athleta is full of amazing store clerks who will help you shop, even if you have a screaming toddler with you. Destination Maternity is a ridiculously wonderful place for new mamas. It is nursing friendly; they sell nursing sport bras. Macy's and Nordstrom have great bra sections where you can get measured for new bras. You will not stay the same size from pre-pregnancy, to pregnancy, to nursing, and frankly, you will be more comfortable and supported in a bra that fits. It's an important expense that will make you feel more comfortable and better about how you look.

If you're looking for great nursing rooms, Nordstrom's second-floor women's restroom has a lovely nursing lounge. Destination Maternity also has a good set-up, complete with a play area plus TV if you have a toddler plus an infant.

Q: Is there anything else to add?

A: Many locals are terrified of going to MOA because their experience is that of a packed Saturday with parking like an airport parking ramp on Thanksgiving. Something I'd like to share is that our classes start before stores open, so there are spaces right up front—no circling ever. Because the stores are closed during classes, foot traffic is limited to mall walkers. Sometimes there are tour buses or school groups, but they're usually headed for a specific destination, so rarely are they in our space.

MALL MAKEOVER

WHILE MALL OF AMERICA has been through its share of face-lifts, truth be told, anyone dreaming of a head-to-toe makeover will find MOA to be the right place. Between wardrobe, makeup, hair, and body treatments, anyone can walk into MOA and leave a different person . . . at least in physical appearance. We haven't heard of any psychiatrists occupying the new office space yet. In the meantime, here are some places to start if you're hoping for a new you.

SPAS AND SALONS

RADISSON BLU'S **Solimar Wellness Spa,** located on the south side of MOA, isn't the largest spa we've seen, but customers seem to walk, or rather float, away happy. You can expect all of the typical treatments of a hotel spa—think stone or wrap massages; facials; microdermabrasion; makeup, hair, and nail services; and wellness consultations. Regarding wellness, the spa is impressively prepared to work on guests being treated for various illness or challenges, including rosacea, acne, high blood pressure, digestive disorders, weight loss, fibromyalgia, depression, and cancer. You don't have to be a guest to book appointments, but hotel guests do get special offers. Spa bargain hunters should keep an eye on the Radisson Blu "Hotel Deals" page at radissonblu .com/hotel-mall-of-america/hotel-deals.

Inside the mall, **Progressions Salon** (W134, ☎ 952-851-9999, progressionssalonspa.com) is an Aveda concept salon and covers the gamut of beauty treatments, including hair, skin, massage, waxing, and nails. Minneapolis-based **Aveda** (W288, ☎ 952-854-0595) provides a number of salon and spa services. **Nail Trix** (E363, ☎ 952-851-9900) and **L.A. Nails** (W364, ☎ 952-854-9102) offer walk-in nail services at average prices, much like the shops in outdoor strip malls. **Relaxing Massage** (N367, ☎ 952-854-4815) is an open-concept massage lounge offering a variety of Asian-inspired treatments.

HAIR SALONS

IF A HAIRCUT OR HAIR TREATMENT is all you need, there are several locations in the mall. As we have discovered, sometimes a trip to MOA is a good opportunity to grab a quick haircut for the kids in between activities. We talked to a former MOA hair stylist, and she said most of the clientele are tourists, mall employees, or local residents from the immediate area. What does this mean for you? Because the stylists are working with a wide range of people, they're more likely to be up with the latest trends and expectations. However, because it's a mall, the turnover is likely a little higher than a salon in the suburbs. Still, we've had good experiences over the years with the occasional haircut. **Regis Salon** (E152, ☎ 952-854-8484) is a traditional hair salon covering all of the basics such as cuts, color, or event primping. Regis Corporation is based in Minneapolis. **MasterCuts** (E368, ☎ 952-854-1414) is an affordable option, especially if your kids need a quick cut.

COSMETICS

TYPICAL DEPARTMENT STORE COSMETIC COUNTERS can be found at **Macy's** and **Nordstrom.** We have frequented both and find both are adequate or comparable to any other department store cosmetic counter. If you need more than a simple blush, we recommend Nordstrom for a number of reasons. Not only is the service always top-notch, but shoppers can also schedule free appointments with beauty stylists, covering everything from

Beauty 101 to makeup tips to big events. This is the place to take daughters to learn proper makeup application and to find the right shades.

In the mall there are two **bareMinerals** locations (E110, ☎ 952-854-9205 and N294, ☎ 952-854-8554). There are also two **Bath & Body Works** stores (S234A, ☎ 952-854-5252 and N172, ☎ 952-858-8377), best known for having a bounty of lotions and fragrant sprays. **LUSH** (E112, ☎ 952-854-9672) is the boss of handmade cosmetics. **IN,** standing for Intelligent Nutrients (S158, ☎ 952-567-1324), is an organic health and beauty brand. Shelves are stocked with aromatics and skin, body, and lip care. **Brow Art** (E362, ☎ 952-854-1270) offers makeup services, eyelash extensions, henna, and the unique practice of body and facial threading.

PIERCINGS

WHILE THERE AREN'T ANY TATTOO PARLORS IN MOA, there are plenty of places to get piercings. Each of these locations has a good reputation for getting ears (or more) pierced. Pay attention to the store's steps for healthy aftercare. **Almost Famous Body Piercing** (E350, ☎ 952-854-8000) will put a hole about anywhere you desire. Rates start at $45 plus jewelry. **Piercing Pagoda** (S103, ☎ 952-853-0843) is a professional service that specializes in children. Little ones can have both ears pierced at the same time by two professionals ($19–$50). All of the **Claire's** (N394, ☎ 952-851-0050 and E292, ☎ 952-858-9903) and **Claire's Boutique** (E179, ☎ 952-854-5504) locations offer free ear piercing with earring purchase ($19–$65).

OPTICAL

THREE MALL OF AMERICA OPTICAL STORES will help you find that new look with improved vision. **LensCrafters** (N304, ☎ 952-858-8410) sees a lot of tourists who have lost or forgotten their glasses thanks to its 1-hour option. Locals can expect a longer order time, about 10 days, depending on needs. **Pearle Vision** (W385, ☎ 952-854-4500) no longer has an express option. Expect a 7–10 day turnaround. **Sears Optical** (NE 2001 [Sears], ☎ 952-853-1143) has a 10–12 business day turnaround.

INDEX

2016 *UNOFFICIAL GUIDE* READER SURVEY

If you'd like to express your opinion in writing about Mall of America or this guidebook, complete the following survey and mail it to:

Unofficial Guide Reader Survey
2204 1st Ave. S., Suite 102
Birmingham, AL 35233

Inclusive dates of your visit: _____

Members of your party:	Person 1	Person 2	Person 3	Person 4	Person 5	Person 6
Gender:	M F	M F	M F	M F	M F	M F
Age:	_____	_____	_____	_____	_____	_____

How many times have you been to Mall of America? _____

LODGING On your most recent trip, where did you stay?

Concerning your accommodations, on a scale of 100 as best and 0 as worst, how would you rate:

- The quality of your room? _____
- The quietness of your room _____
- Shuttle service to the mall? _____
- The value of your room?_____
- Check-in/check-out efficiency? _____
- Swimming pool facilities?_____

CAR RENTALS Did you rent a car? If so, from what company?_____

Concerning your rental car, on a scale of 100 being best and 0 worst, how would you rate:

Pickup-processing efficiency?_____   Cleanliness of the car? _____

Return-processing efficiency?_____   Airport-shuttle efficiency? _____

Condition of the car? _____

DINING Concerning your dining experiences, estimate your meals in restaurants per day?
_____

Approximately how much did your party spend on meals per day? _____

Favorite restaurants at Mall of America: _____
_____

Did you buy this guide before leaving?_____   While on your trip?_____

How did you hear about this guide? (check all that apply)

❑ Radio or TV   ❑ Library   ❑ Internet   ❑ Newspaper or magazine

❑ Bookstore salesperson   ❑ Chose it on my own   ❑ Loaned or recommended by a friend

What other guidebooks did you use on this trip?
Please rate them on a scale of 100 as best and 0 as worst. _____
_____
_____
_____

Using the same scale, how would you rate the *Unofficial Guides*(s)?_____

Are *Unofficial Guides* readily available at bookstores in your area? _____

Which other *Unofficial Guides* have you used? _____
_____
_____

If you like, on a separate sheet include comments about your Mall of America trip or *The Unofficial Guide*.